THE REVOLUTIONARY SELF

ALSO BY LYNN HUNT

History: Why It Matters
Writing History in the Global Era
Measuring Time, Making History
Inventing Human Rights: A History
The Family Romance of the French Revolution
Politics, Culture, and Class in the French Revolution

THE REVOLUTIONARY SELF

Social Change and the Emergence of the Modern Individual, 1770–1800

· LYNN HUNT ·

W. W. NORTON & COMPANY
Independent Publishers Since 1923

Copyright © 2025 by Lynn Hunt

All rights reserved
Printed in the United States of America
First Edition

For information about permission to reproduce selections from this book, write to
Permissions, W. W. Norton & Company, Inc., 500 Fifth Avenue, New York, NY 10110

For information about special discounts for bulk purchases, please contact
W. W. Norton Special Sales at specialsales@wwnorton.com or 800-233-4830

Manufacturing by Sheridan Chelsea
Book design by Patrice Sheridan
Production manager: Julia Druskin

ISBN 978-1-324-07903-3

W. W. Norton & Company, Inc.
500 Fifth Avenue, New York, NY 10110
www.wwnorton.com

W. W. Norton & Company Ltd.
15 Carlisle Street, London W1D 3BS

1 2 3 4 5 6 7 8 9 0

Contents

Introduction: HOW THE SMALLEST THINGS LEAD
TO BIG CHANGES 1

One: TEA AND HOW WOMEN BECAME
"CIVILIZED" 11

Two: REVOLUTIONARY IMAGERY AND
THE UNCOVERING OF SOCIETY 37

Three: ART, FASHION, AND ONE
WOMAN'S EXPERIENCE 64

Four: REVOLUTIONARY ARMIES AND
THE STRATEGIES OF WAR 89

Five: MONEY, SELF-INTEREST,
AND MAKING A REPUBLIC 115

Epilogue: SELF, SOCIETY, AND EQUALITY 148

ACKNOWLEDGMENTS 155

NOTES 157

INDEX 189

THE REVOLUTIONARY SELF

Introduction

HOW THE SMALLEST THINGS
LEAD TO BIG CHANGES

OVER THE COURSE OF THE 1700S, PEOPLE IN EUROPE AND British North America came to have a happier view of human prospects. Previously, most people saw themselves as irreparably tainted by original sin and only kept in line by the terror of higher powers, divine or earthly. Now the idea spread that ordinary people had the potential for autonomy and were capable of exerting their liberty, whether in the choice of spouse, occupation, religious beliefs, or governing bodies. Through education, which enhanced the ability to reason, the person marked by sin became a person defined instead by an aptitude to develop and improve. The modern world of participatory democracy surfaced, not all at once, but ineluctably given such a revolution in attitude.[1]

Another less evident outcome accompanied the independence of the individual: society began to emerge as a distinct entity assumed to have its own rules, and individuals came to be viewed as creatures shaped by social conditioning. This created a paradox: at the very moment when breaking free seemed possible, people began to learn that as individuals they were subtly but nonetheless powerfully molded by social forces. Original sin lost its hold, but seeping into its place was social determinism, the idea that our identities are formed by class, race, ethnicity, sexuality, age, profession, and marital status—that is, all the markers given value by modern bureaucracies and internalized by individuals.

This book is about the origins of that paradox: the simultaneous discovery that individuals had a capacity for autonomy and that society had the power to sculpt that individuality. Although many of the causes of the rise of individualism have been examined, some surprises remain: the unexpected consequences of consuming goods from afar, such as tea; the role of women, although women's individual capacities were often belittled; the challenges created by new ways of fighting wars; and the opportunities unleashed by the invention of new financial instruments, ranging from insurance companies to national debts. These new social practices all extended the reach of the individual's potential. Tea drinking, for example, gave women new roles as tea servers; but perhaps more significantly, in those new roles women now sat at tea tables alongside men, serving them at the same level rather than standing apart in a more subservient position. The tea table brought intimations of gender equality even as it still signaled social status and therefore social disparities.

While white women gained new expectations even though they remained legally dependent on their fathers or husbands, Black enslaved people did not, at least not in theory. Slavery as a condition and as a practice nonetheless infused the new thinking about individual capacities. It defined the contours of freedom and was the opposite of autonomy in every respect. Yet even as the number of enslaved people brought to the Americas ballooned between 1725 and 1800, more than doubling the number of those transported from Africa during the previous two centuries, enslaved people enacted their desire for autonomy in countless ways, from small undertakings of resistance to major exploits of self-emancipation, often through the manipulation of the commercial economy that had brought them into their bondage in the first place.[2]

The aspirations of enslaved people combined with the growing emphasis on individual aptitudes to foster the abolitionist movement, but it only took root once the definition of personhood had changed. Servitude took myriad forms in the early modern era: domestic service, indentured labor, feudal obligations to lords, serfdom, and slavery, not to mention the legal subservience of minors, women, and journeymen in craft guilds. In a hierarchical world, few enjoyed the advantages of autonomy, and as long as the many varieties of servitude remained unchallenged, arguments for the abolition of slavery gained little traction. From the unlimited powers of parents to those of lords over serfs, servitude came into question in the second half of the eighteenth century. The emphasis on capabilities thus helps answer one of the enduring questions about the centuries of enslavement of Africans: Why did abolitionism emerge only toward the end of the eighteenth century but then relatively rapidly win converts?

The historical development of social determinism—the other half of the paradox—is harder to pin down because society is a more nebulous concept than the individual. An individual is presumably located in the body of a single person, but society has no fixed location. It operates through largely unspoken conventions. While the body of an individual may always be changing and along with it an individual's identity, it nonetheless manages to seem distinct and distinguishable. We think we know what a person is, but society is less identifiable. Margaret Thatcher famously insisted, "There's no such thing [as society]. There are individual men and women and there are families." In short, society requires more explanation; it can only be conceived through metaphor. Its rules may appear in print at some point (usually when the rules come into question), but they regulate the space between people as well as how individuals use their bodies—for example, in the ways tea is served or armies train their recruits. Society is nowhere and everywhere at the same time.[3]

Society has always existed, but its existence has only become an issue at certain moments in history. One of the most critical times was the second half of the eighteenth century. Jean-Jacques Rousseau captured that sense of urgency in his 1755 *Discourse on the Origin and Foundation of Inequality among Men*: "The first person who, having enclosed a plot of land, took it upon himself to say *this is mine*, and found people simple enough to believe him, was the true founder of civil society." He continued, saying that this act was the source of endless crimes, wars, murders, miseries, and horrors in human history. Rousseau's *Social Contract* (1762) was meant to solve the problem created by this invention of society. By joining together in a social compact, individuals could protect their persons and property and thus retain their individual freedom. But the contract had a caveat that goes to the heart of the paradoxical relationship between the individual and society; if an individual did not conform to the general will, he (it is always he, never she, for Rousseau) "shall be forced to be free," that is, forced to conform for his own sake.[4]

Rousseau had put society on the intellectual agenda but was not alone in his concern about it. In both English and French, the use of the terms "society" and "social" took off after the mid-1700s, spiking in French in the 1790s with the onset of the French Revolution in 1789. The French Revolution convinced some that society required a new kind of scientific study, called "social science." ("Sociology" only appeared as a term in the 1840s.) The advent of social science in the 1790s signaled a new desire to understand society and social relations.[5]

It is difficult to precisely date the emergence of "social science" as a term. In 1789, Abbé Emmanuel Sieyès used it in his sensational anti-noble pamphlet *What Is the Third Estate?* It also appeared in other writings from 1789 to 1794, often linked to the moral and political sciences. Mathematician and political visionary Nicolas de Caritat, Marquis de Condorcet, employed it on various occasions between 1792 and 1794. His idea of a distinctive social science took root after 1795 among his followers, who were members or associates of the new National Institute, established to organize and disseminate knowledge. (Condorcet himself had committed suicide in 1794 when faced with the prospect of the guillotine.) Institute associate Antoine Destutt de Tracy coined the term "ideology," by which he meant the science of ideas. He argued that social science required "recognized and systematized principles" to become truly scientific and that with them "we would be able to explain and even predict the good fortune and misfortune of diverse societies." From the beginning, then, the scientific study of the social was tied to developing comparisons between societies.[6]

Why did social science arise in France? The term "social science" had appeared in English in a few eighteenth-century poems but solely as a stand-in for social refinement. It took hold in English only after John Stuart Mill studied the writings of the French thinker Auguste Comte, who had been influenced by Condorcet. In 1843, Mill ardently defended the idea of a social science, and though he differed with Comte on how best to pursue it, he developed his ideas in reaction to Comte's work.[7]

The critical element, therefore, was the French Revolution. Destutt de Tracy, like Condorcet and Sieyès, was looking for ways to stabilize French society even while accepting many of the breaks with the past produced by the revolution. Their perceived need to steady the ship reflected a common sense that social relations were in turmoil, but the belief that such relations could be systematically studied to develop better policies indicated something even deeper: the conviction that society was a body regulated by hidden laws.

Such a conviction could only develop over time. One way of tracing it is through language and in particular the term "social organization." It was rarely used in French before 1789 but began to appear frequently in 1790 and the years following, first in speeches in the new revolutionary assemblies and then in more systematic works of reflection. The invocation of social organization followed on the heels of the creation of a new political category, the *ancien régime*, meaning the "former" or "old" regime. "Social organization" signaled that a new regime was in the making. When Sieyès deployed it in *What Is the Third Estate?* he suggested its incendiary potential: "The noble order is not at all included in the social organization; it can certainly be a *burden* for the nation, but it cannot be part of it."[8]

As Sieyès's words make clear, if the political regime was going to be altered, it would necessarily require social transformation. But how much and how fast? The vertiginous succession of upheavals during the French Revolution—eliminating noble titles and privileges, killing the king and queen, fighting much of Europe, repeatedly revising the constitution—made the need for understanding social transformation more urgent. It also provided the most important rationale for social knowledge: the French Revolution showed that a change in regime and therefore in social organization was possible. After that time, everything had to be justified, including any return to tradition. Most of all it was imperative to explain why social and political transformation occurred in some places and not in others and more generally why societies operated in the ways they did.

For society to become an object of study, it first needed to be seen and its density and complexity and the general significance of social relations understood. The French Revolution had ripped apart the fabric that had made social hierarchy seem natural and inevitable, but society did not become immediately visible behind the tear in the curtain. It could not because society is a construct of the imagination. Still, there are ways of signaling the existence of underlying rules of social engagement, and one of the aims of this book is to trace the ways that people in the late eighteenth century visualized their society. I will be considering many sources, some of them less expected, such as the comparison of European societies with those of North America, the rendering of social relations in prints produced during the French Revolution, the depiction of fashion in painting, the regulations for treating ordinary soldiers, the use of actuarial tables to create insurance companies, and the debates over the wisdom of maintaining a national debt. They all concern functions within society and the powerful influences society has on the individuals within it.

The tug between individualism and society's rules profoundly shapes modern life and has many points of origin. In this book, I will be pointing to some of these tensions, especially as cultural practices changed people's lives and their interactions with each other. Along the way you will meet a handful of remarkable individuals who illuminate key features of this duality.

The first of these is the Glasgow law professor John Millar (1735–1801). Originally destined to a clerical vocation like his father, Millar turned instead to the law, which he made into a platform to inquire into the nature of human society. Possessed of a vivacious personality and wide-ranging intellect, Millar drew attention to the correlation between the status of women and the level of civilization achieved in different societies. For a law professor to be writing about comparative civilizations was far from expected. He repeatedly challenged traditional outlooks in other ways: he lectured in English while his colleagues persisted in using Latin; he spoke extemporaneously and constantly revised his lectures in consultation with his students; and rather than drone on about the Roman law codified by the Byzantine emperor Justinian—the assigned curriculum—he quickly branched out into speaking about law, society, and government more generally. Millar embraced the individual's greater sense of self and also provided ways of reflecting on its social causes.[9]

No individual printmaker in the next chapter features in the same way as Millar because French artists who made revolutionary prints often did so anonymously. Much more is known about painters. Marie-Gabrielle Capet (1761–1818) is highlighted here. She exemplifies the new opportunities that the French Revolution afforded, not because she achieved such great renown but rather because she came from humble origins and yet managed to make a notable career for herself as an artist. Capet somehow made her way to Paris and the workshop of one of the best-known painters of the day, Adélaïde Labille-Guiard. The older woman's mentorship of talented young women was one of many examples of how coteries of friends could replace the traditional role of family relationships. Portraits might seem an unlikely place to look for the emergence of concerns with society or the social, but in the eighteenth century, portrait painters aimed at much more than the likeness of individuals, and their attention to fashion often encapsulated, inadvertently or not, social changes that were underway. Capet's vivid works made society visible even when not depicting society as such.[10]

Napoleon Bonaparte might be the most obvious person to spotlight when discussing the role of the army in fostering individual prospects, and his astonishing ascent to power might be considered unusual. It wasn't. It obscures the general accessibility of the path he followed. Many of his marshals came from origins far less lofty than his own minor noble Corsican family. His eventual brother-in-law and king of Naples, Joachim Murat, was the son of an innkeeper; Michel Ney's father was a cooper; André Masséna was the son of a shopkeeper. All rose to the highest rank thanks to their skills, yet at every level, similar trajectories could be found. Structural innovations in the army made it more receptive to individual initiative, even that of newcomers. The institution most likely to suppress individual qualities in the interest of attaining collective goals discovered the virtues of fostering individual talents.[11]

The career of the Swiss-born financial wizard Étienne Clavière (1735–1793) provides the central thread for the chapter on finance. The son of a Genevan cloth merchant, Clavière was forced to leave town because of his association with a democratic revolt there in 1782. He eventually moved to Paris, where he established himself as a stockbroker and learned how actuarial tables could be used to make life insurance companies profitable. His close ties with two future French revolutionary leaders, Jacques-Pierre Brissot and Honoré Gabriel Riqueti, Comte de Mirabeau, brought him into politics even before the French Revolution broke out in 1789. Brissot got him named minister of finance in 1792, and when Brissot fell, so did Clavière. He stabbed himself to death in his prison cell in December 1793.[12]

Clavière's journey is illuminating because it was not at all typical. There were many other financial speculators at the time, but most of them were in it for the money and not for the politics. Clavière wanted wealth, but he also hoped to reshape the world through utopian experiment, the abolition of slavery, and the spread of republicanism. He deeply believed in the new truth of individual potential, starting with his own, and he discovered that by studying society—through actuarial tables, for example—an individual could make money and perhaps even restructure the government.

While giving close attention to individual lives, this book keeps bringing back the conflicts between people and their societies. New social practices, such as the opening up of French exhibition spaces, cleared the way for ambitious individuals to make their marks, but the individuals were still molded and often restricted by the social worlds in which they found themselves. Looking at the late 1700s helps us see a time when society provided more room for people to assert themselves in larger roles. Perhaps it can let us see with a fresher gaze the continuing friction between the self and society today.

TEA AND HOW WOMEN BECAME "CIVILIZED"

INDIVIDUALISM—THE EMPHASIS ON THE INDIVIDUAL'S autonomy—has been traced back to numerous sources but never, as far as I can determine, to tea. Among the new stimulants imported to Europe from the sixteenth century onward, coffee has garnered the lion's share of the attention. The first coffeehouses in Europe appeared in the mid-1600s. Soon patrons read newspapers while drinking their beverages, and not long afterward, public opinion bristled with demands for government accountability and individual participation. Coffee thus paved the way to democracy. Coffeehouses, for the most part, were for men, as was political involvement.[1]

Tea tells a different story, since it mainly involves the private as opposed to the public sphere, yet it is a story with equally momentous implications. Tea overtook the drinking of coffee in Britain, and its popularity, along with the vogue for tea paraphernalia, changed women's roles. Middle- and upper-class women now presided over tea tables, which became the center of conversation in the household. Before the introduction of tea, servants laid out the food, and in those families without servants, the women in the family often served the food and then stood aside while the men ate. Tea brought everyone to the table, and among the prosperous, tea drinking became a ritual in which the highest-ranking woman present (the mother or the eldest daughter, for example) supervised the preparation of the tea and served it herself. At a time when "sitting together at a table" constituted "one of the strongest characteristics of civilization and refinement," the use of silver teapots and teaspoons and porcelain teacups and slop bowls signaled even greater sophistication.[2]

In the second half of the eighteenth century, the status of women took center stage in writings about the supposed superiority of European civilization. "Civilization" was a new term, hardly used in English before the 1760s, and it was given currency in particular by Scottish moral philosophers who began to rank societies along a spectrum that ran from backward to advanced. The status of women was crucial to those rankings. Although it is impossible to prove that tea put these developments into motion, the links are suggestive: tea impacted the position of women, tea had an unusual presence in Scotland compared with England, and Scottish philosophers rather than English ones did the most to compare and categorize societies.[3]

Tea, and especially the appeal of Chinese porcelains that came along with it, had an uncanny relationship with British women. In London, women patronized and even owned porcelain shops, and over the course of the seventeenth and eighteenth centuries, both tea and porcelain evolved from their initial status as luxury consumer goods into everyday objects associated with domesticity and feminine warmth. Where once tea and porcelain hinted at female desire and sensuality, even in the very form of some teawares, the tea ritual at home eventually helped create the ideal of maternal domesticity.[4]

Domesticity may have been the prescribed norm, but to become an effective model it had to assimilate the changes in women's position

Richard Collins, *A Family of Three at Tea*, ca. 1727. Oil painting, 64.2 × 76.3 cm. *Victoria and Albert Museum / Art Resource, NY*

that tea preparation and, in particular, tea tables promoted. Women now presided over tea at a table whose presence encouraged conversation between women and men as equals, at least in relation to their placement at the table. Conversation, in turn, encouraged literacy, a connection immediately grasped by those early broadcasters of eighteenth-century politeness, Joseph Addison and Richard Steele. Their paper, *The Spectator* (1711–1714), lasted only three years, but its daily advice about social comportment from morals to fashion enjoyed wide influence for decades, both in Britain and on the Continent. In the March 12, 1711, issue Addison compared himself to Socrates; if the Greek had succeeded in bringing philosophy down from the heavens to the benefit of mankind, then he, Addison, had "brought Philosophy out of Closets and Libraries, Schools and Colleges, to dwell in Clubs and Assemblies, at Tea-Tables, and in Coffee-Houses." In short, he brought it from the schools to families and the general public.[5]

Addison claimed, moreover, that the paper would be especially useful to women. He wanted to encourage a domesticity fueled by tea and periodicals and recommended "these my Speculations to all well-regulated Families, that set apart an Hour in every Morning for Tea and Bread and Butter; and would earnestly advise them for their Good to order this Paper to be punctually served up, and to be looked upon as a Part of the Tea Equipage." Addison knew that some women's intellectual ambitions went even further. A month later, on April 12, he recounted the story of a country lady who had a remarkable library that included Newton's works and Locke's essay on human understanding. The folios were kept in place by china vases and the octavos by tea dishes. In the middle of the room was a Japanese-style table. An acute observer such as Addison detected the omnipresence of teaware in spaces occupied by women and perhaps also grasped how tea, porcelain, and tea tables worked together to foster silent changes in the status of women.[6]

It took decades, however, for a positive association of tea, reading, and conversation to take root. Originally touted for its medicinal qualities, such as purifying the blood and curing headaches, critics soon found reason for alarm; tea came from a purportedly effeminate nation, China, and would emasculate British men. Tea was an "idle custom," "an absurd expense," according to one denigrator; others insisted that the women who indulged were foolish gossips with an unquenchable taste for luxury. In the 1740s, Eliza Haywood could still publish an anti-tea screed in her widely read *Female Spectator*, though her motives in doing so are not entirely obvious. One letter supposedly from a male reader opined in 1746 that "the immoderate Use of Tea, which however innocent it may seem to those that practice it, is a kind of Debauchery, " especially since "all Degrees of Women are infected with it, and a Wife now looks upon her Tea-Chest, Table, and its Implements, to be as much Right by Marriage as her Wedding-Ring." Was Haywood truly bemoaning the development of tea consumption or ironically depicting a particular stripe of male opinion? In any case, the comments demonstrate that the female fervor for tea and tea things had become commonplace by this time.[7]

TEA AND HOW WOMEN BECAME "CIVILIZED" · 15

In a reminiscence about daily life in Scotland not published in her lifetime, Elizabeth Mure reported that tea tables arrived in the 1720s; "everything was a matter of conversation; Religion, Morals, Love, Friendship, Good manners, dress. This tended more to our refinement than any thing ellse [sic]. The subjects were all new and all entertaining. The bookseller's shopes [sic] were not stuffed as they are now with Novels and Magazines." The 1740s, she insisted, saw another major change. Men had been meeting regularly in their various clubs, playing backgammon and other games for money, buying tobacco, drinking, and often transacting business, too. Tea tables brought them home, for "the Teatables very soon intredused [sic] supping in private houses." Tea domesticated men even as it infused a model of domesticity for women.[8]

Until recently, scholars overlooked the social effects of the consumption of tea, paying more attention to official documents such as the records of taxes paid on it than to the evanescent everyday gestures concerning the handling of foodstuffs. Much more is known about the importation of tea than about its meaning once it arrived inside households, yet even the bare economic figures suggest a revolution in taste. Official tea imports to Britain more than doubled between the 1730s and 1750s, doubling again by the 1760s, and kept increasing. In 1700, Britons drank ten times as much coffee as tea. As the price of tea went down relative to coffee, tea rapidly supplanted coffee as the beverage of choice. By the 1720s, the value of tea imported to Britain was seven times that of coffee.[9]

Tea depended on access to global markets, and its consumption fueled ever more intense global interconnection, not always to the benefit of everyone involved. Europeans imported tea from China in the eighteenth century. But once the British took over Assam in eastern India in the 1830s, they had tea grown for export in order to break the Chinese monopoly. The desire for tea in Britain also promoted British colonization in the West Indies in order to get access to affordable sugar (milk was not usually added to tea in the eighteenth century).

British consumption of sugar jumped from nearly six pounds per capita in the first decade of the century to twenty-three pounds per capita in the 1770s. To produce the desired sugar, the British enslaved Africans to work on their sugar plantations in the West Indies. The gruesome British practice of shipping people from Africa to the Caribbean to enslave them increased exponentially during the eighteenth century, from about 115,000 people in the first decade of the century to 245,000 in the 1760s, reaching a total of nearly two million Africans for the eighteenth century. Tea drinking depended on slavery in ways that were largely overlooked by its consumers until the end of the eighteenth century.[10]

Like tea, porcelain was at first a Chinese monopoly. In the early eighteenth century, the British imported one to two million pieces of porcelain a year from China, and by the 1720s, at least a third of middle-class households owned porcelain. By 1740 this figure may have reached 50 percent. Altogether, the Dutch VOC (East India Company) imported forty-three million pieces of porcelain between 1600 and 1800, and the other European companies, including Britain's, imported another thirty million pieces. In one year alone, 1777–78, the European companies brought in seven hundred tons of porcelain. These official trade figures do not include the private trade carried on by supercargos, the ship owners' representatives who supervised the cargo, and other sailors.[11]

As might be expected, the enthusiasm for Chinese porcelain prompted Europeans to ferret out the secrets of its delicacy and translucence. Research supervised by Augustus the Strong of Saxony led to the establishment of a porcelain works in Meissen, Germany, in 1710, and almost immediately others joined in the hunt to get hold of the Meissen recipes. English manufacturers followed by the 1730s but with an emphasis on less expensive bone china and then creamware that could be marketed to the middle classes as an inexpensive but still desirable alternative to Chinese porcelain. The ultimate master of branding was Josiah Wedgwood (1730–1795), who used commissions from the queen and other aristocrats to give his creamware the kind of social distinction that made it a popular item for social emulation. He wrote to his partner Thomas Bentley in 1767, "The demand . . . still increases—It is really amazing how rapidly the use of it has spread allmost [sic] over the whole Globe, & how universally it is liked.—How much of this general use, & estimation, is owing to the mode of its introduction—& how much to its real utility & beauty?"[12]

By the time he wrote these lines, Wedgwood had expanded his capabilities far beyond the bounds imagined by most of his contemporaries. Born the youngest of thirteen children to a Staffordshire potter who died when Josiah was nine years old, the young lad left school to work for his oldest brother, to whom he was officially apprenticed at age fourteen. A bout of smallpox three years earlier had left him with great pain in his right leg (it was eventually amputated) that made continuing work as a thrower impossible. He turned to molding and studying the effects produced by different clays and minerals for glazes and coloring. As soon as he reached age twenty-one, he left to form a series of partnerships with men more receptive than his brother to his desire for experimentation. By age thirty he had set up for himself and was constantly introducing new tools, materials, and kilns. He became friends with the manufacturer and steam power pioneer Matthew Boulton, who advised him on the expansion of his business. Wedgwood eventually lobbied Parliament for new roads and canals to expedite the import of raw materials from as far away as North Carolina and the shipping of finished earthenware around the country and overseas. In this way, Wedgwood transformed Staffordshire pottery from a local trade carried by peddlers into an international concern selling to buyers all over Europe, North America, and even China and India.[13]

People like Wedgwood knew that palates and lifestyles were rapidly changing, and so was Europe's place within a wider world of trade and colonization. To make sense of this heady combination, philosophers and social commentators often turned to the travel accounts published in the wake of European commerce and conquests overseas. These books eventually inspired a destabilizing cultural relativism that undermined the certitudes of traditional religion, politics, and social life, including long-standing European notions of property, justice, and freedom. Yet even while travel books could knock Europeans off-kilter, they ended up fostering a new sense of European superiority. Europeans craved Chinese tea and porcelain, but as they surveyed the world, they increasingly saw themselves as its potential masters. In doing so, they would make the position of European women central to their sense of superiority.

Comparisons between European social customs and those of discovered lands proved critical both to cultural relativism and assumed cultural superiority. As John Locke said in his second treatise on government (1689), "in the beginning all the World was *America*." By this he meant that all peoples had originally been as "backward" as the Indigenous Americans, who had entirely different conceptions of property and no notion of money, or so Locke and others like him concluded from the travel accounts they read. Money depended on establishing social conventions about its exchange value. Without money, Locke concluded, the value of land depended on the labor that went into it, and the production of surplus was useless because without a system of exchange, the surplus would go to waste. Money allowed that exchange to take place and with it the possibility that some could accumulate more and more property. Travelers' depictions of "America" thus enabled Europeans to see the cultural relativism of their own customs and to recognize that inequality had historical and cultural roots.[14]

Two related conclusions would eventually be drawn by Europeans from these ruminations prompted by travel literature: first, since all the world was originally like America, there must be a trajectory of development of societies, and second, Europe was the end point of that trajectory and therefore by definition superior because "more advanced." So even as travel literature chipped away at European traditions, suggesting to some readers that those traditions were just social conventions and not God-given truths, it simultaneously gave rise to a European sense of superiority. These conclusions depended on the elaboration of a concept of "civilization" and on comparisons of the status of women in different societies.

Although the belief in Western superiority is now associated with "modernity," a condition first supposedly achieved by western Europe, eighteenth-century people did not make this connection. While the term can be traced as far back as 1635 in English according to the *Oxford English Dictionary*, the digital database Eighteenth Century Collections Online yields only one reference in English for the entire eighteenth century. The terms that resonated in the eighteenth century were "modern times" and "civilization." Both date from the second half of the century. Even before then, however, the importance of women as a societal marker had been set out by the French writer Montesquieu. He proposed an influential correlation between types of political regimes and the status of women, suggesting it first in his entertaining pseudo-travelogue *Persian Letters* (1721) and then systematizing it in Book VII of his major treatise *The Spirit of Laws* (1748). In the latter work, he laid out the "consequences of the different principles of the three [types of] government with respect to sumptuary laws, luxury, and the condition of women." He found that in monarchies, women at court enjoy a certain "spirit of liberty," but they bring with them the reign of vanity and luxury. In despotic states, women do not introduce luxury, for "they themselves are an object of luxury" and are treated like slaves. In republics, in contrast, "women are free by law and in the thrall of manners; luxury is banished and with it corruption and vice." This reference to "the thrall of manners" (*captivée par les moeurs*), which Montesquieu equated with the virtue, simplicity, and chastity of ancient Greek women, would prove to be crucial as it was further developed by European thinkers in the eighteenth century. His phrase also captures the tension between new individual freedoms ("free by law") and social determinism ("the thrall of manners").[15]

Despite arguing for a direct connection between these forms of rule, the status of women, and the problem of consumption, Montesquieu did not give that correlation a historical or civilizational arc. In fact, the French term *civilisation* only became more current in the 1770s and 1780s. The civilizational path was provided, instead, by the thinkers of the Scottish Enlightenment, who inserted Montesquieu's categories into a progressive, historical sequence of stages and shifted the emphasis from luxury, vice, and corruption to women as symbols of commercial society, embodying refinement, civility, and conversation.[16]

Scottish intellectuals, among them judge Henry Home, known as Lord Kames, and moral philosopher Adam Smith, used their reading of travel literature to develop an evolutionary history of the stages of civilization. The long-term consequences of this stage theory can hardly be overstated: policymakers, especially colonizers and empire builders, relied on it to explain the "backwardness" of undeveloped parts of the world and justify its control by the developed world, with the terms themselves of "developed" and "un-" or "underdeveloped" having been shaped by the model of stages. Because undoing these associations has taken so long (insofar as they have been undone), it is hard to grasp how inchoate stage theory was in the eighteenth century. The basic elements for it were present, but it was far from codified; it was a set of sometimes conflicting hypotheses rather than a theory. Most of Adam Smith's thoughts on stage theory, and he is widely considered an originator, were to be found in his lectures on jurisprudence at Glasgow University in the 1750s and 1760s. Their message was known only through students' notes.[17]

One of Smith's students, John Millar, can provide a guide through this thicket because he gave increasingly more concrete expression to stage theory during the period of its initial elaboration. Millar's most influential work, *Observations concerning the Distinction of Ranks in Society* (1771), clearly linked Montesquieu's static typology to the development of civilization over time, and in the process of revising subsequent editions, he began adopting the terminology of stages. Millar is not a household name now, but his book had gone into a third edition by 1779, albeit with an updated title, *The Origin of the Distinction of Ranks;*

or, An Inquiry into the Circumstances Which Give Rise to Influence and Authority, in the Different Members of Society. The title of the 1773 French translation of the second edition made the connection with the issues of self and society even clearer: *Observations sur les commencemen[t]s de la société* (Observations on the beginnings of society). In his preface, Millar laid out his interest in social determinants as the key link between individual lives and national destinies: "When at the same time we consider how much the character of individuals is influenced by their education, their professions and their peculiar circumstances, we are enabled, in some measure, to account for the behaviour of different nations."[18]

Like many of his fellow Scottish intellectuals, Millar aimed to offer a "natural history of mankind" by drawing attention to "the more obvious and common improvements in the state of society." Chief among these, for Millar, were changes "in the degree of consideration which is paid to the women as members of society." He traced those changes through the different "ages" of human history. Women "in early ages" (which he often called "rude and barbarous") are "degraded below the other sex" and "usually treated as the servants or slaves of the men." The state of women improves "with the gradual advancement of society in civilization, opulence, and refinement." The term "civilization," which often appears in Millar's book in tandem with either "advancement" or "refinement," reaches its apex in Europe: "The laws and customs of the modern European nations," he opines, "have carried the advantages of liberty to a height which was never known in any other age or country." The causal arrow was evident to him: advancement in laws and customs leads to improvement in the status of women, and the upgrading of the status of women is a sure sign that refinement of manners is taking place, which means a higher level of civilization.[19]

Millar confidently asserted the "natural progress of human society" in the first edition, but it was only from the 1773 edition onward that he specifically drew attention to the steps in that progress from the barbarism of "rude ages" through the introduction of pastoral arts and agriculture to the improvement of useful arts and manufacture. In the third edition, he finally used the word "stages," but only once: "There is thus in human society, a natural progress from ignorance to knowledge, and from rude, to civilized manners, the several stages of which are usually accompanied with peculiar laws and customs." By examining those "peculiar laws and customs," Millar was putting meat on the bare bones of stage theory.[20]

Millar styled himself a follower as well as a student of Smith. "The great Montesquieu pointed out the road," Millar insisted. "He was the Lord Bacon in this branch of philosophy. Dr. Smith is the Newton." Unlike Montesquieu, who favored comparisons with the countries of the Middle East and Asia because he was mainly concerned with despotism, Millar, like Smith, focused his attention on the travel literature about the Americas because of their supposed location at the beginning of the march toward civilization. Millar cites evidence from the Americas more often than that from China, Persia, and the Ottoman Turks combined. Like Smith, Millar was particularly influenced by the writings of the French Jesuit missionary Joseph-François Lafitau, whereas Montesquieu had shown no interest in Lafitau, his contemporary.[21]

Lafitau's eleven-hundred-page work of 1724, *Moeurs des sauvages amériquains, comparées aux moeurs des premiers temps* (Customs of the American Indians compared with the customs of primitive times) proved to be singularly important for Scottish thinkers, in contrast to their French counterparts who either ignored Lafitau or, as in the case of Voltaire, ridiculed him for thinking that the Native Americans might be descended from the Greeks of antiquity. Although Lafitau began with the goal of proving that Indigenous Americans were not atheists, his work inevitably fostered a sense of cultural relativism. By comparing the customs of Indigenous Americans to those of the ancient Greeks and Romans, he effectively affirmed Native Americans as part of humanity and therefore the relevance of their ways of life for Europeans. Having spent five years as a Catholic missionary in Canada among the Iroquois,

TEA AND HOW WOMEN BECAME "CIVILIZED" · 23

Lafitau amassed a trove of relatively unbiased information about Indigenous groups. He did not have an evolutionary history in mind, but by developing an extended analogy with the ancient Greeks and Romans, he suggested that the Indigenous Americans belonged to an earlier time in history; looking at them, the Scots could see themselves at an earlier point in time, at the beginning of the development of civilization.[22]

The Scottish philosophers did not have a particularly rosy view of the Americans, but in this they were hardly unusual. Lafitau himself, though at pains to rescue the Native Americans from the grossest prejudices of Europeans, still found them full of faults: they were vindictive, suspicious, ungrateful, flighty, lazy, "brutal in their pleasures," and "cruel to their enemies." Millar was not departing from Lafitau when he offered the following breezy assessment: "From the extreme insensibility which is so observable in the character of all savage nations, it is no wonder they should entertain the grossest ideas concerning those female virtues which in a polished nation are supposed to constitute the honour and dignity of the sex." Millar marveled at the indifference with which marriages were contracted among the "savages" and their lack of concern with premarital sex. Like Lafitau, whom he cites on this point, he finds parallels to their customs among ancient peoples, but then goes a step further and develops analogies with contemporary tribal groups described in travel literature about the Kamchatka Peninsula of Russia and various nations of Asia (Pegu [Myanmar], Siam [Thailand], Cochinchina [Vietnam], and Cambodia).[23]

Montesquieu had taught that political, military, and sexual differences in different parts of the world could be explained by climate; the relative weakness of Asia and strength of Europe, the slavery of Asia and liberty of Europe, he maintained, followed from Europe's location in a temperate zone, whereas in Asia there was no zone between the very cold and very hot. Montesquieu paid little attention to the Americas because of his focus on the despotic East, but his ideas about climate resonated widely. Yet Millar followed Smith in downplaying the effect of climate, which could hardly explain the relative "savagery" of the North American Indigenous peoples, since their climate was the same as that of Europe. Like Smith, Millar instead emphasized the means of subsistence:

> A savage who earns his food by hunting and fishing, or by gathering the spontaneous fruits of the earth, is incapable of attaining any considerable refinement in his pleasures. He finds so much difficulty and is exposed to so many hardships, in procuring the mere necessaries, that he has no leisure or encouragement to aim at the luxuries and conveniences of life.

The character of the Indigenous people was not different from that of Europeans. Millar insisted that "man is everywhere the same; and we must necessarily conclude, that the untutored Indian and the civilized European have acted upon the same principles." What differed was their level of prosperity.[24]

Neither French nor English intellectuals showed this same concern with civilizational questions and the place of North American Indigenous groups on the trajectory toward "refinement." The Scots may have been influenced by living in such close proximity to their own "savages," those of the Highlands. The Scottish intellectual elite came from the Lowlands, but the Highlands were right next door, as its 1745 uprising in favor of "Bonnie Prince Charlie," the last Stuart claimant to the British throne, made abundantly clear. The opinions of the Lowlands writer John Pinkerton strike a racist note that echoed in the England and Scotland of his day. In his history of early Scotland published in 1789, Pinkerton minced no words:

> The Lowlanders are acute, industrious, sensible, erect, free. The Highlanders stupid, indolent, foolish, fawning, slavish. The former in short have every attribute of a civilized people. The later are absolute savages: and, like Indians and Negroes, will ever continue so. For a

people, which has continued savage from their origin till now, will infallibly remain so till the race be lost by mixture. Their savage indolence forbids all ideas of cultivation.

Millar would never have gone that far, but he did once remark, in a footnote in his 1773 edition, that "it cannot be disputed that an English waggoner has more of an independent spirit than is to be found among persons of low rank in the highlands of Scotland."[25]

Whatever the reason for his and other Scots' interest in stages, the study of "savages" helped convince Millar that the status of women was signally important, a truth that he had already learned from Montesquieu but now could put into an evolutionary historical context. He may also have been influenced by his own life decisions; he took his professorial post because it had a more regular income than private practice and he wanted to marry and start a family, which eventually included eleven surviving children. Smith and David Hume, in contrast, were lifelong bachelors, though Lord Kames married and had two children. (As a young man, Millar briefly tutored Kames's son and became something of a protégé of the judge and philosopher.)[26]

Millar's interest in the standing of women did not derive from his own travels. Unlike many Scots, he had little experience of the world outside Scotland. For a land of at most 1.5 million people, Scotland produced a staggering array of expatriates and emigrants. Tens of thousands uprooted themselves for the British North American colonies, the Caribbean, England, Ireland, and Europe. Thousands more worked for colonial services or far-flung merchant companies. Millar, in contrast, never went to Paris, a favorite destination for many Scottish intellectuals, including Hume and Smith, and only visited London twice; for most of his long life he stayed close to Glasgow and his family.

When he first published his *Observations* in 1771 as a thirty-six-year-old law professor, Millar was just beginning to make his reputation as the most renowned professor of law of the time in all of Britain. He was expected to lecture at length on the Digest of Justinian (Roman law) and on feudal law, canon law, and Scots law. Later he added English law. The lecture notes of his students reveal that he used Roman law as the starting point for his wide-ranging comparisons. Discussion of Smith on moral sentiments and Edmund Burke's differences from Smith appeared in the midst of his discussion of Justinian. Even after publishing the first and second editions of *Observations*, Millar continued to add new material in his lectures and to the book.[27]

Millar maintained a kindly atmosphere in the lecture hall, no doubt facilitated by his decision to lecture in English rather than Latin. He provided his pupils with a clear sense of what he expected of them and even encouraged his students to ask for clarification or raise objections, a rare informality for the time—and so unlike the many law professors who were known for their dry and tiresome lectures.[28]

Letters written by two of his boarders, Frederick and William Lamb, provide a glimpse of his family life. Their mother, Lady Melbourne, sent twenty-year-old William (a future prime minister) to study with Millar in 1799–1800 because it was considered good training for the English bar, to which William was destined. Seventeen-year-old Frederick wrote to his mother describing three other boarders who were also students. Given the number of Millar's own children, the atmosphere in the house must have been energetic. Frederick complained to his mother "that there is nothing heard of in this house but study" and that "all the ladies here are contaminated with an itch for philosophy and learning." He admitted that "one of the Miss Millars is pretty, but they are all philosophers."[29]

The most popular conduct book for girls in Scotland at the time recommended that "if you happen to have any learning, keep it a profound secret, especially from the men, who generally look with a jealous and malignant eye on a woman of great parts." Clearly, then, for Millar, the status of women was not just an abstract scholarly concern. He encouraged his own daughters to learn, even if it meant study at home. (Women were admitted for the first time to the University of London in

1878 and to Scottish universities in 1889. Cambridge University did not permit women to take full degrees until 1948.) He regularly consulted his wife about his writings and often read passages to the assembled family. William Lamb did not comment on women's desire for learning in the same way as his younger brother, but he did notice the similarity between English and Scottish tea rituals: "We drink healths at dinner, hand round the cake at tea, and put our spoons into our cups when we desire to have no more, but exactly in the same manner as we used to behave at Hatfield, at Eton, and at Cambridge."[30]

Millar was not the only Scot to pay attention to the role of women, which raises the question of why Scottish intellectuals put so much emphasis on women as harbingers of civilization. French women supposedly excelled in conversation, and many of the Scottish intellectuals had been to Paris and witnessed this firsthand. Women had gained public notice more readily in England than in Scotland, especially as novelists and painters, if only because they had greater access there to printers and exhibition spaces. Yet neither French nor English philosophers developed the civilizational narrative in the same way.

A peculiar combination of "advancement" and "backwardness" seems to have fostered the Scots' concern with civilization, commerce, and the role of women. While the Scots were always looking over their shoulders at England and finding there a level of sophistication for which they sometimes longed, they also enjoyed some advantages over their southern neighbors. They had much closer contact with the Continent, both in commerce and ideas. Their four universities (England had only two) had evolved from seminaries of Calvinism in the seventeenth century into institutions known for their openness to studies of natural philosophy, medicine, and law in the eighteenth. Moreover, the lingering ambivalence created by the official union with England after 1707 created a space for Scottish intellectuals to follow their own paths of inquiry.[31]

Scottish intellectuals, too, were living through an especially rapid transformation in their economy from a relatively impoverished, largely agricultural society into a much more vibrant commercial society. Between 1700 and 1800, the proportion of the Scottish population living in towns with over ten thousand inhabitants more than tripled, reaching 17 percent; in the same period, the proportion of the English population living in large towns increased by just over half, reaching 20 percent. The value of linen produced in Scotland increased sixfold between 1728 and 1771, the year of the publication of Millar's first edition. Imports to Scotland increased threefold between 1755 and 1771, and re-exports shot up more than fivefold in the same short period. Sugar imports doubled in the same time frame and then increased even more dramatically in the late 1770s, 1780s, and 1790s. About half of the sugar was re-exported. Economic changes in the nineteenth century would be even more dramatic, but those of the eighteenth century gave intellectuals much to ponder.[32]

There are no comparable statistics for tea because Scotland got so much tea illegally from Swedish, Danish, Dutch, and Belgian sources. In fact, tea reveals a great deal about the Scots' fraught relationship with England. Smuggling was more rampant than in England in part because it was supported by local people as a way of putting a thumb in the eye of the English. The Scottish jurist Duncan Forbes railed against this illegal trade in 1744:

> When the Connection which the Dealers in this Country had with many *Scotsmen* in the Service of the *Swedish* Company at *Gottenburg* [*sic*], introduced the common use of that *Drug* [tea] amongst the *lowest* of the People; —when *Sugar*, the inseparable Companion of *Tea*, came to be in the Possession of the very *poorest* Housewife, where formerly it had been a great rarity . . . the Effects were very *suddenly* and very *severely* felt [the excise tax revenue dropped].

Tea drinking had become common in Scotland by 1720 and widespread by 1750 when tea, sometimes mixed with brandy, replaced ale at the breakfast table and was increasingly sipped in the afternoon at ladies' tea parties. The term "tea table" only became common in English after 1750, when the new customs of tea drinking and their elevation of the status of women began to attract extended commentary.[33]

Even in the remotest Highlands, peddlers sold packets of tea alongside imported tobacco and snuff. The budget for an ordinary working family of six in Dumfriesshire from the 1790s showed the greatest expense for the staple of the poor, oatmeal (four times more than what the family paid for rent), but it included the same amount for tea and sugar as was spent on soap, salt, and candles. Tea and sugar had become necessities in Scotland, too, and tea in particular was caught up in the new Scottish enthusiasm for trading with China.[34]

Some of the most important Canton tea traders were Scots, but not necessarily on behalf of British commercial interests. The experience of Colin Campbell is illuminating. He had to flee London after the financial crash of the early 1720s known as the South Sea Bubble left him with large debts as a speculator. First he joined the recently established Ostend East India Company as an assistant supercargo in 1723, and by the time it folded in 1731, he had managed to become one of three founding directors of the Swedish East India Company. He went as supercargo and representative of the king to the Chinese court on the Swedish company's first voyage to China in 1732, and from his diary of the voyage we know that he carefully studied the price and quality differentials of both tea and porcelain, commenting on what the English and French paid. He thought he could get black Bohea tea, the main tea destined for ordinary consumers, for less than his competitors paid but complained that the English took all the good-quality porcelain. The British government in London followed Campbell's activities with great worry about the potential for competition with English commercial interests.[35]

Campbell was far from alone. A recent study has shown that some fifty Britons joined the Swedish company in its first two decades of existence, and the majority of them were Scots. The correspondence of another supercargo reveals that they often carried on a substantial private trade, not registered in official records of either the companies or the customs office. In 1738–39, Campbell's friend Charles Irvine, of Aberdeen, assembled a private cargo in China of 273 chests and 48 tubs of fine teas, 1,424 Indian cotton textiles brought in from Madras, 223 pieces of Chinese wrought silks, and 70 bales of raw silk, as well as various other drugs and souvenirs. Irvine, too, had had connections to the Ostend company, and he used his agents there to sell his goods on the Continent. He no doubt also had personal networks of petty smugglers in addition to his contacts with wholesalers in Britain and on the Continent. Between the 1730s and 1780s, the Swedish and Danish companies together imported almost as much tea from China as the London East India Company, and it is estimated that 90 percent of their tea was re-exported, no doubt much of it illegally to England and Scotland. No wonder Forbes was so agitated about the imports of the Swedish company and their connection to the Scots.[36]

Tea thus played a distinct role in the Scots' relationship with England, the Continent, and the wider world. Even officials responsible for maintaining the official monopoly on tea bought tea that was smuggled. Tea could be sold by peddlers in rural areas and by retail shops, licensed and unlicensed, in the towns. For example, the market town of Crieff, population less than three thousand at the end of the eighteenth century, housed no fewer than nineteen shops selling tea. Tea also facilitated women's crossings between the private and public spheres: not only did women preside over tea tables that reached beyond the private sphere, but they also bought tea for the household. An analysis of one merchant's account books in the market town of Dumfries in the 1750s shows that nearly half the customers for tea were women.[37]

Women entered the public sphere in other ways, too: public concerts took shape in the early 1700s (the Edinburgh Musical Society was founded in 1728); literacy was increasing, though female literacy

TEA AND HOW WOMEN BECAME "CIVILIZED" • 31

was lower in Scotland than in England at mid-century; and theater and balls enjoyed continuing popularity. All these followed from the rising levels of disposable income in Scotland, and the consumption of tea was in many ways the most conspicuous indication of that prosperity as well as being an engine of it.[38]

While it is unlikely that female conversation played a greater role in Scotland than in England or France, it seems to have drawn particular attention from Scottish writers, if only because it was an even more recent phenomenon in Scotland. David Hume described the "fair sex" as "sovereigns of the empire of conversation," and David Fordyce wrote less playfully in his influential *Dialogues concerning Education* of 1745 that "it is the Business and particular Interest of Women to excel in Conversation, and in the amiable Decencies of Life, and to delight and polish the Men by their Softness and Delicacy in Speaking." According to Fordyce's female character Cleora, that was the view taught to her by her uncle and guardian, who also held that "Speech is one of the best Instruments of Female Power, by which they calm the Storms of Passion, and charm our rude Natures into a softer Kind of Humanity."[39]

It is hardly surprising, then, that conversation loomed large for Millar as a sign of civilization. Women in the "early ages" were "seldom permitted to have any conversation or correspondence" with their men. As societies managed to produce more than the bare necessities of life, they became "more refined in their taste, and luxurious in their manner of living." The consequences for women were immediate:

> The fair sex are more universally admired and courted upon account of the agreeable qualities which they possess, and upon account of the amusement which their conversation affords. They are encouraged to quit that retirement which was formerly esteemed so suitable to their character, to enlarge the sphere of their acquaintance, and to appear in mixed company, and in public meetings of pleasure. They lay aside the spindle and the distaff, and engage in other

employments more agreeable to the fashion. As they are introduced more into public life, they are led to cultivate those talents which are adapted to the intercourse of the world.

Yet all was not as rosy as it might seem. As Fordyce's didactic passages make clear, the point of women's conversation was to "delight and polish" men; their function was still defined by their relationship to them.[40]

The association between women and civilization therefore proved to be ambiguous. Because civilization, like tea drinking, was now associated with feminization, effeminacy loomed as a potential limit to the civilizing process. Millar clearly articulates the perceived threat:

> It would seem, however, that there are certain limits beyond which it is impossible to push the improvements arising from wealth and opulence. The love of pleasure, when carried to excess, is apt to weaken and destroy those passions which it endeavours to gratify; and in opulent and luxurious nations, the free intercourse of the sexes gives rise to licentious and dissolute manners, inconsistent with the good order, and with the more important interests of society.

Montesquieu's luxury, corruption, and vice still lurked as a menace, even in advanced nations. In the "eastern nations," such voluptuousness leads to polygamy, Millar asserts; in the West, to prostitution. Most at danger are France and parts of Italy, where "improvements, in the state and accomplishments of the fair sex," have reached their apex. Similar improvements had made their way to England and Germany but had not gone as far because there people paid attention to the "more necessary and useful arts."[41]

In later editions, Millar developed this view even further, but largely by reference to the history of ancient Rome, thus demonstrating that a cyclical view of human history implicitly pulled against the narrative of progress. His key passage, cited earlier, is modified at the end:

The love of pleasure, when carried to excess, is apt to weaken and destroy those passions which it endeavours to gratify, and to pervert those appetites which nature has bestowed upon mankind for the most beneficial purposes. The natural tendency, therefore, of great luxury and dissipation is to diminish the rank and dignity of women, by preventing all refinement in their connection with the other sex, and rendering them only subservient to the purposes of animal enjoyment.

Despite the general Scottish dislike for Rousseau's entirely conjectural history of the origins of society, most figures of the Scottish Enlightenment endorsed views of women's place that were much like his. Women should be educated to at least read and write and be able to converse with men, but they should not be too free. Their primary role was to educate children and soften the more martial side of their menfolk. Montesquieu's "thrall of manners" meant ingrained constraint.[42]

Yet Millar's evolutionary history had a logic that could not be entirely denied. If "advancement" (one of Millar's favorite words) of society inevitably impacted the status of women, then continuing improvement might lead to as yet unforeseen changes. Millar may not have seized upon this in the case of women, but he did ardently advocate the abolition of the slave trade as well as various parliamentary reform causes. From the very first edition of his book (published more than a decade before the formation of the first abolitionist societies in Britain), Millar denounced plantation slavery: "In whatever light we regard the institution of slavery, it appears equally inconvenient and pernicious." He began with the economic argument, that free labor was much more productive, but he concluded with an argument about "good morals." Slavery dehumanized the enslaved ("to cast a man out from the privileges of society, and to mark his condition with infamy"), but it also produced "inhumanity" in the masters. He concluded that "it is matter of regret that any species of slavery should still remain in the dominions of Great Britain, in which liberty is generally so well understood, and so highly valued."[43]

It is thus not surprising that Millar played a key role in drafting a petition from the university in 1792 to support the abolition of the slave trade. By then the case was being made even more explicitly on moral and rights grounds:

> Both in our individual capacity, and as members of a public seminary, we think ourselves called upon, at this juncture, to express our disapprobation of the African Slave Trade, and humbly pray for its abolition as an existing evil of infinite magnitude; as an evil which comprehends in it the most obvious violation of the feelings of nature, of the prescripts of morality, and of those doctrines and duties inculcated in the Gospel, which forms the basis of our most holy religion.

Millar had made no religious arguments for abolition in his published work, but the abolitionist movement in Britain, of which this petition aimed to be part, had strong religious affiliations.[44]

Millar's arguments might seem cautiously moderate to us now, but that was not how they were seen at the time. Many Scots directly participated in the slave trade or indirectly benefited from it, and few Scottish philosophers took an active role in abolitionist societies. Already in 1771, Millar was referring to the "natural rights and liberties of mankind," though not explicitly in reference to slavery. It is perhaps to be expected that he was much more receptive to the French Revolution than some of his compatriots. In 1791, he helped organize a public dinner to celebrate the second anniversary of the fall of the Bastille.[45]

Millar did not support revolution within Britain, but the raising of the political temperature inevitably brought his reformist views into question. British authorities spied on and then began arresting, prosecuting, and ultimately transporting Scottish radicals such as Thomas Muir to Botany Bay, the penal colony in Australia. Muir, a leading member

TEA AND HOW WOMEN BECAME "CIVILIZED" · 35

of the Society of the Friends of the People in Edinburgh (a pro-French revolutionary group), had studied law with Millar for two years in the 1780s, and they had remained friends.

Some sense of the hysteria caused in Britain by the French Revolution can be gathered from the way the chief judge summed up the evidence for the jury in the 1793 sedition trial of Muir:

> *First*, That the British constitution is the best that ever was since the creation of the world and it is not possible to make it better. . . . The *next* circumstance is, that there was a spirit of sedition in this country last winter, which made every good man very uneasy. . . . Yet Mr. Muir had at that time gone about among ignorant country people, making them forget their work, and told them that a Reform was absolutely necessary for preserving their liberty, which, if it had not been for him, they would never have thought was in danger. His Lordship did not doubt that this would appear to them [the jury], as it did to him, as sedition.

Millar had been Muir's teacher at the university, and another student's father claimed that Millar "was, in truth, a most dangerous man in times when young men wished to be set free from every shackle which restrained their turbulent passions." Another went even further: "I would certainly prefer finishing my son's education in a brothel to a school where his political principles were likely to become contaminated. . . . In some instances the teachers in the public seminaries of this kingdom profess themselves Republicans."[46]

An early biographer of Thomas Muir insisted that "every lover of liberty reveres [Millar's] memory." The name John Millar no longer echoes in the same way, and insofar as his work still attracts attention, it is often for his theory of European superiority. While there is certainly no doubt that this notion of superiority went on to wreak havoc in the world, it is less clear that this was Millar's intention. He studied a variety of legal systems and surveyed travel literature in order to grasp the rationales of their differing customs, never losing sight that "Man is everywhere the same" and acts upon the "same principles." His accomplishments in laying the foundations for sociology, especially in relation to political economy, were significant. Millar did not tie any of this to tea because he discussed food only in the most general terms and drink not at all. Yet he did notice which societies allowed women to eat at table with their menfolk and clearly rated higher those societies that did so. In the end, what is most striking about Millar is the consistency of his principles. His concern for his own family, including the girls, for his students and friends, and for a host of reform causes reveals him as a man who put his principles into practice every day, no matter the cost.[47]

REVOLUTIONARY IMAGERY AND THE UNCOVERING OF SOCIETY

INTELLECTUALS IN FRANCE FOLLOWED THE WRITINGS OF Scottish philosophers, including Millar's. Like many books that publishers hoped to get by official French censors, Millar's *Observations* was published in French in Amsterdam in 1773. An anonymous reviewer wanted more development by Millar of the political consequences of his study but considered it a step forward in the ongoing attempt to get free from "the theological spirit" that "explained all sources of corruption by original sin." The "immense machine" that made society run was just beginning to be understood.[1]

Society was coming into view toward the end of the eighteenth century, and then the French Revolution of 1789 gave it new urgency. No one said explicitly at the time that the idea of society had gained in clarity. But the sharp rise in references in French to "social" and "society" in the 1790s, the emergence of "social science" as a term and potential discipline, and the first uses of the expression "social organization" all indicate conceptual ferment among writers and politicians. Others were contributing in a different manner through art. For society is not just a concept; it is a set of relations that are encountered in private and public spaces. Those encounters appear prominently in many of the prints produced during the French Revolution. By their nature as visual depictions in a time of political crisis, prints called on viewers to take conscious notice of the way French people interacted with each other.[2]

Prints produced during this period often depicted social relationships—whether naturalistically, commemoratively, comically, or satirically—and in so doing brought those relationships into question. At the same time, the intentions of revolutionary printmakers were often obscure because little is known about them or about the reception given to their work. Prints did not make society visible all on their own, but they did offer contemporaries a way of seeing and thereby taking distance from their society and customary social relations. The space created by visualization thus fostered new ways of reflecting about society.[3]

The printing of images in France was increasing before the French Revolution but expanded dramatically as the political crisis unfolded after 1787. Although it is impossible to be precise about the figures for print production, the prints currently in the collections of the French National Library can be considered an indicator: the number rises by about half from the 1750s to the 1770s and then more than doubles between the end of the 1770s and the years 1787–1791. This sudden proliferation of prints was almost entirely due to the making of images related to the revolutionary rupture. The French National Library holds six to seven thousand images related to revolutionary events, with the largest single collection, known as the De Vinck collection after the collector, Belgian baron Eugène de Vinck de Deux-Orp (1859–1931), including some 5,200 unique images for the period 1789–1799.[4]

The stream of printed images channeled only part of a sudden demand for portrayal of all sorts. With the loosening of censorship, writers rushed pamphlets and newspapers into production. After the National Assembly abolished theatrical monopolies, the number of theaters in Paris rose from nine before 1789 to fifty during the revolutionary decade; on average, there were twenty-three performances a day in Paris between 1789 and 1799. Similarly, when the assembly opened the biannual art exhibition to all comers, the Salon of 1791 included twice as many works as the Salon of 1789 and three times as many exhibitors. With the reorganization of government, official letters with new seals and letterheads and in particular the introduction of paper money put untold numbers of new images into circulation. There was much more to be seen than ever before.[5]

Although the relaxing of censorship facilitated this outpouring, the frenzy of image making also reflected an underlying crisis of meaning. Would the traditional monarchical and aristocratic regime give way to a different political and social order? What would the new regime look like, figuratively and literally? Images had buttressed the monarchy, but they could also undermine it once the floodgates opened. As the monarchy gave way to a republic and the republic took increasingly radical measures, prints reflected and also interpreted those upheavals. While newspapers and pamphlets gave verbal expression to the hopes and fears prompted by rapidly escalating events, prints compressed and abstracted them and gave them an edge that might, or might not, be consciously grasped by the viewer. Printmakers thus responded to the crisis of meaning and at the same time deepened it. Visualization heightened the sense that the political and social orders were changing in unexpected ways. By rendering those transformations, visual images showed that the rules governing society were not fixed. This evident mutability inspired intellectuals to develop a science of society.

The large number of prints testifies to the astonishment and uncertainty created by rapid changes in the political regime and the social makeovers implied by those changes. Everything had to be depicted in order to be more fully comprehended: the personalities involved (about one-third of the images in the French Revolution Digital Archive are portraits), the unfolding events, the places, and the shifting social customs. The prints did not just describe persons or events; they helped establish the significance of personalities and events.[6]

The supposedly anodyne genre of portraits provides an excellent example of the ways in which visualization could shape political understanding and therefore political outcomes. As art historian Amy Freund has shown, the collections of portraits of deputies that were rushed into print in the summer of 1789 made the implicit but nonetheless potent argument that the deputies represented the nation as much as the king did. They did this visually by framing the deputies the same way they framed the king. The king had prescribed the costume of all the deputies to the Estates General. Only nobles could wear plumed hats, silk breeches and jackets, and gold facings. The deputies to the Third Estate were ordered to wear black cloaks without facings, black jackets, woolen breeches, and unadorned hats. The crown and the court wanted to maintain the visual signs of social difference; the print collections of deputy portraits underlined similarity by putting their heads in the same frames. The Third Estate deputy Michel Gérard, a self-described farmer from Brittany, chose an unusual presentation of self for his portrait; unlike many Third Estate deputies, he does not wear a wig or a cravat at the opening of his coat. With his natural hair and simple dress, he stands for informality and rural virtue, at the opposite end of the spectrum from aristocratic pretense. By offering these series of portraits of the deputies to the public, with both their subtle similarities and obvious differences, the engravers and print merchants helped establish the collective importance of the deputies and their claim to represent the nation, not just their various estates (clergy, nobility, Third Estate), at the meeting of the Estates General that began in May 1789.[7]

By elevating the Third Estate deputies to a visual equivalence with the king and aristocrats, the prints implicitly challenged the stability of the monarchical regime and laid out, less explicitly to be sure, the possible bases of a new regime in which the deputies would claim powers for the nation. The prints did not directly inspire the Third Estate deputies to demand sovereignty for the nation, which the deputies proceeded to do, but the prints did help prepare the way by making palpable to all viewers the equivalence between deputies representing the nation and the king. Since the publisher of these particular prints, Nicolas-François Levachez, hired seven artists to draw the sketches and seventeen engravers to prepare the plates, it is evident that he, and others like him, anticipated a sizable market for such prints. Most people sensed that something momentous was taking place, and they grasped at anything that might clarify the situation for them. Even portraits could prompt viewers to rethink the political and social order and in the process gain greater distance from the one they lived in.[8]

While it is impossible to speak with great confidence about the chronology of print production because so many of the prints are undated or are dated only very generally by the French National Library (for

Portrait of Louis XVI. Etching with tools, 23.5 × 18 cm, engraved by A. Sergent, Paris, 1789. *Bibliothèque Nationale de France*

Portrait of Michel Gérard, Deputy to the Estates General from Brittany. Aquatint, 23.5 × 18 cm, engraved by Antoine Louis François Sergent, drawn by C. Lefebvre, Paris, 1789. *Bibliothèque Nationale de France*

example, 1789–1792, 1793–1799, 1798–1815), the French Revolution Digital Archive provides evidence that seems credible: prints related to revolutionary events appeared in the greatest numbers in the early years, 1789–1791, and then dropped off but remained significant in number for the rest of the decade.[9]

Although many of the prints available in the collections of the French National Library are in color (because collectors preferred them), they were usually colored by hand rather than through the printing process, and the majority of prints published at the time were no doubt black and white. When the Committee of Public Safety, the emergency executive arm of government in 1793–94, decided to commission prints for propaganda purposes in early 1794, it ordered nine hundred to one thousand copies of each, two-thirds of them in black and white and only one-third in color. Colored prints cost about twice as much as black-and-white ones. Prices varied according to the amount of work required to produce a print, but in general the peddlers paid 5 to 10 sous for the cheapest prints and then resold them for 10 to 15 sous at a time when bread, the staple of the lower classes, cost 1 to 3 sous a pound and the daily wages of ordinary workers ranged from 20 to 50 sous (20 sous = 1 livre). Although many could afford an occasional purchase, the displays of prints outside shops and along the river quays proved to be a constant attraction.[10]

Evidence concerning how people felt when they viewed such prints is difficult to find, but there are two contemporary commentators of note, one from the political right and one from the political center left. Both referred to specific images. The first, the journalist Jacques-Marie Boyer-Brun, known as Boyer de Nîmes, wrote about the initial explosion of anti-aristocratic, anti-clerical, and anti-monarchical images from the standpoint of someone who bemoaned their corrosive effects. The second, the writer and deputy Louis-Sébastien Mercier, focused on images produced in the years after the end of the radical emergency regime of 1793–94 (often referred to as "the Terror").[11]

Boyer was a fervent Catholic royalist from Nîmes, a city in southern France that had long been a hotbed of Calvinism, even when Calvinism was officially outlawed. After 1787, when Calvinists gained a measure of legal toleration, the prosperous Protestant elite of Nîmes saw its chance. More than half of the deputies elected from the region to the Estates General were Protestants. During regional elections in June 1790, tensions came to a head when armed Catholics threatened those voting in Nîmes. In response, Protestants organized themselves and more than three hundred people died in street fighting, most of them Catholics. Boyer had founded his own journal in Nîmes in 1786 and was at first favorable to the revolution. He accepted election as deputy attorney general for Nîmes in March 1790, but after publishing anti-revolutionary and anti-Protestant writings in reaction to the June killings, he fled to Paris, where he continued to work as a journal editor and collected caricatures that formed the source for his 1792 book about them. His religious convictions enhanced his appreciation of the power of images, which no doubt also derived from his career as a journalist.

Boyer's *History of the Caricatures of the Revolt of the French* was first announced as appearing in weekly installments beginning April 1, 1792. Each installment was supposed to include two etchings with bister wash (grayish-brown color) of caricatures along with thirty-two pages of analysis. The announced subscription price was 50 livres per year (for four volumes), which put it out of the reach of ordinary people. In fact, Boyer ended up publishing fifty-one reproductions of caricatures (not counting the frontispieces to his two eventual volumes) and six hundred pages of text between April and August 1792, with great variation in the length of analysis for each caricature. Subscribers were meant to organize the book binding themselves and were sent the frontispieces for that purpose, but the volumes could also be purchased separately at the office of Boyer's paper *Journal du peuple* (Journal of the people).[12]

Although he had commissioned almost no illustrations for his journal in Nîmes, Boyer came to see prints as "the thermometer that registers

"They only wanted what was good for us." Boyer's reproduction of the anonymous print "Ils ne vouloient que notre bien," 1789–90, bister etching with tools, 14.5 × 9 cm (the original hand-colored etching was 22 × 33 cm). *Bibliothèque Nationale de France*

the degree of public opinion," and therefore, "those who know how to master their variations also know how to master public opinion." The prospectus for his book made the aim explicit: "The author will demonstrate in the first part of this work that every means was employed to overthrow the altar and the throne and it will be shown that caricatures were one of the means used with the greatest skill, perseverance, and success to mislead and whip up the people." Boyer did not hesitate to show caricatures that demeaned the king and the royal family, but always with the aim of denouncing what he saw as the revolutionaries' goal of fomenting civil war and overthrowing the monarchy.[13]

Boyer displayed particular interest in the psychological effects of prints. He analyzed an anonymous etching with the sardonic title, "They only wanted what was good for us," which showed a kneeling peasant in the foreground being blessed by a grossly fat bishop in exchange for two sacks of money. To the right of the first peasant is another even more pathetic one who is being allowed to kiss his noble lord's hand (the noble, like the bishop, is recognizable by his distinctive hat). This peasant does not see that the lord is holding an iron collar and chain to keep him in servitude. Boyer claims that the third figure in the background is a magistrate taking money from a client in exchange for a few lines of writing and that the overall point is to show the bad faith of the upper classes and the good-heartedness and stupidity of the peasantry. Boyer is right about the first two scenes but the figure in the background looks like a caricature of a Jewish moneylender rather than a judge. He has a hunchback, a hooked nose, and a hat that resembles a fez, all seen in caricatures of Jewish moneylenders. One of the most prominent defenders of the rights of Jews, the Catholic priest Henri Grégoire, nonetheless included page after page about the evils of Jewish moneylending in his prizewinning 1788 "Essay on the Physical, Moral and Political Regeneration of the Jews." Boyer himself accused the Jews of southern France of collaborating with Protestants in encouraging uprisings and argued against giving Jews the right to hold office alongside "Mohammedans, idolators, actors, [and] executioners." (Jews had gained political rights in September 1791, non-Catholics, actors and executioners in December 1789.) Yet Boyer did not see—or want to recognize—the Jewish moneylender in this image.[14]

That the figure depicted might be a Jewish moneylender does not work against Boyer's main point, however. The portrayal of abasement by means of the supplicant postures of the two peasants in the foreground contrasts vividly with the evident grossness of features of those on top. Boyer imagines an ordinary "man of the people" who would "feel humiliated" when viewing this print: "Like the imbeciles that are being mocked here I had respect and confidence in the clergy, the nobility, and the parlements [high courts], who must not be as respectable as I believed since someone dares to denounce them . . . in ways that would be avoided if they did not deserve it."[15]

Although Boyer's assumptions about the humiliation felt by a man of the people might be contested, he makes the important point that etchings like this one are a process of visual communication that includes the artist's, engraver's, and publisher's intentions (not necessarily identical) and the reactions of a viewer. His reproduction of the print adds another layer of ambiguity to the communication process because his intentions are most likely not the same as those of the original printmaker. Boyer wants to show how prints are used to provoke lower-class viewers into seeing the injustice of their subordination, whereas another viewer might simply interpret the image as critical of those same people for their unseeing subservience. Boyer shows, nonetheless, that some observers at the time recognized the power of the printed images that were inundating public spaces. He gives pride of place to the emotions triggered in that viewer and the ways in which those emotions prompt the development of new attitudes. Seeing the humiliation of the lower orders presumably provokes the opposite response in viewers. They experience a kind of revulsion at their previous subservience to those now being mocked. The vulgarity of the upper classes reinforces the social imputation of the image. If the upper classes—the clergy and nobility—are coarse, why are the lower classes thinking of themselves as lesser?

Boyer abhorred the notion of equality, which is why this image and others like it upset him. He believed that Protestants had leagued with the Jansenists (dissident Catholics), Physiocrats (free-trade economists), and Freemasons to spur the French to revolt, which was "a necessary consequence of the insubordinate principles of equality set down by *John Calvin* [his emphasis]." Liberty really meant anti-clericalism, and equality was trumpeted in order "to insinuate that the king was only a man like any other." The "sublime" equality promised in the declaration of rights ended up being "equality of incoherent and illusory systems, equality of absurdities and extravagances, equality of impiety, apostasy and revolt against those in power." Such caricatures could be found on all the quays of the Seine and in virtually every square and intersection, he complained, and they spoke directly to viewers in a way that the written word could not. Through their manipulation of sentiments, the prints compelled viewers to take stock of themselves and their place in the system of social relations. In this way, the prints did more than frame events or create personalities; they encouraged viewers to think socially, to criticize the status quo, to desire social leveling, and even to reflect about the nature of social relations more generally. Boyer would ultimately pay dearly for his views. In May 1794, the revolutionary court in Paris condemned him to death on the grounds that he had encouraged violence against patriots in Nîmes.[16]

Although Boyer devoted much more sustained attention to prints than did other right-wing journalists, he was not alone in bemoaning the influence of them. Toward the end of 1790, the deliberately outrageous royalist journal *Actes des apôtres* (Acts of the apostles) offered a brief story about a pro-revolutionary national guardsman interpreting caricatures for those passing by. This "caricaturo-patriotic professor" pointed to the woman in an image who was breastfeeding a wolf while her son languished next to her. The wolf, the guardsman explained, stood for the ferocity of the aristocracy. The inscription in English, "political affection," must refer to [the Duchess of] Polignac, the guardsman insisted, one of the queen's most notorious favorites. Those listening applauded while guffawing and went away quite happy with his interpretation. "At this level the revolution costs the people nothing," the article concluded, "but they will end up paying hugely for it." The wolf in question was no doubt a fox, however, for the print was most likely Thomas Rowlandson's 1784 etching with the same title. It satirized Georgiana Cavendish, Duchess of Devonshire, for her support of Charles Fox (hence the fox) and the Whigs. The anecdote again underlines the uncertainties inherent in visual communication, not to mention the possible repurposing of prints. Boyer's dismay about anti-monarchical images was shared in June 1791 by the counterrevolutionary *Journal de la cour et de la ville* (Journal of the court and the town). It inveighed against "the atrocious caricatures that the image merchants, especially of the Palais-Royal, spread out before the eyes of every passer-by."[17]

The anti-revolutionaries were not alone in recognizing the appeal of the prints appearing in many public places. In the fall of 1789, *Journal des révolutions de l'Europe* reported that "at all of our illustrators" across the city "you can see prints that are infinitely amusing to the masses and that maintain their hatred for the aristocracy." The anonymous author then went on to describe a pair of caricatures that can be readily identified despite some variation in the titles. One is "I Knew We'd Have Our Turn," one of many prints depicting the reversal of the social order with a peasant sitting on top of a noble who is hanging on to a clergyman. The author did not find these images dangerous or mean-spirited but clearly thought they were designed primarily for the illiterate who could be moved emotionally by viewing them. Such images were meant for "that portion of the public whose imagination is stirred when something hits their eyes rather than speaking to their intelligence."[18]

The pro-revolutionary press reported as well on the conflicts aroused by images, whether in print shops or out in the street. *Révolutions de Paris*, a weekly that offered a print with each issue, complained of the treatment of a print seller in its edition of July 9–16, 1791. The date was significant because the king and his family had just been forcibly brought back to Paris after their failed attempt to flee. The merchant had reported a man to local authorities after the fellow entered his shop and tore to pieces two prints that he found offensive. But the merchant soon found himself arrested for selling an "incendiary print." The editor of the weekly professed surprise that a print about a white elephant that was meant to mock Siamese religion could be found incendiary or lacking in respect to authorities. Yet he admitted that the print was based on one that appeared in *Révolutions de Paris* a couple of months earlier that had been meant as a satire of the king, the mayor of Paris, and Lafayette in his role as head of the national guard. Prints could capture and condense feelings on opposing sides of the political divide, and in so doing

REVOLUTIONARY IMAGERY AND THE UNCOVERING OF SOCIETY · 49

they could themselves become the object of fury. In its edition of May 30, 1792, *Courrier français* noted that "caricatures on the shameful English commerce in human flesh [the slave trade] were posted in every street but no sooner were they stuck up than they were removed from the eyes of the people."[19]

The only other sustained commentator on revolutionary images besides Boyer was Louis-Sébastien Mercier, a centrist republican who expressed his own ambivalence about popular prints in the late 1790s. They could serve valuable purposes by reminding viewers of the horrors of the Terror (1793–94) or criticizing the more outlandish versions of contemporary fashion. Yet they could also illustrate obscene books or simply amuse passersby with their renditions of current customs. Like Boyer, Mercier was unusual in his attention to prints, and like his political opposite, his partisan views only intensified his appreciation for the power of such depictions.

Mercier served as a deputy between 1792 and 1797 and spent more than a year in prison in 1793–94 because of his support for the Girondins, the moderate republican opponents of Maximilien Robespierre and his more radical Jacobin colleagues in the National Convention. The fall of Robespierre and his closest colleagues in July 1794 marked the end of the Terror. Political engagement gave Mercier a firsthand view of the constantly changing situation, and he came to that commitment with an established reputation as a playwright, novelist, and observer of Parisian life. His *Tableau de Paris* (Picture of Paris) of 1781 had not suited everyone when it came out, especially one critic who complained that "this is a book conceived in the street and written in the gutter." In its pages, Mercier had already drawn attention to the licentious prints that had multiplied along the quays and boulevards.[20]

Other than his defense of the Girondins, Mercier failed to make much of a mark as a legislator. Like almost all the deputies of the National Convention, he agreed that Louis XVI was guilty, but he voted against the death penalty on the grounds that the former king would better serve as a kind of hostage whose presence would prevent any other pretender from gaining the throne. Marie-Jeanne Roland wrote of Mercier not long before her own execution in 1793 as a Girondin: "The good Mercier, facile, amiable in company, more than is common among people of letters, was only a zero in the [National] Convention."[21]

When serving as a deputy in the Council of Five Hundred, Mercier attracted attention when he argued in October 1796 against exempting artists from business licenses on the grounds that they could not possibly liken themselves to scientists, writers, or poets. He then found himself the victim of a caricature campaign. In "M . . . r [Mercier], An Ass Like No Other," for example, Mercier's head appears on a donkey outfitted as a vinegar maker with "vinegar" appearing on the side of the barrel. The donkey has knocked over an ancient bust, threatens to disfigure a painting by Raphael, and tramples on the works of Descartes and Racine, showing his disregard for serious art. In general, however, Mercier clearly preferred writing to politics and continued to write plays and poems during the revolutionary decade. He also found time to write articles for various journals and even collaborate in their production. In this sense, he seemed to suffer from an ailment that appeared in his 1801 dictionary of neologisms: "*Scribomanie* [scribbling mania]. Passion for writing. It is sometimes a sickness but at least it makes the one who has it happy."[22]

In *Le Nouveau Paris* (The new Paris), 1799, his revisiting of Paris after years of revolution, Mercier continued to complain about obscene books with their prints that were "equally repellent to modesty and good taste," but now he blamed them on postrevolutionary conditions: counterfeiters who pushed for an unlimited freedom of the press, the institution of divorce, gluttony, dances, and daily attendance at the theater. (This, from a playwright!) He nevertheless granted that the print *Inside the Revolutionary Committee* could make the viewer relive the horror of the "plots hatched in those lairs of Polyphemus [the savage man-eating giant in Greek mythology]" during the period of terror and violence in 1793–94, when Mercier himself languished in prison, threatened with execution.[23]

An Ass Like No Other. Anonymous etching with burin, 24 × 27 cm, Paris, 1798. The text reads: "What do I care about the great works of all the arts, so long as I crush, I raise myself, and I don't lack for [medicinal] thistle. Oh, people of taste, recognize the brute!" A zoom of the image would show excrement coming out of the donkey's rear end. Thistle in cordial form was used for hemorrhoids. *Bibliothèque Nationale de France*

Like Boyer, but without reproducing the illustration, Mercier offered a psychological reading, in this case of a scene depicting someone accused by their local revolutionary committee:

Who does not tremble with horror at the look of this livid president? One hears the croaky snoring of the secretary with a red cap, elbows on the table, who is sleeping off his morning wine. The viewing of these bottles whose label establishes the crime of suspicious relations with foreign countries; the fright which grabs hold of the unfortunate

Inside the Revolutionary Committee: Last Scene. Etching with tools, 43 × 59.5 cm, engraved by Boulet, Paris, 1797. *Bibliothèque Nationale de France*

accused who repeats in a low voice, *Vin de Hongrie* [Hungarian wine, the Austrian Empire being at war with France].

The title that Mercier cites is that of a play by Charles-Pierre Ducancel first performed in Paris in April 1795. Mercier probably had in mind an etching that was published in 1797 as an illustration of the final scene of the play. The print shows the very staging that Mercier describes except that Mercier mistakes the figure under accusation, which in the play is the wife, not the husband.[24]

Mercier remarked on the proliferation of prints, but he was not entirely sure what to make of them. He vaunted their power to capture the dread of the recent past, and in his chapter on "critical prints" he praised the efforts of Carle Vernet, who satirized the *incroyables* (incredibles) and *merveilleuses* (marvelous females), young men and women

REVOLUTIONARY IMAGERY AND THE UNCOVERING OF SOCIETY · 53

who affected outrageous apparel. Still, he could not resist disparaging the caricature vogue. He bemoaned the license that had destroyed the credibility of the political press and reduced to insignificance periodical publications because they could not keep up with fast-moving events. "Caricatures seem to want to replace them [periodicals]," he wrote, "and add to the unlimited liberty of the press. Passers-by crowd in front of the print sellers to look at the *Incroyables*, the *Mérveilleuses*, the fish vendor, the *rentier* [someone who lives off his investments], the *folie du jour* [folly of the day], anarchy, the danger of wigs." These prints were nothing but "naive depictions of our ridiculousness, of our follies, of our idiosyncrasies, of our vices" that "only excites a fleeting smile from a fickle people that sizes itself up by weighing its choices of dress."[25]

Although Mercier scorned the practice—the constant comparison of appearances—he had nonetheless hit upon something significant about visual images and especially the rendering of fashion: it was a way for people to see their society in a mirror and therefore to understand what they were becoming and even to become something else. He went on: "Who would believe it? The print of the *Incroyables* has spread [the style of] 'dog's ears' [two long curls hanging down the side of the face]: that is how inept newspapers, *frondeurs* [rebellious troublemakers] of republicanism, made a lot of republicans." Mercier meant this sardonically, yet in one of his characteristic reversals, he then lauded the many prints portraying French generals, who "saved all Europe from the horrible system of oppression and slavery that the kings had prepared against the people." He also cheerfully reported that portraits of "fat Louis and his daughter" could be bought, if one so chose, or could just be laughed at.[26]

Mercier worried about the effect of prints, sensed the growing preoccupation with social identities after 1794, and clearly understood that something profound had happened to the social order. "The social system has been shaken down to its foundations," he affirmed, but he was not very optimistic about what was replacing it: "From every part of the social body we have seen the appearance of the newly opulent, and with them, gold and riches." Mercier's use of the adjective "social"—"social system," "social body," "social interest," and "social mechanism" all appear—reflects the influence on him of Rousseau and, to a lesser extent, Condorcet. Mercier helped organize the publication of the collected works of Rousseau that came out between 1788 and 1793 and published a two-volume work in 1791, *Jean-Jacques Rousseau Considered as One of the Authors of the Revolution.* He did not write about the philosophical views of Condorcet in the same way, but he learned that he shared many political views with Condorcet when they both sat as deputies to the National Convention and collaborated on the journal *Chronique du mois* (Chronicle of the month), closely identified with the Girondins. *Chronique* brought together leading politicians who saw themselves as intellectuals and experts, including Condorcet, Jacques-Pierre Brissot, and Étienne Clavière. They contributed long articles—the monthly often ran to over one hundred pages—on current issues. Each issue had an engraving of one of its leaders at the beginning. Condorcet adorned the first issue, Mercier the third. Mercier defended Condorcet and the Girondins in 1793, went to prison for objecting to their arrest, and continued to exalt the memory of Condorcet for years afterward.[27]

Alongside other followers of Condorcet, in 1795 Mercier had been named to the new National Institute's class of "moral and political sciences" and to the subsection "morals." His friend Pierre Daunou sat in the subsection "social science"; Abbé Emmanuel Sieyès was named to the subsection "political economy." Mercier had his doubts, however, about scientific approaches to analyzing humans or their societies. He understood that "the social mechanism" was still more or less "a secret for the eighteenth century," but he was not sure that that secret should be unlocked, if unlocking followed from the "reign of those guilty philosophers who wanted to explain everything by the bodily senses, who wanted to reduce everything to purely physical operations." Mercier fretted about the influence of atheism and materialism and wanted no part of either. Yet at the same time, as a close observer of social life, he found himself speaking the language of social systems and social mechanisms, a language that emerged along with and in part in reaction to the increasing visualization of social differences.[28]

What Mercier did not see, but then no one did, was the way visual imagery helped make the notion itself of a social order more intelligible. Consider, for example, the seven prints cited by Mercier as "naive depictions" of ridiculous behavior. Four of them were drawn by or based on paintings by known artists: *Les Incroyables*, *Les Mérveilleuses*, and *The Danger of Wigs* by Vernet and *The Folly of the Day* by Louis-Léopold Boilly. At first glance, they might seem more like fashion plates, though the satirical intent is palpable. As the print *Les Mérveilleuses*

Les Mérveilleuses. Stippled engraving, 32 × 36 cm, by Louis Darcis, drawing by Carle Vernet, Paris, 1797. *Bibliothèque Nationale de France*

demonstrates, men, as well as women, are trying, however preposterously, to follow the latest fashions; but most striking is the competition between the two women to appear the most up-to-the-minute, an ambition that was frequently denounced after 1794. *The Folly of the Day*, for instance, refers to a comedy by that name performed in 1795 that mocked a wife intent on outshining everyone else at a concert. The two women in *Les Mérveilleuses* appear ridiculous because their desire to be stylish is not matched by much in the way of taste or manners. They seem to be flashing ankles at each other, perhaps to show off their slippers, since one aim of the new styles was to expose the feet and footwear.[29]

Yet even these prints, while focused on the desire to appear fashionable, carried deeper political and social meanings. Dress was politicized from the first days of the French Revolution, when the color of one's cockade signaled political allegiance, black for royalism and red, white, and blue for revolutionaries. After the founding of a republic in September 1792, some politicians took the emphasis on simplicity of dress to new extremes and wore the red bonnet associated with radical republicanism or affected the dress of the lower classes. The exception that had been deputy Gérard's insistence on wearing natural hair and simple clothing in 1789 had become the rule in 1793–94, though Robespierre refused to follow the crowd and wore a powdered wig and embroidered waistcoat. By experimenting with fashion, and even exaggerating it, the *merveilleuses* and *incroyables* drew a line between themselves and the Robespierrist regime that had fallen in July 1794. The *incroyables* who resented the message of the play *Folly of the Day* attended its performances and got into fistfights with its supporters. Fashion was not apolitical during the French Revolution.[30]

The other prints specifically noted by Mercier used social cues to convey blatantly political messages. He mentions prints about a fish vendor and a *rentier*, and they can be found together in a 1797 print by Joseph-Laurent Julien, *Poor Ruined Rentier—Fish to Fry, to Fry*. The poor ruined bondholder is forced to accept charity from a humble fish vendor because the government repudiated two-thirds of the national debt in

1797. In his pocket is the receipt for his inscription in the Great Book of the Public Debt set up in 1793, a certificate now worth only one-third of its original value. Mercier frequently mentioned the sad fate of the rentiers, who had invested in state bonds only to find that the republic could not even pay the interest due. As a figure, the bondholder represents the kinds of corrosive social changes that so worried Mercier. The bondholder's upper-class identity, or at least pretension to that status, is signaled by his wig, ruffles at his wrists and neck, sword, and buckled shoes. (Wearing a sword was a noble privilege under the Old Regime.) But his coat is fraying at the elbows and his extreme thinness evokes his reduced circumstances. In contrast, the lower-class fishwife is plump and wearing earrings, necklaces, and slippers, not common clogs. Social identities have gone topsy-turvy.

Poor Ruined Rentier—Fish to Fry, to Fry. Stippled engraving, 27 × 32.5 cm, by Joseph-Laurent Julien, Paris, 1797. Musée du Louvre, Arts graphiques, 5816 LR / Recto © RMN-Grand Palais / Art Resource, NY

The most political of the prints referenced by Mercier, *Anarchy*, is most likely the etching by Simon Petit, *The Anarchist: I Fool Both of Them*, which shows a two-faced man appealing on the one side to a woman of the lower classes and on the other to a young man of the middle classes. The woman on the left is dressed much like the fishwife in *Poor Ruined Rentier* but without the jewelry. She is being solicited by a man with a swarthy complexion, dark hair, and a mustache, traits seen in anti-Jacobin prints after 1794 that depicted lower-class supporters of the Robespierrists. His lower-class status is also signified by his short jacket, the long pants on his leg, and the clog on his foot. He is one of the sansculottes, a man without the breeches of the upper classes. It was not uncommon in the late 1790s to excoriate the followers of Robespierre as "anarchists." Whenever Mercier used the term, he meant those Jacobins who used popular pressure to turn democracy into social disintegration: "They wanted to make us into entirely new men and only made us into something close to savages." The virtually racial depiction of the anarchist's right face resonates with Mercier's reference to savages. Dark skin, dark hair, and facial hair indicated someone inferior, though mustaches did gain in reputation as they became associated with soldiers.[31]

The face turned toward the middle-class young man is brighter, smooth-skinned, with lighter hair and a finer nose. He wears a fashionable frock coat, knee breeches or a tight pantaloon, with either a stocking and slipper or a variation on a buskin (made to look like a Roman laced boot—the lacing is only evident in a close-up). The young man he is importuning is dressed similarly, though he wears a hat and ankle boots and sports the sideburns that developed out of the *incroyable* fashion of "dog's ears." The young man is therefore even more fashionable than the "anarchist" facing him. Ankle boots with pointed toes came into vogue in 1797, and in late 1798 they still were, according to one of the major fashion journals. The young man carries a fancy walking stick in contrast to the club of the man whose face is turned toward the woman of the people. The young man carries a stick because anyone

The Anarchist: I Fool Both of Them. Etching with stippling, 32.5 × 38 cm, Simon Petit, engraver, Paris, 1797. *Bibliothèque Nationale de France*

dressing like an *incroyable* could find themselves involved in a street fight with republicans.[32]

Mercier may have been consistent in his views of the Jacobins, whose meetings he described as "hell on earth" because of the participation of "rabble women," but he could not resist lumping caricatures of them with fashion prints as "naive depictions" of French foibles. Since Mercier's writing often verged on the slapdash, it is hardly surprising that he sometimes contradicted himself from one passage to another; thus, the Vernet prints could be models of critical depiction on one page and examples of French ridiculousness on another. In the end, however, it seems likely that they were both, that is, portrayals of a new obsession with fashion that signaled an underlying uneasiness with the pace and direction of social change.[33]

The mania for the socially picturesque had a logic that was not immediately evident, not even to a discerning observer such as Mercier. Fashion was a key indicator of social change, including the remaking and confusion of social identities, but it also still signaled social status, as *The Anarchist* demonstrates. Without the depiction of dress and appearance in this print, there would be no political message. Fashion communicated social identity, and when portrayed in prints like *Poor Ruined Rentier* or *The Anarchist*, it called on viewers to think about the social order in new ways. The social order was clearly changing, and because it was changing, its rules were coming into question.

The fashion for women of the prosperous classes changed with vertiginous speed during the French Revolution, but men's appearances were more fundamentally transformed. Men were moving toward a more uniform style of self-presentation, without wigs, with frock coats and eventually trousers rather than knee breeches. As Mercier noted, the classic French three-piece outfit, worn in courts throughout Europe, "no longer dares to show itself." In its place, "the old man, like the adolescent, puts on the shortened *frac* [riding coat or frock coat]." The style endured, though knee breeches made something of a comeback under Napoleon, who wanted to emulate court finery and who, as he gained weight, found the tight long pants uncomfortable. While men's hairstyles varied, sometimes from year to year, wigs fell out of favor and increasingly men wore their own hair unpowdered, though women still wore wigs and men did, too, on certain formal occasions. The painters and engravers who collaborated in making images like the ones presented here could barely keep up. Their work shows that people were noticing the changes taking place and trying to make sense of them. Every little detail signified, and how one looked mattered more than ever.[34]

A French royalist commentator writing from exile in England denounced Mercier's book as filled with "blasphemies, obscenities, worn-out and reshuffled declamations against the court and the courtiers," yet he could not resist reproducing some of Mercier's juicier passages, in particular the ones against Robespierre and the proliferation of obscene books and prints. Most of the reviews of the book focused on Mercier's political positions. The prints singled out by Mercier were not analyzed in detail by anyone else, but many of them did have an echo. One of the most influential journals of the time, *La Décade philosophique, littéraire et politique* (the *décade* was the new ten-day week), commented in January 1797 that Vernet had just released "a caricature, or rather an exact portrait of our *incroyables* of the day, which is much in vogue. Everyone is getting this engraving. The author has announced the pendant which will be a portrait of our *merveilleuses*." A month later, a letter to the editor in the same journal observed that "the *Incroyables* and the *Mérveilleuses* of Vernet have made caricatures all the rage, and we have seen appear a host of others." The letter writer went on to complain that the artists could do more if they followed the lead of English caricaturists: "It is not necessary to limit caricatures to the idiosyncrasies of fashion; they could become political satires." Why he did not see that this had happened already in France is unclear. In 1797, during a stay in Frankfurt, the German writer Johann Wolfgang von Goethe assembled notes about many French caricatures of the time. Included among them were every one of the prints specifically cited by Mercier in *Le Nouveau Paris*. As might be expected, the German classified some as fashion prints but clearly recognized the political and social meanings of the others.[35]

The comparison of English and French caricatures nonetheless raises a critical issue: if prints played such a key role in developing social vision in France, why did they not have the same effect in England, where social and political caricatures had a much longer history? Or to put it the other way around, why did social science develop in France first? James Gillray, Thomas Rowlandson, and Isaac Cruikshank overshadowed their counterparts in France, not only in terms of the numbers of prints they produced and their likely public exposure but also their satirical range. Well before 1789, foreign visitors to London had commented on the freedom with which British satirists attacked their

62 · THE REVOLUTIONARY SELF

own elites, and after 1789 this license became even more striking. The Spanish diplomat and friend of Francisco Goya, Leandro Fernández de Moratín, visited England in 1792 and 1793 and wrote in his diary: "I have never seen Royalty more violently demolished than in the English caricatures: there is no sovereign in Europe, however much feared and however powerful he may be, who has escaped being made a figure of fun and providing amusement at the price of two or three *reals* for the population of London." The British Museum collection includes nearly 9,700 satirical prints just for the period 1793–1800.[36]

Social science emerged first in France for one main reason: the French Revolution. Unlike the English revolutions before it, in the 1640s and 1688–89, the French Revolution effected a deliberate rupture with the past. Whether that rupture was as complete as the revolutionaries thought or not is irrelevant; by claiming to be starting anew and to be consciously transforming the future, the revolutionaries opened a space for thinking about past, present, and future political regimes and their social underpinnings. The prints helped them perceive that political regimes depended on social systems. If the "secret" of the "social mechanism," to return to Mercier's words, could be discovered, then a better future could be inaugurated.

Rather than pursue an analysis of "civilization" in the manner pioneered by Scottish thinkers such as Millar, which rested, after all, on armchair reading of travel accounts, in the late 1790s and early 1800s the French aimed for a study of society that was both more theoretical and more empirical. Sieyès, Condorcet, and Destutt de Tracy led the way to the more theoretical understanding, which was based for the most part on the French experience. This strand culminated in the work of Auguste Comte, which helped set the template for sociology. Destutt de Tracy also helped set in motion the second, empirical strand when he joined with other members of the National Institute to set up the Society of the Observers of Man in 1799. Although short-lived, the society announced an ambitious program with lasting influence. It advocated and even organized fieldwork in the form of expeditions to far-flung places to investigate the various physical, moral, and intellectual aspects of human life that it considered part of "anthropology."[37]

The painters, draftsmen, engravers, and publishers who collaborated in the production of prints during the French Revolution did not know themselves that they were advancing social science, but their sense of the market for images led them to produce prints that made it possible to visualize society in new ways. Society became a system of organization or a mechanism—an object of study seen to have its own rules of operation. While the work was done in part by intellectuals thinking about what had happened, what had changed, and what those changes meant, much work was also done by illustrators with no intention of writing a tract or organizing an expedition. Their depictions of personalities, events, and social relations enabled viewers to feel new emotions and think new thoughts.

ART, FASHION, AND ONE WOMAN'S EXPERIENCE

NO ONE EVER REFERS TO JACQUES-LOUIS DAVID OR PABLO Picasso as a male artist. The reference to "woman artist" or "female artist" signals that women artists are somehow unexpected. The term "female artist" had a certain currency in Britain between 1750 and 1850 (in American English only after 1800), with "woman artist" becoming more common in English in general in the twentieth century. Both expressions gained much greater traction after 1970, perhaps because feminism then began to permeate art history and art criticism. In French, references to the "femme artiste" seem more clearly correlated with the political upheavals of 1789 and 1848, since usage peaks in 1800 and 1850, though French usage shows a similar pattern to English after 1950 or so. In short, "woman artist" is not a neutral term, and the fluctuations in its incidence reveal changing interests and attitudes. Women's capacities for autonomy were gaining notice in the eighteenth century and in the case of France would be particularly remarkable, in the arts as in politics, after 1789. Women artists were not alone in their attention to society in their work, but the inevitable precarity of their situation as artists certainly made them sensitive to the power of social relationships.[1]

A few women artists of the eighteenth century have long attracted scholarly attention: the Swiss artist Angelica Kauffman, who worked in London and Rome, and the French painters Élisabeth Vigée Le Brun and Adélaïde Labille-Guiard were all famous in their day and have been the subject of studies ever since. Largely unrecognized until very recently was the increasing presence of women artists in Britain and France in the second half of the eighteenth century. A landmark study by historian Paris Spies-Gans has shown that more than a thousand women exhibited their work in London and Paris between the years 1760 and 1830. More women participated in public exhibitions in London, but in Paris the works of women made up a greater proportion of the works on display (more than 10 percent of Salon entries). Women's participation expanded most strikingly in both cities after the mid-1790s. In France, the reason for this increase is obvious; in August 1791, the National Assembly ended the Royal Academy's monopoly of the biennial Salon. As the art world opened up (the number of works exhibited doubled between the Salons of 1789 and those of 1791), women's participation steadily increased. Spies-Gans has found that at least fifty-two women exhibited publicly in Paris in the 1770s and 1780s but that more than two hundred women did so between 1791 and 1814.[2]

One of those women was Marie-Gabrielle Capet (1761–1818), a painter of modest fame whose trajectory is noteworthy because she came from a lower-class background—her father was a servant—and yet developed a moderately successful career. Unrelated to the royal family whose surname she shared, Capet had to labor within the constraints faced by a woman artist who never had enough reputation or fortune to establish complete financial independence. She is nonetheless considered "one of the best French miniaturists of the end of the 18th and beginning of the 19th centuries."[3]

66 · THE REVOLUTIONARY SELF

Born in Lyon in 1761, Capet somehow made her way to Paris and the workshop of Adélaïde Labille-Guiard, one of only four female members of the Royal Academy in the 1780s. Her relationship with Labille-Guiard and, after the teacher's death in 1803, with Labille-Guiard's second husband, the painter François-André Vincent, proved critical to her career and even to her survival. She was their protégée in the most literal sense, since she lived with them, and for her they were surrogate parents. She even asked in her will to be buried next to her "father" Vincent. Her mentors painted portraits of her, and Capet's own most ambitious painting depicts Labille-Guiard's studio.[4]

Capet began exhibiting work in the 1780s and, like her protectors, she stayed in France during the 1790s. She painted in the Napoleonic era as well, so she had the opportunity to capture some of the most significant developments of the time, in particular a growing preoccupation with the mutability of social roles and with the constantly changing fashions in dress that signaled that volatility. Capet followed the lead of her teachers in specializing in portraiture, but in her case, that often meant miniatures, including miniatures of paintings by Labille-Guiard. Portraiture was the dominant genre choice for French women artists in the 1790s; more than half of the paintings exhibited by women in the Salons of the 1790s were portraits (the proportion of portraits in all paintings exhibited was less than one-third). Grand history painting was considered a male genre while portraits and flower paintings were thought suitable for women.[5]

Art in its various forms was crucial to making society visible, with the French Revolution playing a catalyzing role. The explosion of prints, newspapers, pamphlets, and theater productions—thirty-seven hundred plays and ninety thousand performances in the decade 1789–1799 (doubling in one decade the total for the previous half century)—testified to the deepening crisis over political and social meanings and the need to see social relations depicted. Charles Théremin, a close associate of Sieyès's, observed in 1797 that "everyone generally has been displaced from their original situation, and no one is what he was in 1789 or what, in the balance sheet of his life, he expected to be in 1796."[6]

Capet's "original situation" is best known from Labille-Guiard's *Self-Portrait with Two Pupils*, shown at the Salon of 1785 and now at New York's Metropolitan Museum of Art. In the portrait, Capet, the pupil on the right, stares at the painting being created by her mentor rather than at the viewer. She is joined by another pupil, Marie Marguerite Carreaux de Rosemond, whose look parallels that of Labille-Guiard, toward the viewer or the subject of the painting. Carreaux de Rosemond might have come from an upper-class family, as the nobiliary particle "de" often

Adélaïde Labille-Guiard, *Self-Portrait with Two Pupils*, 1785. Oil on canvas, 83 × 59.5 in. (210.8 × 151.1 cm). Metropolitan Museum of Art, New York. Image copyright © The Metropolitan Museum of Art. Image source: Art Resource, NY

signified nobility, or at least the pretense to such status. Not much is known about her, as she died in childbirth in 1788. Although it might be said that Labille-Guiard has chosen to depict Carreaux's visage as lighter and finer than Capet's, not much can be deduced about Carreaux's dress, as it is largely occluded. Neither she nor Capet wears anything like the fashionable dress of Labille-Guiard, and neither has a hat. Their location behind the chair makes them observers rather than active participants. Still, Labille-Guiard did not have to feature two of her pupils, and the large format of the painting (7 × 5 feet) gives them considerable space. She is underlining her role as a teacher of young women even while also highlighting her skills as a painter and her position as a fashionable woman of society.

In 1783 and 1784, Capet had exhibited her own self-portraits at the local Youth Exhibition in Paris for aspiring painters. She depicted herself in the second of these in the same dress as in the Labille-Guiard portrait. Here, however, her hat was black, her hair lightly powdered, and her kerchief white gauze. In contrast to Labille-Guiard's rendition of her, Capet appears in her self-portrait as much more confident and forthright. Like Labille-Guiard in *Self-Portrait with Two Pupils*, Capet holds the palette, wears a hat, and directly engages the viewer.[7]

In the 1780s, self-portraits by women artists of themselves at work made a political statement by their very existence. Women artists in France only began to represent themselves painting in the last quarter of the eighteenth century, whereas women artists in Flanders and Italy had started doing so in the sixteenth century. The change happened in France when women got more opportunities to exhibit, even if those occasions were still limited, and consequently began to think of themselves as something more than artists of the second rank. Vigée Le Brun and Labille-Guiard led the way, creating "an unprecedented political and psychological shock" when they exhibited portraits of themselves painting in 1782.[8]

Even while depicting themselves as painters, these two artists also

Marie-Gabrielle Capet, *Self-Portrait*, 1790. Black and red chalk drawing heightened with white chalk on tan laid paper, 34 × 29.4 cm. *The Horvitz Collection, Wilmington*

emphasized their stylishness rather than the inevitable messiness of paint. The dresses in their self-portraits hardly seem the likely apparel for someone applying colors to a canvas, though in these earlier self-portraits the effect is not quite as striking as it is in Labille-Guiard's *Self-Portrait with Two Pupils*. Art historian Laura Auricchio has shown that

Labille-Guiard based her elegant costume in her 1785 self-portrait on the fashion prints of that moment. Fashion journals took off in France in the late 1780s as the social and political crisis was developing. Largely disappearing between 1794 and 1796 when political rhetoric and an uncertain war situation made them seem frivolous, they picked up again in 1797 as fashion and social distinctions began to reassert themselves. The fashion press registered the confusion about social identities, even increasing the unpredictability by making fashion more broadly consumable and by highlighting and perhaps accelerating the frequent changes in fashion.[9]

Capet no doubt saw the same fashion prints, which makes her 1790 drawing of herself especially striking. She is once again in the same dress but without the headdress or hat of either previous portrait and without the neckpiece and cuffs of both. The 1790 drawing thus foregrounds Capet as an individual artist. She also broadcasts new values of work, productivity, and individuality, even of a low-born person. Fashion, whether in clothing or furnishings, is present mainly by its absence.[10]

Capet appears to be actively thinking about a new order taking shape and her possible place in it. In a sense, she has stripped away the old social order or taken it down to its bare bones, and she knows exactly how fashion signals social positioning. With a simple ribbon, no hat, an unadorned dress, and a very ordinary chair, she occupies an almost timeless space in which our gaze continuously rotates between her expression, with her slight smile, her right hand about to draw, and her portfolio signaling much work already accomplished. It does not seem far-fetched to affirm that she presents herself as the female representative of the Third Estate, who, like deputy Gérard in his portrait of 1789, is capable and hardworking. When she is at work, she is apparently unconcerned with the supposedly traditional female attentions to appearance and adornment. Or rather, she is intent on showing that they can be bracketed. She can be attractive without a hat, neckpiece, or cuffs, letting her hair fall naturally. Capet also anticipates an important trend: depictions of

ART, FASHION, AND ONE WOMAN'S EXPERIENCE · 71

female artists by women increased dramatically after the opening of the Salon to all women artists in 1791.[11]

The portraits of revolutionary deputies published as prints in 1789 (see chapter 2) effectively reinvented the language of power. Art historian Amy Freund argues that "they speak about authority in a language of modesty, intimacy, and transparency." Although the effect derives in part from the collectivity of portraits, which suggests that sovereignty is transferring from the king to the nation's representatives, individual portraits, such as the rendition of deputy Gérard, set up a clear distinction from the Old Regime; the artist and presumably also the sitter have chosen to deliberately strip away the pretenses of ceremony so often linked with the monarchy and aristocratic privilege. Freund's terms "modesty, intimacy, and transparency" seem apt as well as a description of Capet's 1790 drawing of herself. The artist's choices are not haphazard; she is wearing a reddish ribbon in her unpowdered hair, earrings, and a ring. She looks at the viewer with an open and frank countenance, but she is not posing for the viewer. Her portfolio bulges with the evidence of her efforts. She is at work.[12]

After 1789, Capet continued to live with Labille-Guiard, and both women tried to adapt to the rapidly changing circumstances thrown up by events. At the end of September 1789, they both played prominent roles organizing women artists to make a patriotic contribution to the new government. Even while unsuccessfully urging the Royal Academy to admit more women, Labille-Guiard began to alter her own aesthetic by toning down artistic flourishes and aiming for the most accurate likeness of sitters in her portraits. Having been known for her contacts with the king's sisters, she now painted fourteen deputies in the new National Assembly, among them Maximilien Robespierre. Capet did miniatures of the portraits. Most of the portraits and miniatures are now lost, but one still exists: the portrait and miniature of Armand-Désiré, Duke of Aiguillon, one of the earliest noble supporters of the Third Estate in the struggle to create a National Assembly. Some have read Capet (and Labille-Guiard) as capturing the nonchalance of an Old Regime aristocrat, but the portrait clearly emphasizes his restrained costume. Unlike the prints of the duke as a deputy, the portraits of Labille-Guiard and Capet depict him without a wig, in his own powdered hair. Capet's miniatures in 1791 and 1793 of unnamed young men show them in very similar redingotes and cravats. In short, nothing in the women's depictions of him make the aristocratic duke seem different from the non-noble deputies.[13]

Robespierre was the exception among Labille-Guiard's sitters. Most, like the Duke of Aiguillon, came from the liberal nobility, leading to speculation that Labille-Guiard and Capet were royalists at heart. If they were, it was the kind that was favorable to constitutional monarchy. Among the sitters was Louis-Philippe, Duke of Orléans, who voted for the death of his cousin, King Louis XVI, and supported the new republic until he, too, went to the guillotine. In contrast to Vigée Le Brun, who left France in 1789, Labille-Guiard never joined the aristocracy in emigration. In March 1792, with her lover Vincent and aided by funds contributed by Capet and another pupil, Labille-Guiard invested in a country residence, where they all sat out the period of the fiercest repression of dissidents (1793–94). During this time, Labille-Guiard made use of the new law to divorce her husband, and as soon as circumstances allowed, the household returned to Paris to official lodgings in the Louvre, where Labille-Guiard, Vincent, and Capet painted the new middle-class republican society of lawyers, intellectuals, actors, and artists.[14]

Although Capet earned a reputation as a painter of portraits in oil and pastels, she is now best known for her watercolor miniatures on ivory like the one of Anne Françoise Hyppolyte Boutet Salvetat, who was known as Mlle. Mars. It differs from many of the others, however, in being oval and of larger than usual format; most of her circular ones varied from 2 to 3 inches (6 to 8 centimeters) in diameter. Perhaps this one is 5 by 4 inches because it was meant to capture the attention of

Marie-Gabrielle Capet, *Portrait of the Actress Mlle. Mars*, 1800. Miniature on ivory, 13 × 11.2 cm. *Musée du Louvre, Arts graphiques, RF 30675, Recto* © RMN-Grand Palais / Art Resource, NY

viewers at the Salon of 1800. Critics repeatedly praised Capet for the truthfulness and verisimilitude of her portraits, and her portrayals also captured, as this one does, the presence of the person, seeming about to speak, whether practicing the lines in the script she is holding or commenting to the viewer or artist. The sense of capturing a moment also derives from the artist's close attention to fashion, in this case the white cotton muslin dress and what seems to be a cashmere shawl.[15]

Artists did not just illustrate the current fashion. They helped shape it, as when Vigée Le Brun painted Marie Antoinette in a seemingly simple muslin chemise dress. It caused a scandal at the Salon of 1783 because of the informality of the queen's appearance, and the artist was forced to replace it with another picture. The precursor of the antique-style tunic worn by Mlle. Mars, the chemise dress shocked viewers because a *chemise*—in French it now means "shirt"—was an undergarment worn next to the skin. Marie Antoinette embraced the flowing, sheer dress because it conveyed the new values of naturalness and freedom of movement as opposed to the rigidities of panniers and corsets.

She wore it when entertaining her closest friends at the Petit Trianon of Versailles, where she first installed an English garden and then a model village, including a working dairy farm. The English garden was meant to re-create a feeling of untamed nature in contrast to the usual French garden with its geometrical patterns and precise trimming of the plants.[16]

Just how the antique-style tunic worn by Mlle. Mars evolved from the ruffled chemise dress is unclear. Looking back from the 1830s, the writer Albertine Clément-Hémery claimed that the young women studying with the artist Jean-Baptiste Regnault created the vogue for Greek-style tunics. She was at the studio one day in the summer of 1793 when her friend and fellow student Adèle Tournezy prevailed upon her and other students to parade through the center of Paris in Greek tunics with bright red waistbands and ribbons, setting off a craze. Clément-Hémery gave up painting and in 1797 became one of the first editors of the most influential and long-lasting of the fashion journals, *Journal des dames et des modes.*[17]

The most common explanation for the move toward antique-style tunics is the influence of neoclassicism in art, especially painting and architecture. New archaeological discoveries at Herculaneum and Pompeii inspired a renewed interest in the art of Greece and Rome from the 1750s onward, and neoclassicism offered a compelling alternative to baroque and rococo styles because it emphasized the simplicity, straight lines, and grandeur of Greek and Roman art in contrast to the busyness of its predecessors. In his 1800 unfinished portrait of Juliette Récamier, the leading French neoclassicist painter Jacques-Louis David depicted the society trendsetter wearing a white muslin tunic that is similar to the one worn by a female figure in his 1784 painting *Oath of the Horatii.* In the older painting, the dress referred elegiacally to ancient history; by 1800 it had become the vogue for upper-class women.[18]

White dresses appeared in revolutionary festivals, especially the notorious November 1793 Festival of Reason and the Festival of the Supreme Being, the latter orchestrated by David in June 1794. Both were associated with attacks on Christianity. In the Festival of Reason, a mountain (the supporters of Robespierre were known as "the Mountain" because they sat in the highest seats of the meeting room) was erected to block from view the choir and altar of Notre Dame cathedral. On it sat a small Greek temple with the inscription "To Philosophy." In front of the temple sat a living goddess of liberty wearing a white dress. She was surrounded by young girls also wearing simple white dresses. Contemporary prints show the dresses as high-waisted but not as tunics. David designed the Festival of the Supreme Being to illustrate the annihilation of atheism, associated with the Festival of Reason, and the installation of a kind of natural religion. Now the goddess of liberty was a statue, not an actress, and she was no longer at the center of the pageant. In this case, according to David's plan, white dresses signaled virginal youth.[19]

Recent research has pointed to other sources of the vogue for antique-style tunics: the adoption of the raised waist in the dress of prominent women in London; Vigée Le Brun's decision to wear such a dress herself while painting; Emma Hart (Lady Hamilton, later the lover of naval hero Admiral Lord Nelson), whose performances of poses of antique women took place at the residence of Sir William Hamilton, the British ambassador in Naples, and also in Bath and other European capitals between 1787 and 1799; and finally, the influence of one of the leading fashion pacesetters of the Directory period in France, Thérèse Tallien. Born Thérézia Cabarrus in Madrid but raised in France, Tallien had connections to Bordeaux, the home of an uncle who was active in the slave trade. She moved there in 1793 after divorcing her first husband and soon began a relationship with the man who would become her second husband, the controversial deputy on mission Jean-Lambert Tallien. Although Thérèse did not gain a reputation for wearing transparent Grecian-style white dresses until after the fall of Robespierre in July 1794 (and her own release from prison in Paris at the same time), Bordeaux provides a possible link to the white muslin dress, as it appears to have been the port through which fashion influences from the colonies entered France.[20]

Simple white muslin gowns first came into use by enslaved women in the Caribbean islands, who most likely made them out of muslin imported from India. The muslin was not necessarily cheap and was often purchased by the enslaved themselves, who saved up for this purpose. After 1794, the fashion for the Greek-style muslin tunics was sometimes traced to Creole women, such as Joséphine de Beauharnais, the daughter of a sugar plantation owner in Martinique who married Napoleon Bonaparte in 1796. A traveler to Saint-Domingue on the eve of the French Revolution reported that Creole women there wore skirts over sheer muslin gowns as their daily dress. Josephine met Thérèse in prison in Paris in 1794 and they became fast friends and joint arbiters of fashion upon their release. It is possible, therefore, that the vogue for the dresses also owed something to the prison experience itself because it was virtually impossible to dress otherwise in prison. Marie Antoinette went to the guillotine in a white dress, and in a 1796 portrait by Jean-Louis Laneuville, Tallien is depicted in her cell wearing a high-waisted white dress. Laneuville's portrait had to be withdrawn almost as soon as it was displayed at the Salon of 1796 because of Thérèse's marriage to the increasingly discredited deputy Tallien. As deputy, Tallien had played a key role in bringing down Robespierre, but he himself was considered a leading agent of repression in the Robespierrist regime. Thérèse had married Tallien a few months after her release from prison.[21]

Although the white muslin tunic-style dress was only taken up in mainland France by elite women such as Mlle. Mars, it left a deep impression on the fashion scene. In December 1798, one fashion journal insisted that "white is still the dominant color. The most beautiful Indian muslins, plain or embroidered, are preferred by our rich elegant women above all other fabrics." In 1799, another journal announced that "one sees almost no other fabric" in dresses and that "the form of this dress is that of a tunic, low cut, it goes without saying." Muslin would remain in

ART, FASHION, AND ONE WOMAN'S EXPERIENCE · 77

vogue until it became an issue of state after Bonaparte came to power. He wanted to revive the French silk industry (silk being associated with Old Regime aristocrats) and stop the British from profiting from their control of Bengal and its dominance in the production of muslin. He almost immediately began encouraging the use of silk and wool rather than muslin. His stepdaughter Hortense reported that whenever she or Joséphine came into a room wearing an elegant dress, he would immediately ask if it was muslin. If he suspected that they were lying when they claimed it was linen, he would tear it off. They gave up and reverted to satin or velvet. In the end Napoleon decreed that all members of imperial courts and tribunals must be dressed entirely in silk.[22]

Mlle. Mars may also have taken up another popular style, if her shawl was cashmere. The shawls became the talk of the town when Bonaparte's officers brought them back from Egypt, where they were much prized. Produced in Kashmir and imported at considerable price, the vogue for cashmere immediately prompted French scientists to study Kashmiri methods of shepherding and manufacture in order to attempt imitations, as was already happening in Britain with calicoes and muslin. Savants debated whether the cloth came from sheep or goats and which term in French to use for a shawl, as the word came originally from India (*schall* gave way to *châle* in French, as the former was seen as too English). Joséphine reportedly owned hundreds of them, and all the women trendsetters had themselves portrayed wearing them, usually in a color much like that worn by Mlle. Mars. Shawls provided warmth and perhaps also a nod to decorum when women wore the flimsy and revealing white tunic dresses.[23]

The style of Mars's hair is also susceptible to more than one interpretation. She seems not to be wearing a wig, and her hair is most likely curled. By the end of 1798, fashion journals were announcing the end of the preference for the short flat Titus cut, seen on both men and women, including Bonaparte, and the new mode of curling hair. Bonaparte had originally appeared with long, loose powdered hair tied behind his head but adopted the Titus cut from 1797 onward. He kept a version of it even when fashions changed. The Titus cut signaled an allegiance to Roman-style republicanism, since it first gained popularity from performances by the actor François-Joseph Talma playing the Roman emperor Titus. He had his hair cut short using the model of a bust of Titus. Talma, a close associate of the painter David, and Mars were both among the highest-paid actors of the Comédie Française in the late 1790s.[24]

In the late 1790s, nonetheless, wigs, even with curled blond hair, came in again, though these soon gave way to dark-haired ones. Blond wigs broadcast protest against the repression of the previous Robespier-rist regime, when blond hair was viewed by some as aristocratic and counterrevolutionary (Marie Antoinette was supposedly a natural blonde but wore wigs of various colors). Thérèse Tallien had thirty wigs, it was said, all of shades of blond. Whatever the truth of Mars's hairstyle, it was clearly meant to go along with her exposed neck. The combination of the white muslin tunic and exposed neck (and sometimes also exposed arms) caught the attention of critics such as Louis-Sébastien Mercier. Commenting on winter balls in his *Nouveau Paris* in 1799, he derided the styles associated with the *incroyables* but could not entirely ignore the attractions of their female counterparts:

> In this enchanted place a hundred goddesses, perfumed with oils [and] crowned with roses, flutter about in Athenian dresses, attract-ing and following by turns the looks of our *incroyables* with their tousled hair [and] Turkish slippers; they resemble in such a striking manner that barbed new engraving that carries their names [see *Les Mérveilleuses* in chapter 2] that in truth I cannot view it as a carica-ture. . . . All the women are in white, and white flatters all women. Their necks are bare, their arms are exposed.

Mars was not a *merveilleuse*, but the Greek-style white muslin tunic and an exposed neck no longer surprised viewers by the end of the 1790s.[25]

ART, FASHION, AND ONE WOMAN'S EXPERIENCE · 79

The year that Capet presented to the public her miniature of Mlle. Mars was also the year that Labille-Guiard finally married Vincent, and in 1802 they all moved to new lodgings in the National Institute given to Vincent, who had been named one of its founding members in 1796. Women were excluded from membership. In 1803 Labille-Guiard died. She had demonstrated throughout these turbulent times a remarkable ability to adjust her aesthetic to the political moment, and the same adaptability would characterize Capet's work right through the Napoleonic regime.[26]

Most commentators have emphasized the tightness of the bond between Labille-Guiard and her student Capet, citing elements in Labille-Guiard's paintings of Capet to make their point. The foregrounding of Capet in Labille-Guiard's 1785 self-portrait is taken to express an egalitarian impulse that emphasized talent over birth, since Capet came from a much more modest background than the other student. Many scholars focus on one of Labille-Guiard's last known works, her 1798 oil painting of Capet holding a small palette while working on a miniature. Capet is wearing the same dress as in Labille-Guiard's 1785 self-portrait and Capet's own self-portrait of 1790, though this time the dress has a good-sized white collar and white cuffs, and Capet has a dark velour cap. Labille-Guiard's painting has been interpreted as articulating "a poignant identification between teacher and student" and as "remarkable for the sincerity of its execution." In the picture Capet has turned toward the artist, and her look has been read as "open and agreeable, which is how she must have appeared to her admired teacher." This may well have been Labille-Guiard's intention, but it tells us little about Capet's reaction. It seems hardly accidental that Labille-Guiard depicts Capet painting a miniature, since Capet did many miniatures of Labille-Guiard's pictures and of her own devising, but Capet also worked in pastels and oils. In Labille-Guiard's eyes, however, Capet remained forever the student who did miniature versions of her teacher's portraits. Many other painters known for working in oil and pastel turned to making miniatures in the 1790s after their potential noble patrons fled the country.[27]

It cannot be surprising, then, that there seems to be more than a little resentment expressed in Capet's 1808 oil painting of her teacher at work. *Studio Scene* is not large at 27 by 33 inches, but it includes many figures, and though supposedly centered on Labille-Guiard, Capet makes herself as much the focus of the viewer's attention as her teacher. Capet holds the palette and looks directly at the viewer. She is the only figure in the canvas who looks straight at the viewer, as if to say, look at me, I did this, I'm the painter. She occupies the foreground and is completely separate from the other people depicted; everyone else is either looking at a person or focused on the painting. It is not far-fetched to see in the studio scene a much-delayed riposte to Labille-Guiard's sensational self-portrait of 1785.[28]

The Capet painting confounds expectations. Studio scenes almost never give the assistant this kind of prominence. Capet is not looking at the painting or her teacher or her father figure, Vincent, who has his hand on Labille-Guiard's chair and is pointing at something in the painting that presumably needs Labille-Guiard's attention. Capet solicits our view but with uncertain intention. The description that Capet wrote for the 1808 Salon was quite long but revealing only to someone intent on discovering hidden motives. She refers to Labille-Guiard as "the late Madame Vincent (student of her husband)" and says that the older woman is painting a portrait of Senator Joseph-Marie Vien, count of the empire and also Vincent's teacher. Capet points to herself filling the palette and also placing in this painting Vincent's principal students. She also includes Vien's son and his daughter-in-law on the far right standing behind Vien. Capet is the one establishing the artistic lineage that goes from Vien to Vincent to Labille-Guiard. Even though the older woman is supposedly the subject of the painting, Labille-Guiard is effectively displaced. Instead, she becomes the wife and student of Vincent.[29]

Marie-Gabrielle Capet, *Studio Scene*, 1808. Oil on canvas, 69 × 83.5 cm.
Neue Pinakothek, Munich, bpk Bildagentur / Art Resource, NY

Capet portrays Labille-Guiard as a spectral manifestation in a white cap and a long, rather shapeless white dress, a far cry from the tunic worn by Mlle. Mars. Although women artists were sometimes depicted in such clothing while working, they always appear more stylish than Labille-Guiard is here. Capet, the assistant, is more formally and colorfully costumed. Labille-Guiard's ghostlike quality signals the deliberately disjointed temporal dimension of the painting, which was shown five years after Labille-Guiard's death. Labille-Guiard's only portrait of Vien was a pastel exhibited in 1782, but Capet is not recalling that moment because Vien, who was still alive in 1808, is wearing the formal costume of a senator of the Napoleonic Empire, and all the figures in the painting are wearing styles from the first decade of the 1800s. Capet's own description names Vien as count of the empire, a position to which he was named in 1808, long after the death of Labille-Guiard.[30]

Capet's interest in the social meaning of fashions of the day is particularly striking in her renditions of Vien and Vincent, who appear in their formal institutional dress. Vien is wearing the dress of a senator as prescribed for the coronation of Napoleon as emperor in 1804: coat, mantle, and breeches of blue velvet, gold facings of the mantle, lace cravat, and hat of black felt ornamented with white plumes. His plumed hat, sitting on the table behind him, carried special significance. The official costume for the noble deputies to the Estates General in 1789 included plumed hats, which were forbidden to non-noble deputies. By the late 1790s, however, plumes had been taken over as a middle-class honorific: the directors of the republican Directory government wore them as part of their official costume, with the hope that they would lend authority to a government that labored to establish its legitimacy. Plumes were prescribed by Napoleon for his new elite. Napoleon obsessed over the regulation of official and court costumes, in part because he came from a military background and in part because he knew that his regime rested on fragile foundations.[31]

Vincent's costume as a member of the National Institute is less imposing than Vien's, but he clearly stands out from the rest of those pictured. Like Vien, his teacher, Vincent is wearing a wig, and his coat is embroidered as required of members of the institute. Capet painted a small oil of Vincent at about the same time as the studio scene, perhaps as a study, and in it he wears the same embroidered frock coat and vest worn by members of the institute. His Legion of Honor decoration (to which he was named in 1803) sits on his left lapel, as it does in the painting of the studio scene. Vien also wears his. Capet is saying that after Vien, the sitter for the portrait, Vincent is the highest-ranking person in the room.[32]

Capet's attention to fashion can be seen throughout her career, but comes through most conspicuously in this studio scene, if only because

ART, FASHION, AND ONE WOMAN'S EXPERIENCE · 83

there are so many people, both male and female, in the painting. Her careful and varied choices, from head to foot on the figures present, make several points: known as a painter of miniatures of paintings by her teacher, she shows here that she can execute her own larger-scale oil; known as a student of Labille-Guiard, she both recognizes the debt and establishes her own independence; and by choosing to paint Vincent's students, she simultaneously puts herself in their company and sets herself apart by her placement in the scene. Unlike them, she is participating in the making of a work, an oblique reference to her own position as creator of the painting.

Capet's rendition of fashion also deliberately highlights generational change. Two or three of Vincent's students have powdered hair, which looks much more natural than the wigs on the older men. Vien is ninety-two, Vincent is sixty-two, and the three with powdered hair are fifty-one, forty-four, and forty-two years old, moving from left to right in the picture. The average age of the six other students is thirty-three years old. The younger men all wear their hair in the fashion of the day, unpowdered, falling forward in a variation of the Titus cut, and often with sideburns that had evolved from the "dog's ears" first sported by the *incroyables* in the late 1790s. They have on the frock coats worn closed with ample muslin or linen cravats or jabots that came in after 1800. Since she exhibited her miniatures with success at the Salon of 1801, Capet must have seen Robert Lefèvre's highly regarded portrait of the painter Pierre-Narcisse Guérin with the same hairstyle, frock coat, and cravat.[33]

Capet was no doubt aiming to valorize Vincent's school by bringing his prominent students together in this way. All of them were recognizable at the time, and some, such as Charles Meynier, the figure second from the left, wearing a blue coat and facing away from the viewer, were quite well known. She is underlining Vincent's affiliation with Vien, whose other famous pupil was Jacques-Louis David, long Vincent's rival. Capet was effectively claiming at least three roles for herself: all-knowing assistant to

Labille-Guiard, ardent celebrator of Vincent, and, above all, the painter who could stage this complicated scene. She did not place herself at the compositional center, which is occupied by the easel, but she certainly drew attention to the ambiguity of her place in the Vien lineage: she is the student of Labille-Guiard, who was a student of Vincent, who was a student of Vien; but like her mentors, she, too, became a painter in her own right. In fact, she is painting a portrait of Vien, Vincent, and Labille-Guiard along with the portraits of Vincent's students. She remained close to Meynier and others in the Vincent circle during the remainder of her life.[34]

Because Capet exhibited many miniatures at the Salon of 1798, she no doubt witnessed the enthusiastic public reception that greeted

Fashion plate 608 from *Journal des dames et de modes*, issue 20, January 1805.
Bibliothèque Nationale de France

Louis-Léopold Boilly's *Group of Artists in Jean-Baptiste Isabey's Studio*. Although Isabey was known as a miniaturist, Boilly chose not to render the act of painting but rather to show artists conversing with other men of the cultural elite, including a composer, a poet, architects, and actors. He depicts a homosocial world; no women are present. Among the artists is Charles Meynier, whose portrait Capet painted both in miniature and pastel for display in 1799. Boilly's studio scene is larger than hers but not by much: his is 28 by 44 inches; hers is 27 by 33 inches. Capet could not compete with Boilly in terms of output or commercial success, but she brought a distinctive woman's vision to her version of a studio scene.[35]

In fact, she may have included Vien's son and his wife, Rose-Céleste Bache, in order to feature a third woman in the composition. Like Capet and Labille-Guiard, and unlike most of the men depicted, Bache is actively engaged, pointing to a drawing by Vien. Vien's son, Joseph-Marie Vien the younger, was also a painter. He studied with both his father and Vincent, and his connection to his father is made evident by his hand on his father's chair. He is forty-seven years old, the same age as Capet, and clearly identified with the younger generation by his hair and his dress. His hair is curled and includes sideburns, and he wears the same fashionable cutaway double-breasted coat as some of the other younger men depicted, like that of the model in an 1805 fashion plate, and he wears the same *jabot de point* as the others. He has on boots, which were becoming more fashionable for men with the rising influence of military styles, whereas some of the other men wear slippers, as does the model in the 1805 fashion plate. Other than Vien senior, who wears the old-fashioned knee breeches, the men whose legs are visible are wearing the tight-fitting nankeen trousers (*pantalons*) that partially displaced knee breeches during the 1790s. The model in the 1805 fashion plate is wearing knee breeches, though ones that meld with his stockings, unlike those of Vien.

Vien's daughter-in-law, Rose, is in a fashionable white dress. Her shawl may be cashmere, and it resembles the one worn by Mlle. Mars in the Capet miniature. Like some of the men, Rose's hair and Capet's, too, is curled à la Caracalla (Caracalla was a Roman emperor), or is a wig in that style, another fashion that first appeared in the late 1790s. In September 1798, *Tableau général du goût, des modes et costumes de Paris* (General picture of the taste, fashion and dress of Paris) claimed that "the taste for the antique has begun to take over hair: the persons who like cleanliness and ease see with pleasure the multiplication of heads with short hair, without powder, flat or curled à la Titus or à la Caracalla." Another fashion journal explained in December 1806 why it was so difficult to tell natural hair from a wig: "The height of the art is to make a wig imitate hair and make hair have the look of a wig."[36]

Women artists may have been especially sensitive to changes in fashion, since they were both artists and women, but the difference between men and women in this regard should not be exaggerated. After 1800, fashion increasingly became the province of women, yet it was never entirely so. Men would increasingly dress alike; all classes of men would eventually wear trousers and discard wigs. Capet's 1808 painting comes at a pivotal time for the question of gender and dress. She captures, for example, the tug-of-war between knee breeches and trousers. Trousers would win out, but not right away. Knee breeches would signal attachment to tradition both for the Napoleonic court and the court of the restored Bourbon monarchy.

Women's desire for the neoclassical tunic with its light fabric and flowing form, its escape from the rigors of corsets and panniers, may have proved farsighted, but in 1800 it had a relatively short shelf life. Corsets, panniers, and constraining dresses would come back in, at least for the prosperous classes of women. Napoleon wanted women back in their traditional places, and so did the monarchy that was restored after his fall. Capet foreshadows this change as well when she portrays herself in a dress that reveals little. Though her underdress is white, she is wearing a version of the new style of long redingote for women that could be seen in *Journal des dames et des modes* as early as March 1802. A version of Capet's collar can be seen in fashion prints of the same years. In short, every aesthetic choice made by Capet was deliberate.[37]

Although Napoleon's wife Joséphine resisted his strictures against English muslin, the fashion did change, and he was not alone in desiring such a change. Just a few days after the coup in November 1799 that brought Bonaparte to power, one newspaper complained about official dress of the Directory government, insisting that the directors were wearing costumes that made them look like street acrobats (*un vêtement de saltimbanques*). The new consuls were urged to wear the velour, satin, and embroidery of Lyon. As might be expected, then, in descriptions of fashions of the day, satin, taffeta, velour, and woolens began to dominate.

Fashion plate 369 from *Journal des dames et des modes*, no. 33, March 1802. *Bibliothèque Nationale de France*

Although white muslin had not disappeared, it was being overtaken by French-made fabrics with color.[38]

Fashion was not the only way to signify social difference. In the 1808 studio painting, Capet draws attention to the importance of assistants in the art world, which often meant a changing role for women. Wives and daughters of engravers often did the finishing work. In families of painters, they prepared the palette and probably contributed to the painting itself as well. Capet seized the moment offered by the French Revolution to bring the role of assistants to light and comment on her place in society; she depicts herself as the assistant in the studio scene, but by foregrounding and separating herself, she reminds the viewer that she, not Labille-Guiard, is the painter. Assistants could rise to the top even if they came from modest backgrounds. Capet did not stay at the top forever. She continued to paint and exhibit until Vincent's death in 1816, when she was evicted by the restored monarchical government from the apartment they had shared and lost her government pension that he had arranged. His way of life had rested on the security of official appointments that were closed to women. Capet died in 1818 at the age of fifty-seven, having asked to be buried next to Vincent.[39]

Through her long career of drawing and painting, whether of miniature portraits, pastels, or oils, Capet enabled others to see social relations and therefore society in new ways. She traced evolving fashions and helped give them life. She portrayed, encapsulated, and gave value to individuality, including her own. Seeing society is not just about developing a critical perspective on relations between employers and workers, landowners and peasants, the prosperous and the poor, or even husbands and wives. It is also about painters and their teachers, their students, and their sitters. Social relations were everywhere, but most often taken for granted as part of the background of everyday life. Artists such as Capet played a crucial role in pushing those relations to the forefront, making them visible in new ways and therefore susceptible to categorization and conceptualization.

Four

REVOLUTIONARY ARMIES AND THE STRATEGIES OF WAR

DISCOVERY OF NEW POTENTIALS IN PEOPLE AND SYSTEMS can be a two-edged sword, and nowhere is this more glaring than in the case of the French revolutionary armies. When the French government declared war on Austria in April 1792, France was still ruled by a king, though not for long, and its armed forces faced disintegration. Only 2 vice admirals out of 9, 3 rear admirals out of 18, and 42 captains out of 170 remained in the navy. Two-thirds of the army officers had already emigrated, many of them intent on joining counterrevolutionary armies. Although tens of thousands of volunteers would join the 100,000 who had stepped up in 1791 after the attempted flight of the king, muskets, cartridges, and uniforms were in desperately short supply. The regular army relied on a reserve of some 600,000 muskets, but at the beginning of 1792, only 160,000 were available. Just how the volunteers would be amalgamated with the regular army remained unclear. The government did not even know how many men it had under arms.[1]

The war had begun because of mutually reinforcing miscalculations. The French deputies thought they could not avoid it given Austria's overt hostility and the fact that Marie Antoinette's brother ruled it until March 1792 and then was succeeded by her nephew. The deputies also believed they could limit the war to Austria. The Austrians, in turn, thought the French would back down if intimidated, and gaining the support of Prussia by an alliance in February 1792, they believed that if war came, it would be easy to win given the disintegration of France's officer corps. Already in 1791, a British officer had reported back from France that "an idea prevails that the French Army is not fit for service in their present state." By the French government's own estimates in 1789, the French army of 230,000 men would be outnumbered by the Austrian army of 300,000 soldiers and even more overwhelmed if joined by Prussia with its 200,000 men. Louis XVI agreed to the French declaration of war because he reckoned that if those allied against France won, they would restore him to his full powers, and if they lost, the French generals would turn their armies back on Paris and oust the deputies. When Louis XVI asked the deputies to declare war, 135 of 153 generals in the French army were nobles.[2]

Once war began, it seemed to confirm Austrian and Prussian expectations. The Austrians easily repulsed French attempts to invade Belgium, and the Prussians captured the border fortresses of Longwy and Verdun, opening the route to Paris from the east in early September. In the north, the French army had panicked and fled rather than retreating in good order, further boosting the confidence of the allies. Moreover, Marquis de Lafayette had gone over to the Austrians when Louis XVI was deposed in August, creating even greater anxiety about the aristocratic generals who remained.

The battle of Valmy on September 20, 1792, confounded Austrian and Prussian expectations and immediately lifted French fortunes. The French outnumbered the Prussians (40,000 men at the key site of the battle opposed to 34,000) because the Austrians and French counterrevolutionary emigrants failed to arrive in time, yet the Prussians had twice the artillery (200 cannons opposed to 100). Both sides fired great barrages, with the Prussians even managing at one point to blow up three French wagons filled with ammunition, creating a momentary panic. When the Prussian columns advanced marching in step, the French infantrymen, nearly half of whom were volunteers, did not lose their nerve. Instead, following General François Kellermann's lead, whose horse had already been shot from underneath him, they held their fire, screamed "Vive la Nation!," and prepared their bayonets for a charge. The Prussians stopped when they reached the range at which French cannon fire turned especially deadly in fear of sustaining great losses. At that point the two sides were separated by only a few hundred yards. After yet more exchanges of cannon fire, the Prussians decided to withdraw.[3]

Neither side reported many casualties, and yet everything had changed. The German writer Johann Wolfgang von Goethe, who accompanied the Prussian armies, claims to have said to the soldiers at his campsite, "From here and from this day begins a new epoch in the history of the world." The French volunteers could hold their own with Europe's best soldiers. The Prussians had fought with their backs to Paris in order to cut off the French from the capital, but now the French blocked the way to their food wagons. Rain, disease, and hunger dictated retreat. An apparently minor exchange had turned into a galvanizing victory for the French army and the newborn French Republic.[4]

French forces soon gathered speed. By the end of October, all enemy troops had been chased from French territory, and French armies had pushed into Savoy and Nice in the south, the Rhineland in the east, and once again, but this time successfully, Belgium. The reversal would bring its own problems, in particular a fatal expansion of the war in 1793, but given the weaknesses of the army, its success was nonetheless astounding. Individual soldiers and the army as an institution were discovering new capacities because the exigencies of the war had entered into explosive combination with revolutionary ideology.

Many changes in organization and tactics had been anticipated by Old Regime reformers such as Count Jacques Guibert, a brigadier general and proponent of military reform. His treatises of the 1770s inspired efforts to weed out some of the bloated higher ranks and gradually eliminate venality, the purchasing of commissions. Guibert seemed to foresee a citizen army, but finding that next to impossible given the hold of the nobility on the army, he advocated greater technical education of the officers and more mobility and boldness in operations. To create faster movement, he urged the deployment of divisional formations (combining infantry, cavalry, and artillery in independent units) with reliance on the countryside for provisioning the troops instead of unwieldy supply trains. To encourage boldness, he argued for more autonomy for generals and flexible maneuvering in open columns before deploying in a firing line.[5]

Most of these ideas could only be put into practice once the revolutionaries swept away the aristocratic domination of the officer corps. In 1789, nine out of ten officers in the army were nobles. The abolition of venality, including offices that conferred noble status, in August 1789; the suppression of all noble titles in June 1790; and the mass emigration of noble officers opened a wide path to a wholesale regeneration of the army along the lines of merit and patriotism. The changes began almost immediately but took some time to bear fruit. In February 1790, the deputies of the National Assembly required every soldier to take an oath of loyalty to the nation, the law, the king, and the constitution, thus contesting the king's supreme authority. They declared soldiers to be citizens; corporal punishment and in particular humiliating blows with the flat of the sword were suppressed. The foreign mercenary regiments disbanded, and the volunteers from the National Guard, with their practice of electing officers, began amalgamating with the veterans.

Seniority now mattered in choosing the ranks of colonel and above. Colonels had previously bought their regimental commands, but such purchases were largely reserved to nobles who had been presented at court. Politics now counted, too. Officers were already being monitored for their political loyalty, and the government reserved to itself the right to name most generals. By 1792, the regular army was younger and less experienced than the royal army of 1789, and only 15 to 20 percent of the officers were noble (this dropped to 2 to 3 percent by 1794). As the noble officers fled, others took their place. By 1794, one-third to one-half of the officers below the rank of colonel came from the middle classes, whether clerks, artists, surgeons, or sons of merchants; one-fourth from artisanal and shopkeeping families; and one-fourth from the peasantry. Competitive examinations to find potential officers were introduced in the navy, and these, too, opened the door to social promotion, though less dramatically than in the army. About a third of those recruited as officers in the navy between 1792 and 1800 came from families of nobles, previous naval officers, or officials, yet nearly half had fathers in the middle classes and one-fifth came from artisanal families. Even in the navy, social transformation was underway.[6]

Renovation, especially of armed forces, takes time, and the French had none to spare. The situation of the navy was especially difficult, since the training of naval officers took years. Although the navy's reputation had been bolstered by its successes in the American War of Independence, it never got the same attention as the army. In 1789, the French government claimed to have 72 ships of the line (sailing warships) and 63 frigates but estimated that the British had 108 ships of the line and 80 frigates. In an attempt to catch up, the French launched 38 new ships of the line between 1783 and 1793, but the British retorted with 44. Mutinies, the collapse of discipline, and the flight of noble officers left the navy in a particularly desperate condition, making the French favor action on land.[7]

With an army in the midst of reorganization, the French had to find new approaches. In the heat of battle and under the threat of complete dissolution, they discovered the power of large numbers and the motivating force of the nation. The regular French army, excluding the king's various personal regiments and the militia, had about 155,000 men in 1789. As many as 200,000 volunteered in 1791 and 1792, and another 150,000 were raised by the levy of February 1793. After the general mobilization ordered in August 1793, the size of the army swelled to 750,000 men, at least officially. The recruitment process was far from smooth and orderly: thousands of the original volunteers were probably soldiers of the regular army who left it and "volunteered" in order to get the higher pay and shorter term of service offered to the volunteers. The difficulty of recruiting is underlined by the number enrolled after the levy of February 1793; known as the levy of 300,000, it produced only 150,000 recruits because of draft evasion and even violent resistance. A young man could be declared unfit for service, join others in rioting against the authorities, marry, or buy a replacement. The rate of official desertion in 1793–94 hovered between 4 and 8 percent, but draft evasions could reach as high as 50 percent in some departments.[8]

The rapid expansion of the army put new pressures on discipline, the training that keeps individual autonomy in check. The rank and file of the regular infantry had already proved restive as the nobility's right to dominate—and therefore command—crumbled. Mutinies rocked the royal army in 1790; soldiers demanded to see financial accounts and gathered to discuss the merits of their superior officers. The admixture of volunteers who subordinated their supposedly temporary role as soldiers to their permanent one of citizens only increased the pressure for discussion and explanation. Local Jacobin clubs invited soldiers to their meetings, and after May 1791, the deputies allowed them to attend when off duty. Although the cavalry, which itself tripled in size between 1789 and 1794, retained the habits of the monarchical regime for a longer time, infantry soldiers might now question not only their commanders but even the government itself.[9]

In this situation, soldiers had to be offered new incentives. Patriotism, loyalty to their fellow troops, and more personal relationships with their superiors kept them from disintegrating as a fighting force. One young volunteer from northwestern France, sent to shadow the

Prussians after Valmy, lamented how the enemy had denuded the countryside but also felt the indignity of their political insults: "They beat the poor peasants who wore tricolor cockades, tore out the liberty tree [planted to express enthusiasm for the Revolution]." He reported that he and his younger brother were doing well: "The zeal with which we serve the fatherland has enabled us to brave everything, and not one among us, at whatever price required, would have wished not to have left our homes." Their commanding general, "Citizen Dumouriez," congratulated them on the courage they had shown and as a "reward" chose them to conquer Belgium.[10]

The relationship of the rank and file to their generals could only be ambiguous, however. On the one hand, ordinary soldiers craved a connection with their leaders, but on the other, they could only wonder about the political loyalty of nobles with a long history of insisting on their social superiority. A Parisian volunteer named Louis Bricard recounted that Dumouriez came to their camp a week after Valmy with two agents from the National Convention to announce that the deputies had abolished the monarchy and set up a republic. The troops greeted them with cries of "Vive la République!" and "Vive Dumouriez!" By mid-November the battalion of volunteers was planting liberty trees in Belgian villages and dancing with the locals. But in April 1793, when Dumouriez defected to the Austrians and tried to bring his army with him, Bricard and his comrades did not join him. They straggled back to Paris and were arrested along the route, only to be released to rejoin the army. In July 1793, representatives from the National Convention announced to the troops the arrest of the new head of the Army of the North, General Custine; Bricard affirmed that the army "observed the most glum silence, [and] appeared sad and dismayed to see itself constantly betrayed when facing the enemy."[11]

Custine, a count by birth and veteran of both the Seven Years' War and the American War of Independence, was relieved from his command because his failure to lift the siege of a major fortress seemed to confirm suspicions about his loyalty. He was convicted of treason and guillotined in August 1793. He was not alone. No fewer than 198 generals and admirals were arrested in 1793, and of the 31 sent before the revolutionary court, 16 were condemned, 15 acquitted. More than 2,200 men served as generals or admirals between 1792 and 1815; of these, 124 were condemned to death, half of them in 1793 and 1794, at the high-water mark of distrust of noble officers. It is therefore not surprising that generals sometimes tried to refuse promotions, from brigadier general to major general, for instance, fearing that increased responsibilities would also make any shortcomings more visible to political authorities.[12]

Bricard's account draws attention to three key aspects of the soldiers' experience in the early years of the French Revolution. He identifies with "the army" as a whole, though his own decisions are shaped by the reactions of those closest to him (they flee together). He feels allegiance to the nation but has trouble understanding just what that might mean. And faced with the unreliability of many generals, ordinary soldiers like him had to rely either on rumor or on the explanations offered by officials sent by the national government. To address the uncertainties of soldiers like Bricard, cheaply printed newspapers destined for specific armies had begun to appear in April 1792, and in the spring of 1793, the government began distributing copies of national political journals to the soldiers. To show their personal concern for the troops, the deputies of the National Convention ordered that their official *Bulletin* be circulated among the soldiers, and it was often posted on battalion billboards. But even though the war ministry bought up literally millions of copies of different patriotic newspapers and sent them to the front, a surprisingly large number never reached the men, in part because of difficulties with the postal system and the armies being in constant movement, but also because some commanders resented the intrusion.[13]

War almost always boosts patriotism in the civilian population, but combating the enemy has an even more galvanizing effect on soldiers, so although the government's propaganda efforts necessarily fell short of

REVOLUTIONARY ARMIES AND THE STRATEGIES OF WAR · 97

their aims, those doing the fighting embraced defense of the nation as their raison d'être. A battle-hardened volunteer such as Sergeant Jacques Fricasse, son of a gardener from northeastern France, usually only noted the ups and downs of combat in his journal, yet he could wax eloquent in late May 1794 about the patriotism of his comrades: "I saw in this fighting brave republicans covered with wounds gather all their force at the moment of breathing their last breath and hurl themselves forward to kiss the cockade, the sacred token of our conquered liberty. I heard them offer to heaven ardent wishes for the triumph of the armies of the republic."[14]

A volunteer from eastern France, François-Xavier Joliclerc, captured more of the ambivalence of those around him even while underlining his own sense of patriotism. In December 1793, he wrote to his widowed mother with some irritation because she wanted him to get out of the army at any cost. He responded with three obstacles to his doing so: it was hard to find replacements, even if you offered them enormous sums; the age-group of those called up was soon to increase from eighteen to twenty-five years old to include those up to thirty-five years old, so you would lose the money paid out for a replacement in any case; and finally: "When the fatherland calls us to its defense, we should fly there as I would run to a good meal. Our lives, our goods and our skills do not belong to us. All that belongs to the nation, to the fatherland." He granted that many in his hometown did not share the same sentiments, but for him, "who was raised with freedom of conscience and thought, who has always been a republican in spirit even if obliged to live under a monarchy, these principles of love for the fatherland, for liberty, for the republic, have been not only engraved on my heart but have become embedded there and will remain there as long as it pleases that superior Being who governs everything to maintain in me a breath of life."[15]

Joliclerc may have tried to rise above the divided feelings of many of his fellow soldiers, but lurking beneath the positive spin in many of the combatants' letters were a whole host of necessarily conflicted emotions. As historian Thomas Dodman has argued most forcefully, ordinary men cannot have found the sudden refashioning of themselves as revolutionary citizens to be easy or stress free. For all their lives, they had been subjects of a king and members of a society dominated by noble privileges. While clubs, newspapers, and even the novelty of voting in national elections surely affected the outlooks of people (including women) at home in France, the volunteers learned as much or more from their army experiences. They shared quarters and food with eight to ten comrades, drilled together, stood guard and fought alongside one another. Their views developed in interactions with their comrades, their officers, local people, agents and communications sent out from Paris, and in letters exchanged with those at home.[16]

Still, they had anxieties in coping with the ever-changing political situation. On July 17, 1792, Gilbert Favier, an officer in a volunteer battalion from the middle of the country, wrote to his mother complaining of the growing attacks on Lafayette, who was admired by many volunteers for his early support of the revolution. "I want to see proofs to show that Lafayette is guilty," he insisted: "The majority of our army thinks like me, it has the greatest confidence in the general, we do not want a two chamber [legislature], we do not at all want a republic, we want our constitution, we will die before letting someone harm it; and we would ourselves turn against Lafayette if he was capable of thinking of changing it." Lafayette would only defect to the Austrians on August 19 after the uprising of August 10 resulted in the king and his family being put under house arrest. The mood promptly changed. As soon as the troops got word of the proclamation of a republic in September, Favier added a new heading to his letters; now "the 4th year of liberty" was joined by "the 1st of the Republic." A few months later, Favier was prepared to believe the worst of Dumouriez, who went over to the Austrians on April 5. He blamed him for every calamity besetting the republic. By now Favier had adopted—or at least claimed to have adopted—the ever more pervasive language of "the terrible plots being uncovered."[17]

In such circumstances, the new generals, especially those who had

REVOLUTIONARY ARMIES AND THE STRATEGIES OF WAR · 99

risen rapidly through the ranks, quickly grasped the need to remain accessible in new ways to their men, from whom, unlike Lafayette and Dumouriez, they differed little. Lazare Hoche provides a particularly striking example. The son of a royal kennel guard in Versailles but raised by his aunt, who sold vegetables, he had enlisted in the French Guards of the royal army at the age of sixteen in 1784 and five years later was still a lowly corporal. After 1789, he ascended from sergeant to captain (1792) and then adjutant general (1793), all by the age of twenty-five. At the end of 1793, he was named divisional general in charge of the Army of the Moselle. He laid out his principles to his officers in a letter of November 1793: "See the troops every day, provide their most pressing needs, rekindle confidence, maintain discipline and accelerate its progress, raise the degree of current patriotism—these are, I believe, the things with which we must ceaselessly occupy ourselves." He insisted on a sense of care for the men. "Greet the complaints of the soldier with kindness: this respectable class is the purest of the army, [so] do right and, in every case, severely punish the guilty of whatever rank they might be."[18]

Even battle-hardened aristocrats such as Custine quickly learned to gain the affection of their troops. One of Custine's planning staff, Laurent de Gouvion Saint-Cyr, remembered years later that Custine's successes on the battlefield in 1792 and 1793 won him the "entire confidence of the troops." Custine inspired real affection: "his way of haranguing them, his familiarity, his military bearing, even if a bit grotesque due to his enormous mustache, contributed not a little to exciting the enthusiasm of the soldiers for his person. I never saw generals who were as loved." Saint-Cyr had enrolled as a volunteer in fall 1792 after unsuccessful careers as a painter and actor. He was almost immediately elected second lieutenant and soon after captain. Within a year he made the rank of adjutant general. He went on to considerable fame as a general under Napoleon, was named count of the empire and field marshal, and after the restoration of Louis XVIII was elevated to marquis and minister of war.[19]

The most ordinary soldiers gained multiple opportunities to rise through the ranks. Advancement started immediately for the early volunteers like Saint-Cyr who elected their officers. In a region of northwestern France, for example, the elections in September 1792 of a battalion's officers produced as lieutenant colonel Guillaume Guiut, a thirty-three-year-old man who had served in the royal army for fifteen years without going beyond the rank of sergeant. A battalion was commanded by two lieutenant colonels and comprised nine companies. Elected captain of the company of grenadiers was Pierre Verger, a thirty-seven-year-old former soldier who had served ten years in the royal army before retiring in 1784. He distinguished himself in battle and was named major within the year and then adjutant general. Serving in a variety of different general staff positions, he ended up a brigadier general in 1797. Although half of the lieutenant colonels elected from the volunteers in 1792 had military experience, half did not. Guiut's second-in-command, for instance, was Jean-Jacques Duboys, the twenty-three-year-old son of a notary whose only previous experience was with the national guard, a militia formed spontaneously across France in 1789 to maintain order.[20]

In early March 1795, Lazare Carnot, the chief military expert on the Committee of Public Safety and a former army engineer, found it possible to sum up French successes in glowing terms:

> All the old routines, all the military prejudices have been overturned in the course of this war. It will be beautiful to see in the register of the Republic's greatest events how badly armed recruits unaccustomed to military drills, without any training other than confidence, and often lacking clothing or food, stopped the flood of the legions united against them by all the countries of Europe; how good farmers, who wanted only love and candor, forced to combat for the defense of their hearths, led by leaders chosen from amongst them, and singing together hymns to Liberty, have vanquished and dispersed those silent and cunning hordes driven by nobles supposedly distinguished in military science.

French triumph depended on the leadership of their generals, "these modest men, who were born in a formerly disdained class" but who nonetheless "suddenly surpassed" all the great generals of preceding centuries. Needless to say, the generals and their men prevailed thanks in part to the organizational skills of men like Carnot.[21]

More was involved, however, than just confidence, camaraderie, or leadership. Strategy and tactics were evolving to make the best use of the growing numbers of men serving. This evolution took place in the hothouse of battle as newly appointed officers tried to cope with an expanding army made up of a volatile combination of volunteers and regulars left from the previous regime. Given the uncertainties of the situation, however, it is perhaps not surprising that the new republican government often intervened in questions of strategy and even tactics and intruded most frequently in the crisis years of 1793–94, when deputies were sent out to the various armies to supervise everything from supplies to the decisions made by generals. Governmental interference gave rise to a paradox. The generals had to answer to politicians and administrators who often worked at cross-purposes even to each other, thus creating confusion and disarray. But despite or perhaps because of the turmoil, government officials were able to exert more power than ever before over military decision-making.

Because the National Convention, elected in September 1792, had not replaced the king with an alternative executive power, military affairs could fall under the jurisdiction of an array of different officials, including the minister of war, who was appointed by the convention; the Committee of Public Safety, made up of twelve deputies of the convention; the military committee (folded into the war committee after September 1792); deputies sent out on mission; and the deputies meeting as a whole back in Paris. France had thirteen different war ministers between July 1789 and April 1794. As a consequence of the number of different hands stirring the military pot, it is hardly surprising that the organization of the army remained for many years a work in progress. The most basic arrangements were constantly debated and only gradually settled. Guibert's crucial suggestion that the army be composed of divisions that combined infantry, cavalry, and artillery in independent units was only partially instituted before 1789, and in 1789 he was still having to defend it against complaints from the officer corps.[22]

Once the monarchy had been replaced with a republic, uniformity could finally win out. In early February 1793, deputy Edmond Dubois-Crancé, himself a former soldier, laid out the plans of the war committee for reorganizing the army in "exact forms." This meant amalgamating every battalion of the regular army with two battalions of volunteers to make up a "demi-brigade," each of which would have attached an artillery company. They were called demi-brigades to avoid the Old Regime connotations of "regiment." Every brigade would have a brigadier general and every division would now have a lieutenant general, adjutant general, two aides, and a war commissioner. These officers were responsible for ensuring that orders from higher up were executed. The most important innovation was the attaching of artillery companies to the demi-brigades rather than leaving them together under control of army commanders.[23]

Dubois-Crancé's report also called for an expansion of horse artillery to twenty companies, another example of how the revolution swept away previous obstacles to reform. Horse artillery had been introduced in Prussia by Frederick the Great in 1759, but French officials only authorized their creation in 1792. The numbers rose rapidly from two companies of six guns each in January 1792 to thirty companies by the summer of 1793. Horse artillery offered several advantages over the traditional foot artillery. The crews were mounted on horses or on the ammunition wagons rather than marching alongside on foot, so the equipment could be maneuvered more quickly, making it possible to bring up a reserve cannon in the midst of battle, as happened at Valmy.[24]

Horse artillery made much more effective all the improvements in guns launched by Lieutenant General Jean-Baptiste Vaquette de Gribeauval. As inspector general of artillery after 1764, Gribeauval had reduced the caliber and weight of most field artillery without sacrificing range by changing the ways the guns were manufactured. He also introduced howitzers and improved mortars. He had not pushed for horse artillery despite favoring it because his other reforms had met such resistance over the years. The revolution removed that obstruction, and though horse artillery had its own problems—at first using cavalry officers with little artillery training—it soon gained a brilliant reputation, especially for countering the cavalry of the enemy, which was almost always superior in number and training to French cavalry. Replacing emigrating cavalry officers had proved difficult due to the preparation required, and requisitioning horses for the cavalry was especially challenging once war cut off foreign markets. When he joined a regiment of light cavalry (*chasseurs*) in 1792, Joachim Murat, the future aide to Bonaparte and eventual king of Naples, had to pay 2,000 livres to equip himself, a considerable sum for the time. Horse artillery also proved critical to French success because the infantry volunteers lacked the training necessary to fire in a predetermined order. As Custine complained at the end of 1792, "The fire of our infantry counts for nothing, our cannon and our bayonets, those are our sole arms."[25]

Sieges and wars of position gave way to wars of movement with their reliance on local sources of provisions. The change was best explained by Antoine-Henri Jomini, a Swiss military theorist who served as a general under both Napoleon and the Russians. Wars of position—huge army camps besieging or defending fixed, often fortified, locations—had dominated military strategy from the Middle Ages to the French Revolution, he wrote. The war began in 1792 in the same spirit but abruptly changed when the French Republic found itself attacked in 1793 on multiple fronts, both from within the country and without. With a million men (Jomini's exaggeration) and multiple armies with no tents, no supply depots, and no money, the necessity for mobility turned out to be an advantage. Tactics also changed: relatively compact columns were preferred over widely dispersed lines in part because skirmishers could be used to cover the columns' movements. "This system," Jomini concluded, "born thus from circumstances, succeeded at first beyond all expectations; it disconcerted the methodical troops of Prussia and Austria."[26]

Defense, most evident at Valmy, no longer seemed sufficient, and in 1793, officials in Paris began to insist that generals take the offensive. In a letter of April 1794 most likely composed by Lazare Carnot, the thinking was clear: "The defensive posture was always baleful to French values, as it is the comportment of cowardly troops or lazy nations. The offensive posture is the only one that suits the national temperament, and the *furia francese* [French fury] cannot be limited to defending citadels and entrenched camps." "French fury" was not a new term—it dated back to the end of the 1400s—but it was now expected to take new forms.[27]

Despite Jomini's insistence that the French relied primarily on columns with skirmishers in support, even their opponents recognized that they alternated, depending on the rapidly shifting context. The German officer Gerhard von Scharnhorst marveled, "the French armies, compelled by the situation in which they found themselves and aided by their national genius, had developed a practical system of tactics that permitted them to fight over open or broken ground, in open or close order, but *this without being aware of their system.*" Contrary to von Scharnhorst's assessment of French lack of awareness, some French officers grasped the necessity of this system of tactical alternation, which had been anticipated by Guibert many years before. Saint-Cyr explained the emphasis on skirmishers as a logical response to the inability of raw recruits to adapt to the traditional practice of firing in three lines. He criticized the *Regulation concerning the Drill and Maneuvers of the Infantry* of August 1791, which remained in effect until 1831, because "it was better suited to make the troops shine in ceremonial maneuvers than it was practical when confronted with the enemy."[28]

According to the 1791 regulation, the first line was supposed to fire while kneeling and the second while standing behind them; the third was meant to reload the guns for the second. Loading the standard musket required twelve steps according to the regulations. All this flew out the window during intense combat, Saint-Cyr insisted: "In war soldiers fire wherever they are without passing their guns to their comrades and without kneeling." As a result, "During the first campaigns, we only undertook a war of skirmishers, . . . [and] the novelty of this system produced some success." The soldiers, especially the volunteers, complained of the obsessive attention to drill. A volunteer from eastern France, Gabriel Noël, wrote home to say, "I don't believe they help to develop the intellectual faculties of those who practice them all their life." He described his second lieutenant, a veteran, as a "good lad," but insisted that though the officer "certainly knows how to perform the drill . . . that is all he knows."[29]

Flexibility, varying between open or close order or different forms of close order, did not mean lack of coordination, however. In a detailed study of the tactics employed by the Army of the North between 1792 and 1794, historian John Lynn has shown that this crucial army used every tool at its disposal and chose the most appropriate ones depending on circumstances. These included the use of skirmishers in independent action but also in support of troops in close order, killing gunners of the enemy artillery, for instance, or preparing the way for a mass bayonet attack. But the choice was not limited to skirmishers; the line, column, and square were all deployed, just as Guibert had advocated in his insistence on a pragmatic "mixed order." The infantry stood in line when on the defensive or waiting for the battle to be engaged. The square, which required training, served to repel cavalry (and could on occasion be formed by artillery). Positioning in columns facilitated rapid advance. The attack column with bayonets was used to turn the tide of battle, but it could only succeed if the columns could reach the enemy before it could get off a deadly barrage of fire.[30]

Although the French may have relied on improvisation and individual initiative, the most astute observers could see what was needed: a mass war, that is, the development of a huge army in which soldiers could react both individually and collectively. At the end of 1792 or early in 1793, the royal military officer, Count Philippe de Grimoard, sent his assessment to the National Convention. Given the desire of many deputies to add Great Britain, the Dutch Republic, and Spain to the list of enemies, which they did in early 1793, the French had to figure out how to use men who lacked training, discipline, tents, and sustenance to fight armies numbering 750,000 men. Grimoard believed the way to succeed was "to make a war of masses, that is, to always direct as many troops and artillery as possible at the points of attack." Generals, he insisted, had to remain at the head of their men to urge them on by personal example. Firing in lines and the usual maneuvers would be useless, given the lack of training. The soldiers had "to throw themselves suddenly [on the enemy] with bayonet blows." Even as the soldiers gained training, bayonet assaults remained central.[31]

The idea of a "war of masses" may have been vague at first, but it soon gained adherents among the generals, deputies, and ministers because it resonated with revolutionary principles while also meeting the immediate challenges of making war. The national mobilization ordered in August 1793, for example, was famously called the *levée en masse*. In a major speech on October 10, 1793, the deputy and ardent follower of Robespierre, Louis de Saint-Just, explicitly referred to the French "war system": "If in this war the French nation is pushed by all the strong and generous passions, the love of liberty, the hatred of tyrants and of oppression; if, in contrast, its enemies are mercenary slaves, automatons without passion; the war system of French arms must be *l'ordre du choc* [the method of shock]."[32]

Although Saint-Just did not say so, French armies now often undertook massed bayonet shock assaults as a way of substituting for cavalry, which remained ineffective until 1794. The integration of cavalry into divisions diluted its force at first, and it only gradually recovered its surveillance functions and ability to charge the enemy at great pace, sabers in hand. When muskets were lacking for the new infantry recruits, the

REVOLUTIONARY ARMIES AND THE STRATEGIES OF WAR · 107

government even temporarily resurrected the pike, long since abandoned by the French armies. Carnot argued for the move in July 1792 as a deputy in the Legislative Assembly. He reminded his colleagues that the pike was as good for offense as defense because it reached longer than a bayonet, and he insisted that it was particularly suited to the French because they wielded a bladed weapon (*arme blanche*) more capably than they shot their muskets. The pike disappeared as the supply of muskets improved, but the use of bayonet assaults continued to be vital to French tactics.[33]

Faced with green troops and covering ever larger distances, generals had to make do, and tactical improvisation would continue over the years. The guns had not changed since the end of the Old Regime; the mentality had. Improvisation can be traced in the ways that new recruits were instructed. A faster pace of march would make greater maneuverability possible, so instructors moved almost immediately from the 76 steps per minute set out by the 1791 regulations to 90 steps per minute, making it the routine marching rhythm. Acceleration to 120 steps per minute had always been prescribed for charging the enemy, but now it was also ordered for changing positions or forming columns.[34]

Tactical innovation and individual initiative reached their height in the person of Napoleon Bonaparte, whose exploits in the Italian campaign of 1796–97 galvanized attention. Even before then, however, he had stood out as an artillery captain during the siege of Toulon in the fall of 1793. As the son of a minor Corsican noble family, Bonaparte had attended military school in France and was commissioned as a second lieutenant in 1785. Having once dreamed of serving in the navy, he chose artillery in part because it was one of the few branches of the military where merit could prevail over patronage and wealth under the Old Regime. Bonaparte did benefit from political connections once the revolution began, in particular his ties with certain deputies on mission and political figures in Paris. But the contacts would have counted for little if he had not shown remarkable capabilities. At Toulon he took over the artillery when the previous captain in charge was injured; Bonaparte had been passing nearby with a convoy of military supplies. With an astute placement of batteries, he broke the English hold on the harbor and was promptly promoted to brigadier general. Wounded twice during the action, his leadership accorded with Grimoard's insistence that commanders should motivate their men by personal example.[35]

Named commander in chief of the Army of Italy in March 1796, only five months after his elevation to divisional general, Bonaparte had carefully studied the terrain during an earlier tour with the Army of Italy and now developed his signature campaign strategy: aim for an early decisive battle to prevent the armies of his enemies (in this case the Austrians and Piedmontese) from joining together; fight them separately to maintain superiority of numbers; concentrate forces at critical places by marching at a fast speed; and pursue the defeated relentlessly. In a few weeks he took a ragtag army of less than 40,000 and conquered Piedmont and Lombardy. The Austrian chancellor Thugut complained in November 1796, "When one realizes that Bonaparte, a young man of twenty-seven years, with no experience, with an army that is only a heap of brigands and volunteers, with half the strength of ours, defeats all of our generals, one must naturally bemoan our decadence and debasement."[36]

Success would bring new problems to the French military and government. As they pushed back their enemies, the French promised liberation to those on the lands they conquered on the model of the French Republic, but that promise soon rang hollow. Although the French army made efforts to repress ad hoc pillaging by the soldiers, it displayed no compunction about appropriating works of art or demanding cash, gold, and silver, often taking local hostages until they were paid. Requisitioning of horses, mules, oxen, and grain frequently aroused peasants to revolt, especially in the Italian states in 1796. The French soldiers themselves recognized the damage inflicted by their passage. The same artillery volunteer who reported dancing with the locals in Belgium in 1792 commented sadly on the damage done by the army's advance through the Rhineland in 1796: "Our march ravaged the crops that were already well along; with sorrow I saw that the pillage turned the inhabitants into so many enemies that would undoubtedly cause us setbacks."[37]

Wherever discontent turned into armed resistance, harsh French repression created lasting bitterness. When the people of Cairo rose up in October 1798 and killed about three hundred French soldiers, the French retaliated with cannonades, killing at least three thousand, and hacked to death several prominent prisoners. After the French took Jaffa in Palestine in March 1799, they executed four thousand Turkish prisoners; the governor of Jaffa had responded to their demand for capitulation by cutting off the head of the French envoy. French soldiers felt little kinship with the local inhabitants, who provided cover for those who stole from the French camps or mutilated their comrades who had become separated from their units. One second lieutenant wrote, "These fanatical and fatalistic peoples only respond to force, which is their supreme law." French atrocities in the Middle East prefigured those of General Leclerc in Saint-Domingue in 1802, who recommended a "war of extermination" against the Blacks of the mountains, not unlike the one waged against rebels in the Vendée at home.[38]

The invasion of Egypt ultimately bogged down the French army, but not its commander. As soon as the Anglo-Turkish fleet left Egyptian shores, Bonaparte secretly gathered three of his leading generals— Murat, Louis-Alexandre Berthier, and Jean Lannes—his new Mamluk servant, and about two hundred soldiers and left for France on August 22, 1799, in a small squadron of frigates. After delays caused by unfavorable winds, he arrived in Paris on October 16, basking in the recently arrived news of his victory over the Turks at Aboukir. The thirty thousand men he left behind only managed to return two years later.

Within a month, and despite bungling his part in a plan to remove the Directory government, Bonaparte became First Consul in the new government that he would soon dominate. The events that produced the regime change on November 9 and 10, 1799, did not constitute a military coup but were a coup nonetheless. Elements of the civilian government had allied with some of the military men to install an authoritarian government led by a general but manned almost entirely by civilians. Bonaparte was an obvious choice because of his popularity after the Italian and Egyptian campaigns. He had burnished his image of conquering hero and even savior by cunningly crafting his bulletins from the front. The relatively inexperienced commander of a supposedly secondary army in Italy had become the most famous man in France. But Bonaparte was not the only possible option, and he could not have come to power without the assistance of Berthier and Murat, who helped win over other officers in Paris, and Lannes, who took command of the troops in Paris.[39]

The coup brought to power a general who would steadily claim for his civilian government an array of dictatorial powers. Bonaparte capitalized on weaknesses in the republican government, but his quest for power ultimately grew out of changes that had taken place within the army itself. In the early years after 1789, civilians had feared the potential for counterrevolution within the armed forces, but increasingly after 1794, the military came to view itself as superior to a civil society seen as driven by self-interest.[40]

The amalgamation of volunteers had democratized and to some extent civilianized the army between 1791 and 1794, but as the army spent more time outside France and on the battlefield, it became more professional and identified more with the generals and with military honor. By 1798, only 3 percent of the soldiers had served in the royal army; 28 percent had volunteered, while the others had been called up. Although some, like Bonaparte, might have believed that the military needed to regenerate civil society, the professionalization of the army also ensured its political passivity in response to the November 1799 coup. Most of the officers who knew that something was brewing simply waited to see what would happen. Authoritarian populism—the reliance on plebiscite, propaganda, police spies, and strict control of the press rather than brute force or terror—was the ad hoc creation of Bonaparte and his closest advisers, but its emergence had been facilitated by changes in military culture.[41]

The trajectories of Bonaparte's three closest military advisers reinforce these points. Murat's support at the moment of the coup was decisive, for he led the troops, sword in hand, who dispersed the legislators denouncing Bonaparte as a "tyrant" and "dictator." "Throw the buggers out," he ordered, and the deputies fled. A rump legislature named Bonaparte one of three leaders of a new government, but it soon became apparent that Bonaparte had taken charge. Three months later Murat, who had been made divisional general during the battle of Aboukir in Egypt in July 1799, married Bonaparte's eighteen-year-old sister Caroline.

The thirty-two-year-old general had been born the son of innkeepers in southwestern France. The youngest of a family of eleven children, Murat had been destined for the Catholic Church, but when he was expelled for bad behavior, he joined the cavalry in 1787. Having received a solid education in the seminary, he rose rapidly from private to quartermaster sergeant when the outbreak of revolution brought him home. He helped train the local national guard and rejoined the cavalry in 1791, just at the moment when many higher-ranking officers were emigrating. Promoted to lieutenant in 1792, captain and then major in 1793, Murat managed to combine hard work and a reputation for bravery in battle with an aptitude for being in the right place at the right time. In May 1795, his unit tamped down a last revolt from the left in Paris, and in October he provided key assistance in defeating an insurrection from the right. The man in charge in October was Bonaparte. Murat's reward was promotion to colonel and a place on Bonaparte's general staff for the Italian campaign. There his boldness and magnetic hold on his men gained him constant attention. Bonaparte used him repeatedly as his personal envoy, and at age twenty-eight Murat was already a brigadier general.[42]

Unlike Murat, who suffered few battle injuries, Lannes was covered with battle scars and eventually died in battle in 1809. The son of a farmer in southwestern France, he was apprenticed to learn the trade of a cloth dyer when he volunteered for the army in 1792. He was immediately elected second lieutenant in the grenadiers, the elite unit of the infantry. Despite beginning with little learning and no training, his almost reckless daring in leading the avant-garde of any unit to which he was assigned enabled him, too, to rise quickly to brigadier general in 1796 and divisional general in 1799. Bonaparte began referring to Lannes's courage in his dispatches from Italy to the Paris government in May 1796 when Lannes was still a colonel, and he soon gave him tasks the equal of those assigned to brigadier generals. By the end of May, Bonaparte had attached him to his general staff as the officer in charge of security. After keeping an eye on Paris during the coup in 1799, Lannes was named commander of two divisions in the southwest tasked with repressing any resistance to the new regime, but he soon reported little dissension.[43]

The career of Bonaparte's chief of staff from 1796 onward, Louis-Alexandre Berthier, is the exception that proves the rule. He was older—thirty-six in 1789—and from a more prestigious family. His father, though not noble, had close contacts with the royal family because of his position as a topographical engineer in the army; he made maps for Louis XV and Louis XVI and rose to the rank of lieutenant colonel. His son joined the army as a teenager and fought in the American War of Independence, rising to the rank of lieutenant colonel himself in 1788. Berthier's service as chief of staff to Lafayette in spring 1792 and the family's history with the monarchs prompted suspicion, however, and Berthier was suspended from his functions for a time in 1793–94. He was reintegrated as a brigadier general, the rank he had obtained before being suspended.

By early 1796, when Bonaparte picked him as chief of staff, Berthier had become a divisional general. His ability to grasp the complexities of any situation in order to pursue as offensive a strategy as possible made him an invaluable right-hand man, and his shared battlefield experiences with men such as Lannes and Murat created lasting bonds. At the

Battle of Lodi in May 1796, for example, he and Lannes were among the generals who jumped to the head of a column of light infantry that had begun to waver in its attack on a key bridge. After the battle, Bonaparte reported to the government in Paris that "intrepid Berthier . . . was, during this day, gunner, cavalry man and grenadier." During the coup that brought Bonaparte to power, Berthier continued to play the role of chief of staff, keeping careful notes about those likely to sympathize with a coup and providing moral support at every decisive moment. As soon as he came to power, Bonaparte named Berthier minister of war.[44]

An army in crisis opened up new spaces for individual initiative, but those individual capacities were bent to new ends, as the army was transformed by distance and constant fighting. Thanks to his leadership qualities and his skills at magnifying his image, Napoleon Bonaparte became first a cultlike figure for his soldiers and then a credible ruler of France despite his Corsican origins (Corsica had become an official province of France in the year of Bonaparte's birth, 1769). He could rise to these heights because the French army was increasingly fighting for long periods of time outside France, and after more and more years of service the soldiers, in particular the volunteers, stopped thinking of themselves as ordinary citizens temporarily taking up arms and instead identified as professional soldiers. Lannes, himself a volunteer, captured a feeling that was no doubt widely shared among Bonaparte's closest aides when he wrote to Bonaparte in December 1799: "One of the characteristics of the revolution of 18 Brumaire [the November 1799 coup] is that you alone could have done it. . . . In all the countries I have traveled, we shout neither 'Long live Moreau!' nor 'Long live Sieyès!' but 'Long live Bonaparte!'"[45]

Lannes frequently wrote to his wife about longing for peace, but only after 1805 and when he became personally disenchanted with Napoleon, finding him fickle in his attachments and unwilling to share his glory. The state of government in France hardly ever crossed his mind after 1799. Lannes did not live long enough to get much benefit from

Napoleon making him Duke of Montebello in 1808 with a small fortune in revenues. Napoleon never relied just on his personal charisma. From his first days with the Army of Italy, he had learned the importance of patronage, and over time, his gifts only became more and more stupendous. Merit still mattered, but Napoleon's fragile sense of his own legitimacy as supreme ruler required constant bolstering.[46]

Individual initiative and social belonging often worked together but sometimes operated at cross-purposes in the revolutionary armies. The French succeeded against all odds because revolution created new expectations about individual capacities, and ordinary men rushed forward to demonstrate them. In the end, however, success also depended on having the biggest army in the field during a given battle; strategies that could make the most of both individual initiative and mass formations; and novel forms of requisitioning, manufacture, and mobilization of men. Armed with these new resources and aptitudes, the French eventually got the upper hand but found that they could not then rein in the forces that had been unleashed. Liberation turned into occupation, defense of the homeland metamorphosed into imperial aggrandizement, and the result after seven years of nearly constant fighting and more than a million deaths was the elaboration of a fateful political form: populist authoritarianism directed by a general, Napoleon Bonaparte. This new regime diverted the prospects of individual initiatives and state resources to the ends of national and Napoleonic glorification. The tension between autonomous selves and ubiquitous social conditioning thus reached excruciating levels during wartime. Ordinary soldiers could achieve previously unimaginable advancement through the exercise of their individual initiatives, but their newfound allegiance to the nation and to their charismatic superiors also facilitated their acceptance of an increasingly dictatorial authority.

Five

MONEY, SELF-INTEREST,
AND MAKING A REPUBLIC

THE RELATION BETWEEN INDIVIDUAL AUTONOMY AND social belonging might be most fateful in the case of the armed forces, since life and death were often on the line, but the relation was (and is) even more conflicted when financing government. No one wants to pay taxes, yet states habitually encroach on individuals in the name of the collective good by demanding levies of various sorts. The slogan "no taxation without representation" captured the British North American colonists' grievances about their relationship with Great Britain before independence, and it pointed to an underlying democratic revolution in the making: increasingly, governments had to justify taxation by claiming to be in some fashion representative of and accountable to the nation. Reinforcing this elementary connection between individuals and the state was the establishment of a national debt when it was supported by individuals buying bonds or shares—rather than states simply borrowing from bankers—and by governments that provided relatively transparent balance sheets to their citizen creditors. With a national debt supported by ordinary citizens, it could be said that the people owned their government or at least invested in its operation. In this way, individuals pursued their financial self-interest while also tapping into their social belonging by sharing in the risk of supporting a nation's debts.

We now take national debts almost as much for granted as taxes, as national debts have been shown to be vital to the historical development of representative forms of government. However, most eighteenth-century Europeans and North Americans did not see national debts as desirable. This averseness is perhaps not surprising if we consider that even today the size of the national debt is an issue. Everyone supposedly wants to reduce it to avoid burdening future generations and limiting their options. In 1752, the philosopher David Hume reviewed the various defects caused by the national debt: it drew riches to the capital at the expense of the provinces; public bonds (Hume called them stocks) were a form of paper money and pushed out gold and silver, rendering everything more expensive; taxes had to be increased to pay the interest on debt, thus raising the cost of labor and oppressing the poor; foreigners could buy into the national debt and make the nation tributary to them; and the ownership of public bonds encouraged idleness because it rewarded those who owned paper rather than working in some productive capacity. He concluded, "Either the nation must destroy public credit, or public credit will destroy the nation."[1]

Hume was echoing the views of the French jurist and philosopher Montesquieu, who offered his own list of "inconveniences" in *The Spirit of Laws* in 1748: foreigners took their interest on the debt out of the nation; a nation perpetually in debt had a low exchange rate; taxes raised to pay the interest on the debt hurt manufacturers by inflating the price of labor; and, in an argument echoed by Hume, the debt took the state's revenue out of the hands of the industrious and gave it to the indolent. "These are its inconveniences," Montesquieu maintained, "I know of no advantages." Citizens of the new United States and revolutionary France shared these views. In his second annual address to Congress in

MONEY, SELF-INTEREST, AND MAKING A REPUBLIC · 117

1802, Thomas Jefferson referred to repaying the national debt as "the emancipation of our posterity from that moral cancer." For their part, the French revolutionaries immediately began discussing the king's debt when the Estates General convened in May 1789. They spoke of the liquidation, discharge, and amortization of it, only rarely of guaranteeing it. They hoped that they could pay the debt down over time, not have it be permanent.[2]

As Hume's analysis makes clear, public debt was problematic because it required an investment in some form of paper money. Paper money had a long and very vexed history in Europe and particularly in France. Some sense of the mountain to be climbed can be seen in the experience of the United States, which did not make federally issued notes legal tender until 1862 and then only because the Civil War was draining the treasury. "Legal tender" meant that public and private creditors were required to accept the notes as payment. France had experimented with paper money in the early eighteenth century when a Scottish financier, John Law, set up a bank in 1716. With government approval, it became a national bank issuing notes. Law then tried to pay off the monarchy's debts with a complex series of maneuvers: he combined all the commercial companies set up to develop the colonies into one megacompany; the company then took over most forms of tax collection and the crown's debts, sold shares at 3 percent dividend, and arranged for the crown to pay 3 percent per year interest (much lower than its usual rate). The shares skyrocketed in value at first but then collapsed in 1720, leading to the failure of both the company and the bank. Bad memories of the "Law system" haunted the financial discussions of the 1789 French Revolution. The explosive combination of debt, paper money, and speculation seemed destined to destroy the king's (or nation's) credit.[3]

Still, paper money of a sort had long been in use by merchants. Called bills of exchange, these instruments of long-distance trading relied on the trustworthiness of the individuals and the commercial houses involved. The payment demanded when exchanging them for specie (gold and silver) depended, like the interest on state bonds and annuities, on the perceived risk, that is, the creditworthiness of those issuing and trading commercial paper. Bills of exchange were not always converted to specie; they became freestanding vehicles of credit that could be passed from one hand to another. Bills of exchange were therefore like paper money except that they were not legal tender. They circulated only within private commercial networks.[4]

Compared with its rival Great Britain, the French government had to pay higher interest rates to gain access to these private credit markets (5 to 6 percent in France as compared to 3 to 4 percent in Britain). The British crown got funding through the Bank of England, a private corporation founded in 1694 that raised money from private investors, loaned money to investors who then bought government securities, and advanced money directly to the state. In 1776, after decades of ignored proposals, the French government authorized a privately funded Discount Bank (*caisse d'escompte*) in Paris. In exchange for a 10-million-livre deposit in the crown's treasury, which was effectively a loan reimbursable over thirteen years, the Discount Bank gained various privileges: it sold shares as a joint stock company, redeemed bills of exchange, served as a currency exchange and bank for individuals, and circulated its own notes. Bills of exchange were customarily discounted in France at rates varying from 4 to 6 percent, depending on the reputation of the holder and issuer of the paper, but the Discount Bank was required to redeem at 4 percent to facilitate the lowering of interest rates in general. Some hoped the Discount Bank would become a national bank like the Bank of England.[5]

At the same time, even while most politicians still rejected the idea of a permanent national debt, risk itself was becoming a kind of commodity, especially in new forms of insurance, such as life insurance. Like bills of exchange and marine insurance, life insurance originated in Italian cities and was at first closely connected to moneylending and commercial risk. Seen as a form of gambling, life insurance was banned in

MONEY, SELF-INTEREST, AND MAKING A REPUBLIC · 119

much of Europe, including France, but it took root in England in the eighteenth century. The French government authorized a life insurance company in November 1787. The way was paved, in a terrible irony, by the practice of insuring the lives of the enslaved on the voyages of the slave trade, and was considered a form of marine insurance. The study of social—in this case demographic—trends was crucial to life insurance; enterprising individuals learned to make money by attracting investment in premiums and calculating life expectancies through actuarial tables. Death, like taxes, might be certain, but the when and the how of death were not.[6]

The organizer of that first life insurance company was the Genevan-born financier Étienne Clavière, and his spectacular rise and fall provides an especially illuminating example of the connections between risk and debt, self-interest, and the fiscal foundations of the new French Republic. He was the son of a French Protestant cloth merchant who, like many other French Calvinists, had moved to Geneva after the criminalization of Calvinism in France. Étienne joined his father in establishing business contacts in Amsterdam, London, and Paris after spending four years of apprenticeship in the German states with French Calvinists who had fled there. An earlier temporary episode of deafness had cut him off from most social relations, so he had spent his youth studying instead. Working with his father in a business with extensive international connections meant that he had to learn the essentials of "banking," that is, the trading of bills of exchange. He married a cousin who was the daughter of a wealthy merchant in Marseille. In 1780, their daughter, an only child, married Pierre-François Vieusseux, a licensed broker in Geneva.[7]

Even while developing his own commercial interests as a wholesale merchant and financial investor, Clavière grew increasingly involved in Genevan politics and took a lead in agitating for a more representative government. In 1782, finding himself on the losing side of an uprising in Geneva, he fled to Neuchâtel with his family. In the last days of the Genevan revolt, Clavière had grown close to Jacques-Pierre

Brissot, a twenty-eight-year-old Frenchman already known for his fiery writings advocating wholesale reform of law and government. Brissot had raced to Geneva hoping to witness a revolt firsthand, and he saw in the older man—Clavière was forty-seven—a possible mentor. Once in Neuchâtel, Clavière resumed his friendship with Brissot and met Mirabeau. Mirabeau and Brissot would go on to play starring roles in the early years of the French Revolution. Clavière, according to a Genevan associate, was timid and lacking in personal courage, yet all his life he put himself in situations that required boldness: "He liked trouble, he took delight in an anxious situation, and he dreaded the consequences."[8]

After fleeing Geneva and failing to attract enough followers to the watchmaker colony he proposed to set up in Ireland, Clavière decided to make Paris his base of operations in 1784. The man whom Brissot later described as having "an inexhaustible supply of new ideas" soon played an unanticipated role in the Parisian financial markets, using the pen of Mirabeau to ensure the success of his short-selling schemes and supporting Brissot both financially and politically. He was not the biggest player in the financial markets, but he learned quickly and promptly grasped how to leverage public opinion to achieve his financial goals.[9]

Clavière's learning curve shot up when he faced financial collapse. Even before the failure of the Genevan uprising of 1782 sent him fleeing, he had been in close contact with Étienne Delessert, a financier born in Lyon into a Swiss Protestant family in the textile business (Clavière's father had a similar business). Delessert had moved to Paris in the mid-1770s to set up a branch of the family business but quickly shifted his interest to banking and became an administrator of the new Discount Bank. Many of the biggest stakeholders in it were of Swiss Protestant origin. In June 1781, Clavière wrote to Delessert in Paris asking his advice about his shares in the Discount Bank bought on Delessert's recommendation: should he sell them after the dividend was paid or keep

MONEY, SELF-INTEREST, AND MAKING A REPUBLIC • 121

them to borrow against? At that point the dividend was 7.17 percent, but by early 1783 the Discount Bank had issued notes worth seven times what it could pay out in gold and silver. When the government ordered the suspension of payments in September 1783, Clavière found himself with 275,000 livres in payments due on his investments and no way to reimburse them without selling his shares of the Discount Bank at a great loss.[10]

He managed to hold out until the government removed the suspension and confidence in the bank returned, but Clavière's temporizing threatened his relationship with Delessert. On December 20, 1783, he wrote to Delessert a long, rather self-pitying letter that reveals the importance of mutual trust in these financial transactions:

> I would rather live the life of a convict who owes nothing to anyone and who could count only on his own arms than to solicit favors that cost me so much in return . . . you have not done more for me than you would have done for anyone, I have corresponded with you as an honest man, negotiating correctly, corresponding peaceably, and I have taken more care in protecting you from any risk than I have had for taking advantage of the services that I had reason to expect.

Once installed in Paris at the beginning of 1784, Clavière would find new ways of ensuring his fortune, while still relying on the services offered by Delessert.[11]

Shocked by the French government's attempts to directly influence markets, Clavière transformed himself into a short seller and advocate for a more moral commercial environment; he did not consider short selling unethical because it was a way of undermining speculation that irrationally inflated assets. In early 1785, Clavière bet on a decline in the Discount Bank's dividends, which he and some others considered overvalued, and at first the government seemed to favor the short sellers when it insisted that dividends must be based on real revenues, not speculation. But when the government found itself accused of aiding the short sellers, it promptly annulled all previously negotiated futures and premium contracts. In a premium contract, the seller paid a premium to the buyer that basically insured the seller against a loss when the futures contract came due; the seller would not have to sell at a disadvantageous rate and would only forfeit the premium. Some investors then refused to reimburse the premiums on the annulled contracts. In the midst of the agitation over the dividends, Clavière confronted one of the opponents of the short sellers on the floor of the Paris exchange and either slapped or punched him, according to the most widely circulated underground newsletter of the time. Clavière's trepidation had its limits, and he was now a controversial figure.[12]

He was not about to go away quietly. In March 1785, Mirabeau agreed to write a tract criticizing the government's intervention with sections contributed by Clavière, Brissot, and the French Protestant economist Pierre Samuel du Pont de Nemours (father of the founder of the DuPont company in the United States). It became the talk of the town. Mirabeau set out his collaborators' arguments against excessive financial speculation, meaning speculation that increased the value of assets beyond the real revenues being produced. He struck all the usual notes of alarm about financial speculation and did so with brio:

> We know what the deadly system of financial speculations has cost in terms of the happiness and innocence of societies; we know what the action of greed aggravated by the ease of gaining very considerable and accelerated profits can and must produce; we know that the mania or rather the furor of gambling infests all the ranks, creates turmoil, contaminates morals, isolates and hardens men; we know in particular that gambling on public funds, by facilitating the loans that it makes easier, favors the passions of the administrators, exaggerates, misleads, [and] intoxicates power, foments, tightens, [and] confirms slavery, [and] aggravates oppression and degrades the human race.

No wonder that Mirabeau and his collaborators published without the name of a place or publisher.[13]

Clavière now looked farther afield. Next up was the Bank of Saint Charles, the first central bank created in Spain. Founded in 1782, it had the monopoly of commerce in Spanish silver and was soon the subject of speculation in France, where shares in the bank cost much more than they did in Madrid. Clavière sold his Parisian shares and asked Delessert to buy shares in Madrid in anticipation of a general decline in value. Mirabeau published *On the Bank of Spain, Called Saint Charles* in July 1785, but Clavière and Brissot were the true authors, once again denouncing corrupt speculators and the governments that encouraged them. The value of the shares in Paris soon plummeted. Clavière knew precisely what he was doing, for he wrote to the Delessert branch in Lyon on July 16, "A very small work is going to appear that could well cause again some sensation," and since its effects would be felt more promptly and more deeply in Lyon than in Paris, he asked the branch to buy the Saint Charles shares when they reached a certain low level (so that he could pocket the difference when he used them to fulfill term contracts). The government's decision to suppress the pamphlet only drew more attention to it and to a follow-up.[14]

While still involved with the Saint Charles Bank, Clavière, again using Mirabeau's pen, went after the Paris Water Company, founded as a private concession in 1778 to deliver water to Paris. The publication of *On the Shares of the Water Company* in October 1785 ignited a pamphlet war with Pierre Caron de Beaumarchais, the author of *Marriage of Figaro*, an administrator of the Paris Water Company, and one of the early shareholders in the Discount Bank. In fact, the water company proved to be an easy target, as speculation had repeatedly pushed its share values far beyond what the company could actually deliver. Moreover, Clavière had developed a new project to establish both life insurance and fire insurance companies, and he would face direct competition from the Paris Water Company, whose founders wanted to move into insurance as well. The fortunes of the Paris Water Company ebbed and flowed, with Clavière alternately gaining and losing money, but in the end it was pushed toward bankruptcy and government takeover.[15]

Losing money on some investments when his timing was off, Clavière thought he had found a better way. Writing in January 1786 to his new favorite banker, Pieter Stadnitski, in Amsterdam, he said that in the future he was going to invest principally in life annuities (*rentes viagères*) offered by the French government. "It is my wet nurse, my savior," he affirmed. "I find that it is not yet understood how well it compares to everything else. People let themselves be dazzled by more brilliant objects, but the life annuity is the turtle whose slow steps lead to the goal; the others are the hare that loses himself running after his enthusiasms."[16]

The life annuity offered by the French monarchy was a peculiar investment. The investor took a risk by giving up a family's fortune in return for yearly payments during his or her lifetime. The payments ceased on death, so the crown would benefit if the investor died before recouping the initial investment. Conversely, life annuities could be lucrative to buyers who lived long lives and financially disastrous for the French crown, which put no limits on the lives or "heads" that served as the basis of the investment. From 1771 onward, Genevan investors had developed a system of syndicates investing in thirty heads, using the lives of thirty carefully chosen Genevan girls under the age of seven. The annual income (about 10 percent) was pooled and shared proportionally among the investors. Clavière could use the dividends he gained to pay the lower rate of interest on the loans he had taken out to invest in life annuities in the first place. And shares could be bought and sold on the market. By his own account, Clavière had invested nearly 1.5 million livres in life annuities as of April 1786, but he owed 2 million livres to his creditors in Paris, Lyon, London, Amsterdam, Genoa, and Geneva. Clavière stayed afloat by balancing loan repayments against dividends and further loans. He knew how to make the most of risk and debt in the short term but also kept digging deeper into their workings.[17]

MONEY, SELF-INTEREST, AND MAKING A REPUBLIC · 125

When issuing the life annuities, state authorities made only crude estimations of life expectancy, so investors began to see the advantage of the more precise knowledge that could be gained from actuarial tables, in particular those published by Richard Price in England in 1783. Actuarial tables were useful for investing in life annuities, but they were even more vital for establishing life insurance companies. Clavière quickly grasped their significance and the possible connection between life annuities and life insurance, both based on life expectancy.[18]

Before 1785, insurance, other than marine insurance, was largely unknown in France. A few plans had come to nothing before the Paris Water Company proposed a fire insurance company, which the government authorized in August 1786, but without an exclusive privilege. In September, consequently, a new group, almost surely organized by Clavière, published its prospectus for a similar fire insurance company, and the government allowed it to compete with the Paris Water Company. The Paris Water Company then proposed a life insurance company to insure the payments of life annuities in case of premature death. Clavière upstaged them again in November 1787 when the crown granted an exclusive privilege for a life insurance company to his group's fire insurance company. Six months earlier, the Academy of Sciences had announced its approval for such a project based on a report presented by two of its members. Condorcet, who would become one of the founders of "social science" and was already known for his mathematical prowess, was one of the two.[19]

The Royal Life Insurance Company, as it was called, combined Clavière's financial self-interest with his long-standing utopian streak. He believed that commerce could serve moral purposes and help shape a better society. His attempt to set up a watchmaker colony in Ireland on the model of Geneva was an early effort in this direction. His enthusiasm for the new United States, for the abolition of slavery, and for republicanism would emerge at the same time as his plans for a life insurance company. Although Clavière's company would flounder in the turmoil of the French Revolution, his innovation anticipated the eventual successful establishment of such companies in France by more than thirty years. So convinced was he that he published a one-hundred-page prospectus explaining how insurance worked and just how premiums would be determined, with elaborate tables to illustrate his points. "The general utility" of insurance "cannot be doubted," he insisted. "In every country where one cares about the happiness of individuals," men who have invented insurance are considered among the "benefactors of society." He emphasized the company's efforts to help those of modest means, and while administrator of the company, he also proposed in 1790 the founding of a mutual aid society for servants at a time when such societies were known only among skilled artisans.[20]

To get exclusive rights, the insurance company promised to raise 16 million livres as a guarantee through share offerings that would be deposited with the government in return for 5 percent interest payable every six months. Clavière was named administrator with a monthly salary of 1,200 livres, a house, and a loan of 150,000 livres on favorable terms. Although the Clavière group successfully fended off an attempt led by the formidable Swiss banker Isaac Panchaud (the original backer of the Discount Bank) to organize a competing company, which Mirabeau this time supported with a pamphlet against the Clavière group, the fire and life insurance companies barely survived until 1792–93. The fire insurance company was facing liquidation, and the life insurance company had given up the insurance part of the business when both were suppressed, along with all financial companies, including the Discount Bank and East India Company, by decree of the National Convention on October 8, 1793. But this unraveling could not have been predicted in 1787.[21]

Because Clavière witnessed firsthand the crown's incessant efforts to borrow money, it is not surprising that state debt intrigued Clavière and eventually pulled him into politics. In April 1786, in addition to his 1.5 million livres in life annuities, he had nearly 700,000 livres invested

MONEY, SELF-INTEREST, AND MAKING A REPUBLIC · 127

in French government loans that were not life annuities, and in the fall of 1786, with his Amsterdam bankers Cazenove and Stadnitski, he organized a syndicate of Dutch bankers who proposed to buy the entire French debt of the new United States and sell it to investors. They would pay France 20 of the 24 million livres owed and profit from the sales. In the end, after a long wait, the US government decided against their proposal. The proposal was not far-fetched, since the United States depended on Dutch investors to cover its interest payments to the French; the United States' government expenditures far exceeded its domestic revenues.[22]

Clavière had more than a passing interest in the United States, an enthusiasm he shared with Brissot. With the French consul in New York, J. Hector St. John de Crèvecoeur, they set up a Gallo-American Society in early 1787 to encourage trade and relations between the two countries. A few months later, Brissot and Clavière published a tract in which they provocatively argued that freedom of the press was essential to maintaining a country's public credit. France had prepublication censorship, and dissidents often faced exile or imprisonment. Brissot and Clavière suggested, though they did not dare say so very explicitly, that the United States could serve as a model of republican virtue for France. They had been deeply influenced by Crèvecoeur's *Letters from an American Farmer* (1782), which lavished praise on American morals and customs in ways that recalled classical republican virtues. In their treatise, Brissot and Clavière also defended the Americans' use of paper money, arguing that it was only problematic when it could not be exchanged against gold and silver. Clavière would go on to play a central role in the French revolutionary debates and policies concerning paper money.[23]

Clavière and Brissot's excitement about the United States included potential utopian projects. Clavière still dreamed of setting up a Genevan-style colony, and Brissot seriously considered moving to the United States. In any case, Brissot wanted to visit in person. His journey of six months there in 1788 was financed by Clavière, Cazenove, and

Stadnitski, who asked him to gather as much information as possible about the solidity of the federal and state debts, with a view to their investing in them. They also wanted him to investigate buying lands newly offered for sale in the territory northwest of the Ohio River with paper based on loans to the American government. Any plans for moving were shelved after Brissot's return to Paris in December 1788; events in France would now rivet both Brissot and Clavière.[24]

Brissot and Clavière had irritated French authorities by publishing a series of pamphlets in 1787 and 1788, *No Bankruptcy, or Letters to a Creditor of the State.* In rejecting the argument for a crown bankruptcy, they insisted that the government would have to call the Estates General to consider new financing and favorably compared English finances to those of the French monarchy: "Profoundly exhausted by a war that lasted seven years [the American War of Independence], supporting a national debt bigger than ours with a population half as numerous, [the English] have nonetheless found the secret, with a less fertile soil and less varied resources, to annually retire a part of their debts." Even the Americans, they contended, were able to maintain the public's faith in their debts despite their many problems. The American Revolution "has singularly enlightened peoples about their rights," that is, all peoples, including presumably the French. The authors attributed a discovery of individual capabilities to the Americans: "They learned that to let a man develop freely is to create genius, talents, riches, [and] that consequently freedom is the true source of their treasures."[25]

To exit from the crisis in France, the authors concluded, the demands of the *parlements* (high courts) had to be met: call the Estates General to consider new taxation, reveal the true extent of the deficit to the public, and abolish *lettres de cachet*, the extrajudicial orders used to imprison dissidents. The authors also demanded a national constitution. Fearing a *lettre de cachet* in retaliation, Brissot fled to London, where Clavière joined him between November 1787 and February 1788. Brissot had already experienced life in the Bastille for a few weeks in 1784 and

MONEY, SELF-INTEREST, AND MAKING A REPUBLIC · 129

was not interested in another stay. Wasting not a moment, the two men pursued contacts with leading English abolitionists and joined the Committee for the Abolition of the African Slave Trade.[26]

When they returned to Paris in early 1788, they set up a sister group, the Society of the Friends of Blacks. In its opening statement, Brissot and Clavière inserted their theme about developing individual potential in this French context: "In a free society, man is drawn by his personal interest to develop his faculties to the highest degree." In a free society, necessarily governed by "universal reason," people must see that slavery violates "the first of truths: *all men are born free*." The nation is bound to be convinced therefore that "the slavery of Negroes is a crime." In roundly condemning slavery while also praising the new American republic in previous tracts, Brissot and Clavière were invoking the new language of freedom and rights and giving it a social and economic dimension. Slavery contradicted the fundamental principle that all men are born free, and freedom, when guaranteed, allowed individuals to develop their potential so they could create knowledge and wealth. The Friends of Blacks attracted such leading lights as Lafayette, Condorcet, renowned chemist Antoine Lavoisier, Mirabeau, and various other aristocrats and churchmen. Without the Friends of Blacks, there would have been no debates about slavery.[27]

In setting up this political action group, Brissot and Clavière clearly intended to further an international antislavery movement that would include the United States and Great Britain as well as France. More was involved than the abolition of slavery, as important as that goal was. Behind their interventions in favor of increased trade with the United States, greater transparency in French government finance, and this nascent movement for the abolition of slavery was an underlying interest in fostering republican virtue across national borders. Geneva was the original model, especially as understood in the writings of Rousseau (himself a Genevan), with the new United States providing a second, and in some ways even more compelling, model because it had successfully demanded its independence. Brissot and Clavière were true visionaries in seeing the transnational connections between slavery, trade, access to credit, constitutions, and the potential for republican virtue in the citizenry. After war broke out in 1792, their transnational vision would get them into trouble.[28]

Clavière was elected the first president of the Friends of Blacks and took an active role in its discussions. In April 1788, for instance, he insisted that it had no interest in fostering a violent revolution to achieve its ends but rather hoped to gather the facts and explain to everyone that justice and humanity demanded the abolition of slavery. Condorcet took over as president in January 1789, but Clavière still attended regularly and intervened frequently in discussions. The Friends of Blacks followed Brissot and Clavière in pursuing international contacts, not only with Britain and the United States but also with the Dutch Republic. In early February 1789, the Friends of Blacks voted to send a letter to all the regional meetings held to elect deputies, asking them to request that the forthcoming Estates General take up the cause of the Blacks and consider suppression of the slave trade, which a few of them did.[29]

The Friends of Blacks monitored discussions in the Estates General and then the National Assembly, and though it got some support, it frequently found itself on the losing end of decisions about colonial matters. Already on September 1, 1789, Clavière complained that he had been personally threatened; he urged the Friends of Blacks to send a deputation to the Minister of the Navy and Colonies demanding to know if the ministry was feeding the rumors that the society was working on behalf of English interests. The presence of the English abolitionist Thomas Clarkson at the meetings of Friends of Blacks between August 1789 and January 1790 added fuel to the allegations. In response to the blowback, the Friends of Blacks focused on arguing for the abolition of the slave trade but not the immediate outlawing of slavery itself. This did not satisfy their proslavery critics. In March 1790, Mirabeau's younger brother denounced them as "these enemies of France, who want to expose to an

MONEY, SELF-INTEREST, AND MAKING A REPUBLIC · 131

almost certain death the planters of our colonies, who want to reduce to inactivity [and] plunge into misery that multitude of workers, sailors, artisans, merchants, capitalists, even farmers that the commerce of the colonies keeps busy, enriches, [and] renders prosperous."[30]

Even before the Estates General began meeting in May 1789, Clavière had continued to write about the national debt, arguing against the proposal for repudiation put forward by Simon Linguet in early 1788. Clavière insisted that renunciation would destroy public confidence in the nation's credit. In his lengthy riposte, Clavière was clearly defending his own self-interests as a holder of French debt, but he also had bigger fish to fry, including a statistical defense of France's ability to pay the interest on the debt and more general considerations about debt, constitutions, and the nature of French rule. The moment was critical because in early August 1788, Louis XVI had agreed finally to call the Estates General, which had not met since 1614, and soon after suspended until the end of 1789 all payments in cash for nonessential services and offered instead interest-bearing paper.[31]

Clavière now assumed that events would lead to the development of a constitutional monarchy and that the new constitution, which he insisted could never be based on a state bankruptcy, would be one in which "the nation would discover all the sacred and imprescriptible rights of social man." The king did not rule for his own profit, Clavière maintained, but rather "for the advantage of the individuals who compose the society of which he is the chief." The monarch governs as "supreme administrator," and that means that "he is not the master who can change certain laws that society wanted to make immutable for its own security and which as a consequence have become fundamental." Clavière's republican political principles, developed in Geneva and honed by thinking comparatively about Britain and the United States, were now finding resonance in France as demands for financial and political reform boiled over in 1787–88. He was already using the language of the "social" and "society," positing society as an entity of its own, separate from the monarchy and with its own underlying laws. He did this as someone reflecting on state finance and political economy but with a distinct background as a Genevan who had supported greater political participation at home. For him, constitutional government required transparency about the debt, which could only be national once its contours were known to the nation's citizens.[32]

Once the Estates General began meeting, Clavière's country home at Suresnes, five miles from the center of Paris, soon became the meeting place for Brissot, Mirabeau, and others elaborating plans for the work to come, including discussions of declarations of rights. Mirabeau was elected a deputy for the Third Estate (the commoners), since the nobles of his home region would have nothing to do with him; his younger brother was elected as a deputy from the nobility and would go on to oppose the revolution. Brissot and Mirabeau rushed to set up newspapers to report on unfolding events. Both papers were suppressed at first and then allowed after the attack on the Bastille prison in July 1789. The Estates General had opened in early May but did not begin serious consideration until late June, after the Third Estate deputies had successfully recast the meetings as those of a national assembly. The three separate estates—the clergy, the nobility, and the commoners—evaporated in favor of one assembly bringing together all the deputies. For his part, Clavière produced another pamphlet on financial matters in June 1789. Once again he argued against bankruptcy, but now he also put forward the reasons for issuing paper money as a temporary measure without connecting that paper to a national bank. The state would issue the paper. He also insisted on a complete revamping of the tax system and annual meetings for the National Assembly.[33]

Clavière's views on paper money gained urgency in the fall of 1789 as the National Assembly and the crown both scrambled to find new sources of revenue. Faced with uncertainty about the future, taxpayers simply stopped paying taxes and the monarchy's usual creditors held back from subscribing to new loans. In a long letter to Mirabeau's newspaper

Courrier de Provence in early October 1789, Clavière tried to shore up his argument against paper money issued by his old target, the Discount Bank, which Jacques Necker, the finance minister, wanted to turn into a national bank on the model of England's. Clavière still promoted paper money as long as it was issued by the state itself. His paper money would be guaranteed by gold and silver held by the state, which would be augmented by loans in the form of tableware or valuables from citizens. The interest on the loans would come from the Catholic Church's tithe revenues. In his proposal, the tithe revenues would be compensated as the paper was retired from circulation and the national debt paid off. Although he continued to operate on the assumption that the debt would be discharged, Clavière was taking the lead in thinking of ways to convert the crown's debt into a truly national one.[34]

Clavière's views were frequently drowned out in the cacophony of voices expressing wildly varying opinions on how to meet the financial crisis, but the first major decision taken in December 1789 concorded at least partially with his—and Mirabeau's—opinions. The Discount Bank would not become France's national bank, though its paper would continue to have currency for another six months. A special treasury office controlled by the National Assembly would issue notes called assignats, whose value was guaranteed by the properties confiscated from the Catholic Church. A portion of them would go to reimbursing the Discount Bank for money it had loaned the crown, and the rest could be held for interest payments or used to buy church properties and thus in principle retire the debt. In April 1790, the National Assembly abolished the tithe, gave the state direct responsibility for the assignats, and increased their number in circulation while also making them legal tender by requiring that they be accepted in any financial transaction.[35]

The disagreements were far from resolved, however, and Clavière published his opinions at a hastening pace in part because he hoped one day to become finance minister. He developed his own views of pressing issues, most prominently the notion that the sale of church properties afforded a unique opportunity to diminish social inequalities. He therefore opposed any measure that might block the access of ordinary people to them. He continued to defend the assignats as paper money in 1790 and 1791, arguing that unlike all previous experiments with paper money, the assignats were solidly supported by the mass of church lands and that they would be retired as the lands were sold off. He advocated an increase in the number of assignats in circulation and insisted that more borrowing was justified to establish a system of national education. With a major new issue, interest payments to creditors that had been suspended in 1788 could be resumed, he insisted, not without self-interest.[36]

He even responded directly to Necker, who in August 1790 had rejected any further creation of assignats beyond the 400 million livres already printed. Clavière reasoned that paper money had just as much value as gold or silver because even the values of gold and silver were determined by their circulation, not by any supposed intrinsic value of the metal. Paper money would only lose its value if it fell into discredit, and this would only happen if the enemies of the revolution or self-interested speculators made it so. Even if 2 billion livres in new assignats were distributed, this would not exceed the value of the goods confiscated from the church, which, he claimed, surely equaled at least 2.4 billion livres. Clavière also responded to worries publicly expressed by Condorcet and Du Pont de Nemours. In short, he was taking upon himself the role of the assignats' chief defender. In doing so, he referred to Adam Smith in particular and to England in general, maintaining that the English had three or four times as much paper money in circulation as gold and silver with no ill consequences for their economy. He cited the English example, as well, to argue for the printing of small denominations of assignats so they could be used by ordinary people in their daily commercial transactions.[37]

By September 1790, the *Courrier de Provence* was referring publicly to Clavière as he no doubt saw himself: "Mr. Clavière, who can be called the creator of the assignats, and who rises well above his critics and his partisans . . . ; Mr. Clavière defended them [the assignats] with an unshakable courage." This judgment is hardly surprising, since the paper, though officially Mirabeau's, was in fact in the hands of Clavière and various of his friends and associates from Geneva.[38]

Mirabeau's role proved decisive on the question of the assignats. He had expressed reservations previously, but on September 27, 1790, three weeks after Necker resigned, he firmly took Clavière's side, repeating his own earlier argument, derived from Clavière, that assignats were not paper money but rather state notes (*billets d'État*) made necessary by the fiscal crisis. In one of his characteristic rhetorical flourishes, Mirabeau blamed the lack of cash, by which he meant gold and silver, on the excesses of the monarchical regime: "A vampiric government has for more than a century sucked the blood of peoples in order to surround itself with ostentation and excessive abundance." Two days later the deputies voted to immediately issue 1.2 billion assignats. Mirabeau wrote to a friend that he considered this one of his greatest accomplishments and that the assignats would be "the hallmark of the Revolution."[39]

As the National Assembly wrestled with the seemingly intractable issues of the budget and began to think about the future administration of tax collection and government payments, Clavière offered his own reflections on these matters. He argued that disorder in state finances would cause the "social system" to "decompose." Once again he pointed to the "great superiority" of English commerce, which was made possible in part by the "imbecility" of the French regime of protection that was stifling talents and outraging "the sacred rights of man." What France required in addition to free trade was a simplification of the tax system and rationalized administration of finances beginning with a public treasury. It would be "public" in the sense of being subject to the scrutiny of the nation (only true at that moment in the United States, he conceded); salaried functionaries would answer to the legislature, not the king. Although some simplification of the tax system was achieved, at least in theory, the financial administration remained byzantine in its complexity well after Clavière's death. Once again, he had foretold innovations that would prove to be inevitable but difficult to introduce.[40]

Clavière continued his work on antislavery alongside financial matters. As debate had shifted away from abolition to the question of the status of free people of color, Clavière took up his pen to defend the Friends of Blacks against increasingly vociferous denunciations. In March 1791, he signed two short pamphlets from the Friends of Blacks in which he refuted the accusations by General Arthur Dillon, a noble deputy from Martinique, that the writings of the Friends of Blacks had fomented the troubles in the colonies and that journalists among the members might be in the pay of foreign powers, meaning the English. Dillon opposed any granting of rights to free people of color. Shortly thereafter, Dillon's colleague from Martinique, Médéric Moreau de Saint-Méry, repeated the claim that the Friends of Blacks had provoked the recent troubles in the colonies that included a rebellion of free men of color in Saint-Domingue, France's richest Caribbean colony. The free men of color had revolted against the white planters in October 1790, but they were defeated, and their leaders were executed in February 1791.[41]

Clavière had to respond not only to defend the Friends of Blacks' positions but also because Moreau de Saint-Méry had named specific members, including Brissot, when suggesting that the Friends of Blacks were secretly coordinating with English abolitionists to destroy French commerce. In his lengthy rebuttal, Clavière made clear his visceral rejection of the slave trade without bringing slavery itself into question: "nothing reasonable can be said in favor of a commerce where all the crimes are necessary instruments." He defended the "natural right" of the free men of color to determine their future because they had a direct attachment to the land. So much had opinion turned against the Friends of Blacks that Clavière found himself insisting on the potential usefulness of the free men of color to the white planters. As property owners, whites and people of color could join together to maintain order among the slaves. He published this pamphlet in March 1791 after the defeat

MONEY, SELF-INTEREST, AND MAKING A REPUBLIC · 137

of the armed uprising by the free men of color but before the great slave revolt that began in August 1791. In May 1791, the National Assembly agreed to grant political rights to free men of color but then rescinded its decision in September.[42]

In early April 1791, Mirabeau died unexpectedly at age forty-two. Clavière's political fortunes then depended even more on Brissot and the political faction that would be identified as Brissotins or Girondins (so called after the Gironde department or administrative region that some of them represented). Brissot and Condorcet were elected deputies to the Legislative Assembly that began meeting in October. Clavière, now officially a French citizen, was elected as a substitute deputy and set up the new monthly *La Chronique du mois* (The chronicle of the month) with Brissot and Condorcet. The Friends of Blacks apparently stopped meeting at this time, perhaps because news of the massive slave rebellion on Saint-Domingue, which began in late August, arrived in Paris in late October. Given that the news took two months to arrive in Paris, confusion and uncertainty prevailed for months to come. Brissot tried to hold back the reaction by arguing to wait for more information and even suggesting that the other islands were peaceful because of the armed presence of the free men of color. As the news grew more alarming, the "philanthropists," or "friends of humanity" as their opponents sarcastically called them, were often blamed. On November 9, 1791, Brissot insisted on responding to such critics that he favored the "humanization" of the colonial regime and the softening of the lot of the Blacks without favoring bloodshed or revolt.[43]

It is perhaps not surprising, then, that Clavière subsequently devoted all his efforts to the financial situation. The first pages of *Chronique du mois* in November 1791 incorporated a report by Clavière that made it clear that the first assembly (1789–1791) had not resolved the major financial issues. Needed still were an exact statement of the amount of the national debt, an inventory of national lands yet to be declared as such and evaluated, a transparent accounting of revenues and expenses, a restructuring of the financial administration, and forceful measures against paper money other than the assignats and against speculation on gold and silver. While still composing his list, Clavière rushed off to the new Legislative Assembly to petition it against issuing any more assignats until the amount of the debt was determined and to suspend payment on all those Old Regime offices previously held as property and now declared as reimbursable.[44]

By this time Condorcet had been won over to Clavière's arguments about the assignats and in particular the virtue of producing them in small denominations for everyday use by ordinary people. The accord of Condorcet meant that Clavière, thanks to his many writings and long association with Brissot, had become the chief financial expert for the Girondins, the party that would now argue most vehemently for war with Austria and for a republic. Clavière certainly favored a republic and quickly accommodated his opinions to the prospect of war. In November 1791, he affirmed that vigorous work on the financial situation would be needed to counter potential enemies: "Moreover, it is necessary to take against the politics of foreign powers, at times menacing, at times uncertain, measures that will secure all the parts of the empire." War was not declared for another five months, but Clavière wanted to be ready. He was preoccupied by estimations of the national debt, worrying that the most cited figures were either too optimistic or too pessimistic, but that even the most pessimistic evaluation could be managed if the assignats could be protected.[45]

The next month Clavière was back to defend his idea of provisionally suspending reimbursement of offices owned by Old Regime officials and of feudal dues, while arguing to protect the value of the assignats on which any repayment of the national debt depended. Clavière's original suggestion to suspend payment proved to be so controversial that he felt it necessary to write a pamphlet defending the idea against those who saw in it a partial bankruptcy of the state. He refuted the claim, saying that the reimbursements had never been fixed, either in terms of the

MONEY, SELF-INTEREST, AND MAKING A REPUBLIC · **139**

amounts to be paid or the dates at which they would be due. He also felt it necessary to denounce speculation on the French exchange rate, especially short sellers who would stop at nothing to "weaken or destroy public credit." Clavière certainly understood the practice: "This interior enemy feeds therefore on anything that could be either disastrous or create fear of disasters. [This enemy] will pay, if necessary, writers who are skilled in the art of false calculations in order to frighten the public about the financial situation." The shoe was now on the other foot, and it was definitely pinching Clavière. Despite repeated interventions by Brissot in favor of Clavière's proposal for suspension of certain reimbursements, the Legislative Assembly voted against the proposal on December 9, 1791.[46]

Clavière did not cease trying to influence decisions on finances, and his tone became increasingly alarmist. In January 1792, he railed against French bankers and "external enemies," calling out the former finance minister Charles-Alexandre de Calonne, who was collaborating with other anti-revolutionary aristocrats who had emigrated and financing one of the leading anti-revolutionary journals being published in England. Clavière also denounced British prime minister William Pitt for using English money to undercut the French assignats. He again insisted that the depreciation of the assignats could only be based on perfidy because their value was tied to the national lands up for sale and nothing was more solid than land. Clavière's desire for war had ramped up, and he wanted to go further than most of his colleagues by urging war against all the princes and not just Austria. One possible solution stood out for Clavière: a new finance minister, "an enlightened and firm patriot," "a national minister," whose actions could save the Legislative Assembly and the king and forestall a war. It must have been obvious to his readers whom he had in mind.[47]

In March 1792 Clavière finally realized his long-cherished dream of being named finance minister. The circumstances were less than propitious, however, as many assumed that the king had been willing to name him alongside other Girondins who favored war with Austria because

Louis XVI hoped to blame them for any failures to come. After the declaration of war on Austria in April, the first military defeats, and increasing tension between the Legislative Assembly and the king, Louis XVI fired the Girondin ministers in June. When the uprising of the people of Paris on August 10, 1792, culminated in the house arrest of the king and his family, the fired ministers were reinstated by the deputies. They continued to serve after the election of a new assembly, called the National Convention, which officially abolished the monarchy and instituted a republic for the first time in France's history.

Clavière's initial experience as minister had already revealed the depth of the financial problems to be confronted: tax payments dribbled in while the expenses of fighting a war required yet more resources, so the printing of assignats steadily increased; bronze, gold, and silver could not be confiscated quickly enough from the churches to provide the currency needed for the armies; and technical problems in printing small-denomination assignats opened the way to private exchange brokers. In his second tour, which lasted ten months, Clavière exercised more authority in theory because in the absence of the king, he now sat on a provisional executive council, but in reality his position remained fragile.[48]

Clavière's past financial machinations had not been forgotten, and his connection with Jean, Baron de Batz, who had helped him set up the life insurance company, could only be dubious, since Batz was an ardent royalist suspected of involvement in various conspiracies, including a doomed attempt to prevent the execution of Louis XVI on the day itself, January 21, 1793. The Girondin deputies had agreed that the king was guilty of treason, but many of them, including Brissot, supported a punishment other than an immediate execution. The defection of General Dumouriez in April 1793 made matters even worse. He had been the Girondin minister of foreign affairs and had pushed the king to name Clavière minister of finance. Having returned to the battlefield but disagreeing with many of the policies decided in Paris, Dumouriez

MONEY, SELF-INTEREST, AND MAKING A REPUBLIC · 141

tried to turn his army against the republican government, as we saw in the previous chapter. When that failed, he went over to the Austrians. His desertion cast a shadow over all the Girondins.[49]

Despite these gathering thunderclouds, Clavière labored frenetically to initiate the reforms he had been advocating for years. He sent a stream of letters to the deputies about his work and published long reports on the issues he faced in order to bring public opinion to his side. His most fundamental concern, the immediate problems of the assignats aside, was with the financial administration itself. Because the deputies had become very suspicious of the king's motives, they had put six commissioners in charge of the treasury in March 1791 and separated it from the finance ministry. The four changes in the title of the finance ministry between 1789 and 1793 and the frequent turnover in ministers—there were seven different finance ministers between July 14, 1789, and August 10, 1792—give an indication of the challenge. In addition, the various finance committees of the National Convention had to be consulted on most matters, and they often refused Clavière's requests.

It is hardly surprising, then, that the first line of one of Clavière's reports complained, "The ministry of public contributions [the name of the finance ministry] is an ill-considered dismemberment of the former ministry of finance." It was in charge of tax collection, but the money once collected went to the treasury, over which the finance minister had no authority. It was supposed to report on the obstacles facing tax collection, but without personnel on the ground, the minister had to rely on guesswork. It was supposed to supervise the properties confiscated from émigrés, but this task was shared with the minister of the interior, which led to inevitable delays and conflicts. The finance ministry was responsible for maintaining the national forests but had no personnel to do so. The list of other responsibilities was long: supervise the liquidation of the previous tax farms, oversee the national lottery, maintain the mint, authorize expenses for the postal system, supervise the office for gathering saltpeter and gunpowder, manage the production of assignats,

142 • THE REVOLUTIONARY SELF

maintain the land register, and liquidate the debts left from the civil list of the monarchy.[50]

To meet all these demands, a more professional administration was required, Clavière insisted, and that meant ending the practice of allowing ministers and deputies to place their friends where they wished. Each administration should be in charge of hiring, talent and virtue should be the only criteria, and those employed should not consider themselves in positions for life. In short, Clavière anticipated the reforms that would be instituted bit by bit over the decades to come. He did not achieve them during his short time in office, much of which was spent chasing after tax revenues that failed to materialize and trying to suppress speculation on the assignats. The task was impossible, as he complained publicly, yet he persisted.[51]

The new republic's financial difficulties forced Clavière to turn over every possible stone, from criticizing regional governments by name for not sending in their tax rolls to asking the Americans to pay back their debt ahead of time. The first won him no friends, and the second dragged on for months, even years, with the United States offering some advanced payments but not the entire sum and only completing the reimbursement in 1795, one year ahead of time, long after Clavière's disappearance from the scene. Having to work through the legislature, Clavière found that many of his proposals languished. He recommended raising taxes on the rich and requiring registration fees on the exchange of commercial paper. Only the latter was enacted. He advised closing the stock exchange, which happened after his time in office. He presented a plan for the reminting of coins that included very precise instructions for the figures that should now replace the king; the 20 sous coin, for example, would have a figure representing the spirit of France engraving the constitution with the end of a pike. The constitution would sit on a bronze table placed on the altar of the fatherland, all this on the face of a coin. The deputies sent the proposal to the committee on assignats, and when they finally decided to act in the spring of 1793, they ignored most of Clavière's overly fastidious recommendations. In fact, the question of reminting was put off because the deputies wanted to link it with a general reevaluation of weights and measures (the eventual metric system), which only developed piecemeal over time, and to an overhaul of the minting system itself (reducing the number of mints, for example). The franc was finally introduced as the new unit of money in April 1795.[52]

Looming over all of this and causing by far the most anguish to Clavière and the deputies was the fate of the assignats. In the fall of 1792, Clavière prevailed upon Pierre Cambon, the intellectual leader of the finance committee and often his adversary, to introduce a law prohibiting the circulation of any paper other than the assignats. In the absence of small-enough denominations of assignats, aid societies, in particular, had issued their own paper; the Paris municipal aid society had distributed upward of 10 million livres' worth even though they had far less than that in their coffers. In vain did Clavière then try to resist the extensions offered for the use of paper other than the assignats, which pushed their final extinction to later in 1793.[53]

Although the indefatigable minister insisted that the value of the assignats could be maintained and even restored, he was pushing a boulder uphill that was gaining weight by the day. Within months of the beginning of hostilities, the generals, supported by demands from ordinary soldiers, insisted that all payment to the armies be in coin. War inevitably caused inflation, and as government expenses ballooned, revenues could not keep up, even though tax collection had improved from its low point in 1790. One scholar has estimated that the proportion of tax revenue to expenses fell from 25 percent in 1792 to 9.5 percent in 1793, mainly as a consequence of an increase in expenses. Because everything was changing all at once, from the structure of government to the face shown on coins, it is, if anything, surprising that the assignats retained as much value as they did. The most comprehensive study on them has shown that the number of assignats in circulation increased from 1.8 billion livres in August 1792 (when Clavière began his second turn as minister) to 3.2 billion livres in May 1793 (the end of his time in office), an increase of nearly 75 percent, but the number doubled again by October 1794. During the same period, August 1792 to May 1793, their value against gold and silver declined from 72 percent to 58 percent. Still, they continued to decline between May 1793 and October 1794, to 35 percent. These general numbers mask incredible local variation, as near the frontier the rates were even lower.[54]

As if all these burdens were not enough, Clavière also attended to the situation in Geneva, where the success of French arms in the fall of 1792 provoked fear of a French invasion and annexation. The man who bitterly resented his exile in 1782 now concluded that neutrality, when it came to the French Republic, was a way of supporting France's enemies—the enemies, that is, of equality. Geneva must recognize the French Republic, he concluded. Clavière opposed General Anne-Pierre Montesquiou-Fézensac's willingness to accommodate the Genevans. As commander of the Army of the South, Montesquiou had occupied Savoy and could have taken Geneva. Clavière's allegations against Montesquiou, one of the many noble generals, led to the general's firing and flight to avoid prosecution in early November 1792. Clavière supported those who wanted to take Geneva in a more democratic direction but stopped short of advocating outright annexation, which occurred only in 1798.[55]

Clavière's eagerness to refute every criticism could not hold back the increasing barrage. He was, after all, a foreigner, a financier, a former speculator, an ally of Mirabeau (now revealed as an agent of the court) and of Brissot and the Girondins, and therefore increasingly a target of the "Mountain," those deputies closest to Robespierre who had supported the immediate execution of the king and now urged increasingly radical measures to get control of the economy and the political situation. The Genevan made matters worse by refusing to give up his

MONEY, SELF-INTEREST, AND MAKING A REPUBLIC · 145

position as administrator of the life insurance company when he became minister. In February 1793, the deputies heard complaints about his oversight of the printing of assignats. In early March, the Jacobin club in Paris listened to demands that he be removed from office as either "incompetent or treacherous"; by late March he was being accused of holding on to his post in order to squander the nation's finances "by his inertia and his insouciance." In mid-April Robespierre denounced him as "the artisan of all our misfortunes, the protector of speculation." Over the night of June 1–2, he was arrested at the same time as Brissot and the leading Girondins. On September 8, he was sent to prison; on September 19, his interrogation began.[56]

Clavière did what he always tried to do: defend himself in print. In his *Summary Account of the Conduct of Clavière, ex-Minister of Public Contributions [Finance], Done by Himself, Addressed to His Judges, His Fellow Citizens and His Enemies*, he answered all the possible charges against him, starting with those laid out during Jacobin club meetings. He could not have plundered French finances or speculated with money from the ministry or his own money because he had no access to the treasury and had so little personal credit. He was not named minister because of his connection to the Girondins, since his appointment was unanimously approved. He could hardly be accused of inertia, for he worked as hard as anyone might. As for the ludicrous charge that he failed to alert the convention to the prospect of civil war in the Vendée, which broke out in March 1793, how could he have known more than the local authorities or the agents of the minister of the interior? Finally, he was not in a position to order the interception of mail.[57]

He also answered the charges against him that had appeared in official accusations against other deputies and ministers. He did not use government monies to publish pamphlets against the revolution of August 10. He only supported the idea of fleeing the capital with the monies in the treasury to safeguard them in case the invasion of the Austro-Prussian armies in September 1792 reached Paris. He did not concert with General Montesquiou to betray the republic; after all, he reminded readers, Montesquiou had accused Clavière of provoking his removal from command. From there Clavière went on to deplore the various slanders that had been uttered to ruin his reputation: that he was a supporter of "federalism," the wave of revolts against the convention led in some cases by Girondin deputies under arrest; that he wanted a republic for the rich; that he enriched himself with counterrevolutionary monies; that he invested money abroad; that he favored the flight of gold and silver; that he was a creature of the Brissotins or Girondins and supplied them with assignats; and that he deliberately named underlings of suspect loyalty. He marshaled all the facts of his writings and his actions to refute the charges, including recalling his role in demanding abolition of the slave trade.[58]

Although he stoutly denied any wrongdoing about the assignats, Clavière could hardly disavow his relationship with Brissot and the Girondins such as Condorcet. Brissot had never asked for any favors once Clavière became minister; they each pursued their duties in their separate domains, Clavière insisted. Despite his valiant efforts, Clavière understood that his connection with Brissot might well doom him: "Far from considering me as the *creature* of a party that has succumbed to accusation, as having conspired against *the unity, indivisibility, liberty and security of the French people*, no one can doubt that I have been true to myself and that I have constantly preached union."[59]

His appeal fell on deaf ears. On December 8, he saw the official accusation against him and was ordered to appear the next day at the Revolutionary Tribunal. That night he killed himself with a knife taken from the supper service. Brissot had been executed on October 31; Condorcet committed suicide the following March. Clavière's wife took an opium overdose, but his daughter and son-in-law, who had followed him to Paris, survived, moving back to Geneva in April 1794. His brother Jean-Jacques, who had joined him in Paris in 1784, was arrested in the fall of 1793 and remained in prison until October 1794. Étienne Clavière's

MONEY, SELF-INTEREST, AND MAKING A REPUBLIC · 147

notoriety was too great to escape the fate of the Brissotins/Girondins. As he wrote, "no one can deny that the revolution has reached a height that had to leave behind the first apostles of liberty." He was neither the first nor the last apostle, but he did try as hard as anyone to anticipate the financial requirements of that liberty.[60]

Epilogue

SELF, SOCIETY, AND EQUALITY

EQUALITY BECAME THINKABLE IN THE 1700S WHEN INDI-viduals began to see each other as potentially autonomous and as joint participants in and makers of society. The claim seems simple, but it is actually big and complex and therefore requires some unpacking. Extending back for as long as anyone could remember, only elite men could act as autonomous individuals. Children, most women, servants, people without property, and certainly enslaved people could not shape their lives according to their own reason and will. Over the eighteenth century, the space for autonomy expanded as the age of majority, the rights of women and propertyless men, and the increasing demands of enslaved people for freedom all came up for discussion, legislation, and, in some cases, revolt. The vertical and hierarchical organization of society in which those on top demanded deference and obedience from those below was increasingly challenged by horizontal conceptions, including equality and rights. The emergence of social science and the increasing visibility of society and social relationships testified to this development and quickened it.

SELF, SOCIETY, AND EQUALITY · 149

Most people had little conscious awareness of these developments, though their actions reflected the animating force of new notions of autonomy and social belonging and renovation. Among them were the British women who sat at tea tables, read the new publications, and shaped social conversations; the creators and buyers of prints mocking the upper classes; the female artists, like Marie-Gabrielle Capet, who found new places to exhibit their works and new clients to buy them; and the hundreds of thousands of ordinary soldiers who dreamed of glory and advancement and sometimes attained them both. The more intellectually inclined, such as the Scottish philosophers and the French founders of social science, conceived new notions—the meaning of civilization and social science—and helped foster more conscious attention to these developments. The financier and finance minister Étienne Clavière found himself somewhere in between, reading the philosophers rather than writing philosophy himself, grasping the new emphasis on individual capabilities and the need for political reform, but using his insights to play the markets, establish new financial vehicles, and desperately try to right the new republic's financial ship.

Equality often tiptoed in by the back door. The law professor John Millar said nothing about the equality of the sexes, and with his ladder of civilizations he certainly did not promote any sense of the equality of different cultures. Yet he built his system around the central pillar of the status of women, and he paid close attention to the logic of different cultures. His ideas gained him a reputation in his time for dangerous radicalism.

French revolutionary prints proclaimed equality, most often by depicting scenes of inequality. Personifications of the concept "equality"—always a female because the French noun is feminine—were most often demure, as in the print *Égalité*, with the female statue holding a level, the symbol of equality, in the background of the scene. She oversees a moment of stronger feelings about equality in which two very different social groups come together. In his print, the artist François Quéverdo

François Quéverdo, *Égalité*, 1793. Etching with burin, 21.5 × 31 cm. The legend reads: "The coal porters, like the *chevaliers de St. Louis*, are required to deposit the distinctive symbol that they got from the Old Regime at the secretariat of the municipality; they will be given a receipt by the clerk, and to make a rapprochement worthy of equality, the same register that is used to record the deposits of the cross of St. Louis will also receive the deposits of the medals of the coal men. Decree of the Municipality of Paris, August 17, 1793, year II of the Republic." *Bibliothèque Nationale de France*

shows coal porters in their long pants and sturdy shoes handing over the distinctive medals of their occupation while upper-class men in their knee breeches, frock coats, and boots or fancy shoes give up their decorations from a special royal order. The legend of the print cites a decree of August 1793 that required everyone to hand over any insignia that had been distributed under the Old Regime. The law was meant to efface emblems of social difference, yet the print's portrayal of the differences in dress and demeanor reminded viewers of the inequalities at issue.

SELF, SOCIETY, AND EQUALITY · 151

Like many Old Regime artists, Quéverdo managed to pivot from book illustrations and portraits of the royal family in the 1780s to patriotic letterheads and revolutionary scenes. Marie-Gabrielle Capet left us nothing as obviously political, though she made a similar conversion in subject matter. Before 1789, she did pastels and miniatures of female members of the royal family. Continuing to do miniatures of aristocrats, including a presumed portrait of the son of Louis XVI in 1792, she shifted to more generic topics in 1793, such as *Portrait of a Woman and Her Child, Young Man in a Blue Jacket and Yellow Vest*, and *Portrait of a Woman*. At the same time, she also painted miniatures of specific individuals, including her patrons Vincent and Labille-Guiard, as well as two self-portraits.[1]

Capet might not have wholeheartedly embraced all the values of the new regime, and she certainly never put equality front and center in the way that Quéverdo did. Yet the audacity of her personal journey to Paris, to painting, and to exhibiting reveals that same aspiration for being seen as equal. The way she worked her way up from the position of apprentice to assistant and then to artist in her own right resembles those trajectories of the countless soldiers who rose meteorically through the ranks of the army. Capet's sense of individuality and social significance coalesced around the depiction of fashion, including her own fashion choices, since fashion is a prime locus for the meeting of self and society. In a miniature self-portrait from the late 1790s, for example, Capet depicts herself wearing the same dress and black cap as in Labille-Guiard's portrait of her from 1798, with her hair again powdered and styled in the fashion of the day. But she portrays herself sitting on a simple chair without the tools of her trade. Instead of a white neckpiece and cuffs, she highlights a green lapel that matches the green ribbons on her cap and a white neck scarf not unlike some of the cravats that will appear on the men in her 1808 painting of Labille-Guiard's studio. With these variations she establishes her individuality and equality.[2]

Soldiers were also dealing with a new sense of self. From letters written by soldiers to their families, we know that one of the recurrent themes, aside from homesickness, boredom, hunger, and fear, was the sense of equality to be found in the units, especially those of volunteers. One volunteer from eastern France wrote home in January 1792, months before the declaration of war and even longer before the establishment of the republic, now "we are all equal, all soldiers of the *patrie* [fatherland]." In November 1793, a lieutenant in charge of a company of artillery wrote to his town magistrates about recent fighting and concluded, "I am, citizen magistrates, with the respect due to the magistrates of the people and your equal in law." At times, soldiers headed their letters with the slogan "Liberty, Equality" or even "Liberty, Equality, Fraternity or Death." Slogans such as these might not seem to mean much, except that they were for family and friends to see. Even when "equality" had become an official value celebrated in festivals, speeches, and prints, it still had to be lived and felt to make sense, and the armies provided countless ways for feeling its impact. The experience of equality flowed from the increasing potential for individual initiative and from the emotional comfort, excitement, and reinforcement of belonging to a mass army. That this understanding of equality within the army did not necessarily translate into acknowledging the equality of peoples in occupied lands does not make it any less significant. The army was the school of the nation and nationalism and as such provided a growing sense of equality among the social classes.[3]

Étienne Clavière believed in equality even though his personal circumstances might have dictated otherwise. He was prosperous, thought himself of superior intelligence, and was always impatient to see his dreams realized. Still, his early years in Geneva, home, after all, of the greatest eighteenth-century theorist of equality, Rousseau, set him on a path of opposing privilege, detesting aristocracy, and actively working for the abolition of slavery. In 1787, he and Brissot included a typically provocative footnote in their tract advocating trade between the new United States and France:

SELF, SOCIETY, AND EQUALITY · 153

These words *noble, nobility, nobly,* can only produce false ideas when applied to facts that concern a republic because they always present themselves in the bad envelope given them by the prejudices of monarchy. They recall the idea of men or orders that are superior to other men and other orders which would make one believe that a similar distinction exists in a republic that is founded only on equality. This reflection confirms what we have said moreover about the necessity to develop a new political and moral vocabulary for the American republics.

Clearly, Brissot and Clavière intended to eventually develop such a vocabulary for France as well.[4]

The French Revolution gave them their opportunity as it did others in so many realms. Equality did not triumph in the short run (has it yet?) any more than did human rights. But some things did change. Women artists gained new opportunities to exhibit that paralleled other gains for women: Labille-Guiard was able to divorce her husband in 1800 and marry Vincent because divorce had been instituted for the first time in French history in 1792. Printmakers could satirize the clergy and nobility because censorship fell away after 1789. It came back, in various forms, after 1793, and especially after 1800, but the opening, however brief, showed that yearnings for equality could be galvanized by the prospect of change and could be given concrete expression by artists willing to venture onto new terrain. The outbreak of war in 1792 opened dramatically new prospects for advancement even as it created seemingly insuperable challenges. In the midst of trying to set up a government on new foundations, men such as Clavière found themselves having to think about the nation's debt and finances in new ways, trying out new procedures and new kinds of money, figuring out how to make the debt truly national and how to make financial administration more transparent and hence more credible.

Still, new conceptions of self, society, and equality did not just come from megaton explosions such as the French Revolution. New conceptions derived from new practices, which could be as different as drinking tea at a table, reading a newspaper or novel, setting up a fashion magazine, opening new exhibition spaces, painting a self-portrait as a woman artist, marching at a faster pace, learning to drive the carriage of horse artillery, or dreaming up a new financial instrument such as life insurance. Our frame of life is shaped by big events but also and in the end most persistently by what we do day to day, which alters over time, sometime very subtly, and brings us to new understandings.

Acknowledgments

AS I HAVE WORKED ON THIS BOOK OVER MANY YEARS, I have acquired more debts than I can even remember. May all those who have been willing to listen and have helped me on my way know that my gratitude is heartfelt. Sometimes the ideas fly in an official presentation, but often as not, the intellectual excitement builds in the corridors, over lunch or dinner, walking through a museum together, or just walking down a street in Paris, Edinburgh, Bielefeld, Los Angeles, Evanston, or Colorado Springs—the full list is too long and would be tedious. My former students, now friends and colleagues, have been a special source of inspiration through shared interests and especially shared lives. If this book resonates for any reader, it will be largely due to the unerring eye of my editor at W. W. Norton, Amy Cherry, who has saved me from myself countless times. It has been a privilege to work with her. Although I do not let Peg Jacob read the pages ahead of time, as criticism close to home is hard for me to take, she is present everywhere in this book and in my life.

Notes

INTRODUCTION: HOW THE SMALLEST THINGS LEAD TO BIG CHANGES

1. In *The Post-Revolutionary Self: Politics and Psyche in France, 1750–1850* (Cambridge, MA: Harvard University Press, 2005), Jan Goldstein emphasizes the reaction to the French Revolution and discusses it in the terms of intellectual history. I focus more on cultural practices and the experience of revolution itself. I do not offer a definition of "self" in these pages but find Goldstein's discussion of this very illuminating (esp. her p. 2). On the rise of individualism and autonomy, see Charles Taylor, *Sources of the Self: The Making of the Modern Identity* (Cambridge, MA: Harvard University Press, 1989), and J. B. Schneewind, *The Invention of Autonomy: A History of Modern Moral Philosophy* (Cambridge: Cambridge University Press, 1998). On original sin, see Matthew Kadane, *The Enlightenment and Original Sin* (Chicago: University of Chicago Press, 2024).
2. I drew the figures on the slave trade from the database available online at Slave Voyages. For a recent account of resistance among the enslaved, see John D. Garrigus, *A Secret among the Blacks: Slave Resistance before the Haitian Revolution* (Cambridge, MA: Harvard University Press, 2023).
3. The transcript of the Thatcher interview with Douglas Keay of *Women's Own* (September 23, 1987) can be found online at the Margaret Thatcher Foundation website.
4. Jean-Jacques Rousseau, *Discourse on the Origin and Foundations of Inequality among Men*, ed. Helena Rosenblatt, with related documents (Boston: Bedford/St. Martin's, 2011), 70 (the quote from *Discourse on . . . Inequality*), 143 (the quote from *Of the Social Contract*).
5. The growth of the terms "society" and "social" can be traced with Google Ngrams for English and French. According to the *Oxford English Dictionary*, "sociology" appeared for the first time in English in 1842. Auguste Comte introduced the term

in French as a neologism in 1839 in his *Cours de philosophie positive*, vol. 4 (Paris: Bachelier, 1839), 252.

6. On early appearances of the term in the French Revolution and crucial developments after 1795, see Robert Wokler, "From the Moral and Political Sciences to the Sciences of Society by Way of the French Revolution," *Jahrbuch für Recht und Ethik / Annual Review of Law and Ethics*, vol. 8 (2000): 33–45. See also Thomas Lalevée, "Three Versions of Social Science in Late Eighteenth-Century France," *Modern Intellectual History*, 20:4 (2023): 1023–43. I traced the references to Condorcet and social science by Destutt de Tracy using the ARTFL-FRANTEXT database. For the definition of social science by Destutt de Tracy, see "Mémoire sur la faculté de penser," in *Mémoires de L'Institut national des sciences et arts*, vol. 1 (Paris: Baudoin, Thermidor an VI [1798]), 389. The series of papers on the subject were first read in 1796 and then reformulated in 1798. All translations from the French, unless otherwise noted, are mine.

7. Mill's "Logic of the Moral Sciences" forms Book VI of his *A System of Logic, Ratiocinative and Inductive*, 2 vols. (London: John W. Parker, 1843), 2: esp. 531–624. Mill and Comte exchanged eighty-nine letters in French between 1841 and 1847. In them Mill explains his indebtedness to Comte, but also develops his differences over method. In a letter to Sir Edward Bulwer-Lytton on March 27, 1843, Mill explained, "I do not always agree in his [Comte's] opinions but so far as I know he seems to me by far the first speculative thinker of the age." Francis E. Mineka, ed., *The Earlier Letters of John Stuart Mill, 1812–1848*, 2 vols. (Toronto: University of Toronto Press, 1963), 2:579.

8. Emmanuel-Joseph Sieyès, *Qu'est-ce que le tiers état?*, ed. Edme Champion (Paris: Société de l'Histoire de la Révolution française, 1888), 31. The use of "social organization" in speeches can be traced through the *Archives parlementaires* section of the French Revolution Digital Archive. The first use I could find was in a speech by Maximilien Robespierre in January 1790. The importance of this term was first pointed out to me in the work of William Max Nelson, which I saw in manuscript, *Enlightenment Biopolitics: A History of Race, Eugenics, and the Making of Citizens* (Chicago: University of Chicago Press, 2024).

9. On the life of Millar, see the essay by his nephew John Craig, "Account of the Life and Writings of the Author," which prefaces the 1806 edition of John Millar, *The Origin of the Distinction of Ranks: Or, An Inquiry into the Circumstances Which Give Rise to Influence and Authority in the Different Ranks of Society, to Which Is Prefixed, An Account of the Life and Writings of the Author, by John Craig, Esq.*, 4th ed. (Edinburgh: William Blackwood, 1806), i–cxxxiv. See also William C. Lehmann, *John Millar of Glasgow, 1735–1801: His Life and Thought and His Contributions to Sociological Analysis* (Cambridge: Cambridge University Press, 1960).

10. For Capet's origins in Lyon, see Christophe Marcheteau de Quinçay, "Marie-Gabrielle Capet, artiste et modèle dans l'atelier des Vincent," in *Marie-Gabrielle*

Capet (1761–1818): Une virtuose de la miniature (Caen, France: Musée des Beaux-Arts de Caen, 2014), 11–25.

11. Following the customary practice, Napoleon Bonaparte is called Bonaparte before 1804 and Napoleon when he has himself named emperor (officially Napoleon I).

12. Jean-Marc Rivier, *Étienne Clavière (1735–1793): Un révolutionnaire, amis des Noirs* (Paris: Panormitis, 2006). In the course of writing, I was sent by the author a recent doctoral thesis on Clavière, which has proved invaluable: Mathieu Chaptal, "De Genève à la France, la pensée républicaine d'Etienne Clavière: Réforme financière, souveraineté populaire et révolutions (1735–1793)" (PhD diss., Aix-Marseille Université, December 2020). It was an incredible act of generosity to have shared this deeply researched work with me. It has now been published as a book. Mathieu Chaptal, *D'une révolution à l'autre: Étienne Clavière (1735–1793)* (Paris: Éditions Mare & Martin, 2023).

CHAPTER ONE: TEA AND HOW WOMEN BECAME "CIVILIZED"

1. The literature on coffeehouses has grown exponentially since Jürgen Habermas drew attention to their role in fostering public opinion in *The Structural Transformation of the Public Sphere: An Inquiry into a Category of Bourgeois Society*, trans. Thomas Burger with the assistance of Frederick Lawrence (Cambridge: Polity, 1989). See, for example, Brian Cowan, *The Social Life of Coffee: The Emergence of the British Coffeehouse* (New Haven: Yale University Press, 2005).

2. The quote is from Sir Frederic Morton Eden, *The State of the Poor: Or, an History of the Labouring Classes in England, from the Conquest to the Present Period*, 3 vols. (London, J. Davis, 1797), 1:524. Eden was bemoaning the treatment of the enslaved who could not eat with their families at table. I was first alerted to this work by Keith Thomas, *In Pursuit of Civility: Manners and Civilization in Early Modern England* (Waltham, MA: Brandeis University Press, 2018), 81. The significance of the way women served food in the household appears in G. J. Barker-Benfield, *The Culture of Sensibility: Sex and Society in Eighteenth-Century Britain* (Chicago: University of Chicago Press, 1996), 159. There is a large literature, now, on this subject. On tea tables and the role of women, see Markman Ellis, "The Tea-Table, Women and Gossip in Early Eighteenth-Century Britain," in *British Sociability in the Long Eighteenth Century: Challenging the Anglo-French Connection*, ed. Valérie Capdeville and Alain Kerhervé (Rochester, NY: Boydell Press, 2019), 69–88.

3. A Google Ngram of "civilization" in English shows that it takes off as a term in the 1760s.

4. David Porter, *The Chinese Taste in Eighteenth-Century England* (Cambridge: Cambridge University Press, 2010), esp. 133–53.

5. *The Spectator*, no. 10, March 12, 1711, p. 1.

160 · NOTES

6. The quote is from *The Spectator*, no. 10, p. 1; for the lady's library, see no. 37, p. 1.
7. Erika Rappaport, *A Thirst for Empire: How Tea Shaped the Modern World* (Princeton, NJ: Princeton University Press, 2017), 23–56; Eliza Haywood, *The Female Spectator*, vol. 2 (Dublin: Printed for George and Alexander Ewing, 1746): 63–64. Patricia Spacks concludes that Haywood is against excessive tea drinking. Patricia Meyer Spacks, ed., *Selections from* The Female Spectator (New York: Oxford University Press, 1999), xv. For a more nuanced view, see Catherine Ingrassia's analysis of Haywood's earlier work from 1725 in "Fashioning Female Authorship in Eliza Haywood's 'The Tea-Table,'" *Journal of Narrative Technique* 28, no. 3 (1998): 287–304. On the tea trade and consumption, see Troy Bickham, *Eating the Empire: Food and Society in Eighteenth-Century Britain* (London: Reaktion Books, 2020), esp. 28–87.
8. Elizabeth Mure, "Some Remarks on the Change of Manners in My Own Time, 1700–1790," in *Selections from the Family Papers Preserved at Caldwell*, 3 vols., ed. William Mure (Paisley, Scotland: A. Gardener, 1883–1885 [1854]), 1:269, 271. Mure thought that the custom waned later in the eighteenth century when the Scots adopted the English separation of women and men after dinner. In her view, this separation led to increased emphasis on education for women, who could no longer rely on men for knowledge (p. 272). Most scholars who have commented on the diffusion of tea tables have emphasized their role in polite society. See, for example, Katharine Glover, *Elite Women and Polite Society in Eighteenth-Century Scotland* (Woodbridge, Suffolk, UK: Boydell Press, 2011), 82–87.
9. Annual imports from China by the East India Company in Derek Charles Janes, "Fine Gottenburgh Teas: The Import and Distribution of Smuggled Tea in Scotland and the North of England c. 1750–1780," *History of Retailing and Consumption* 2, no. 3 (2016): 223–38, esp. 226; Cowan, *The Social Life of Coffee*, 75.
10. On Assam, see Rappaport, *A Thirst for Empire*, 85–119, and Carole Shammas, "Changes in English and Anglo-American Consumption from 1550 to 1800," in *Consumption and the World of Goods*, ed. John Brewer and Roy Porter (London: Routledge, 1993), 182. The figures about slavery come from the Slave Voyages online database.
11. Maxine Berg, "Britain's Asian Century: Porcelain and Global History in the Long Eighteenth Century," in *The Birth of Modern Europe: Culture and Economy, 1400–1800. Essays in Honor of Jan de Vries*, ed. Laura Cruz and Joel Mokyr (Leiden: Brill, 2010), 133–56, esp. 139, 141, and 145.
12. For the early development of porcelain in Europe, see Suzanne L. Marchand, *Porcelain: A History from the Heart of Europe* (Princeton, NJ: Princeton University Press, 2020), and Katherine Eufemia Farrer, *Correspondence of Josiah Wedgwood*, 3 vols. (London: Women's Printing Society, 1903–6), 1:197.
13. Samuel Smiles, *Josiah Wedgwood, F.R.S.: His Personal History* (London: J. Murray, 1894). Smiles was the apostle of "self-help" in his time. On the impact of

NOTES · 161

Wedgwood's marketing, see N. McKendrick, "Josiah Wedgwood: An Eighteenth-Century Entrepreneur in Salesmanship and Marketing Techniques," *Economic History Review* 12, no. 3 (1960): 408–33.

14. John Locke, *An Essay concerning the True Original Extent and End of Civil Government*, paragraph 49, in *Two Treatises of Government*, 4th ed. (London: John Churchill, 1713), 218.

15. I traced "modernity" in the online edition of the *Oxford English Dictionary* and in Eighteenth Century Collections Online; a search of the French language database ARTFL-FRANTEXT shows the term appearing from the 1820s onward. "Modernité" in *Dictionnaire de la langue française* (Littré), vol. 3, can be found under the "Dictionnaires d'autrefois" tab in ARTFL-FRANTEXT. A Google Ngram shows that "modernity" only takes off in the 1980s. A Google Ngram shows that "modern times" became more current in English beginning in the 1750s. *De l'esprit des lois, par Montesquieu. Précédé de l'analyse de cet ouvrage par D'Alembert*, 3 vols. (Paris: Pourrat, 1831), 1:191, 205–6. I have translated the original French myself because of the importance of the passage and the variability of the English translations.

16. ARFTL-FRANTEXT gives the first occurrence of "*civilisation*" in 1755 and a Google Ngram shows the most significant increase in the 1770s and 1780s. On the Scottish Enlightenment and the influence of Montesquieu, see Silvia Sebastiani, *The Scottish Enlightenment: Race, Gender, and the Limits of Progress*, trans. Jeremy Carden (New York: Palgrave Macmillan, 2013).

17. For a discussion of various writers' use of stage theory, see Karen O'Brien, *Women and Enlightenment in Eighteenth-Century Britain* (Cambridge: Cambridge University Press, 2009).

18. John Millar, *Observations concerning the Distinction of Ranks in Society* (London: Printed by W. and J. Richardson for John Murray, 1771), ii. Millar is far from the only Scottish intellectual interested in this question. See, for example, H. M. Höpfl, "From Savage to Scotsman: Conjectural History in the Scottish Enlightenment," *Journal of British Studies* 17, no. 2 (Spring 1978): 19–40. There is a considerable literature on Millar and a burgeoning one on the Scottish Enlightenment. My aim is not to cover all those writings or to give a full account of Millar's views but to link together things usually kept apart: tea and the status of women in civilizational histories. For a good overview of earlier work, see John W. Cairns, "John Millar's Lectures on Scots Criminal Law," *Oxford Journal of Legal Studies* 8, no. 3 (Winter 1988): 364–400. The most recent account, one that emphasizes Millar's interest in family forms, is Nicholas B. Miller, *John Millar and the Scottish Enlightenment: Family Life and World History* (Oxford: Voltaire Foundation, 2017).

19. Millar, *Observations* (1771), vi–vii, 18, 37, 232. There is a growing literature on the question of women in the Scottish Enlightenment. An essential point of departure for me was Jane Rendall, "Clio, Mars and Minerva: The Scottish Enlightenment and the Writing of Women's History," in *Eighteenth Century Scotland: New*

162 · NOTES

Perspectives, ed. T. M. Devine and J. R. Young (East Linton, UK: Tuckwell Press, 1999), 134–51.

20. Millar, *Observations* (1771), xii; John Millar, *Observations concerning the Distinction of Ranks in Society*, 2nd ed. (London: Printed for J. Murray, 1773), xix–xx, 3; John Millar, *The Origin of the Distinction of Ranks; or, An Inquiry into the Circumstances Which Give Rise to Influence and Authority in the Different Members of Society*, 3rd ed. (London: J. Murray, 1779), 5. The same phrase appears in the editions of 1781 and 1793.

21. For the quote on Montesquieu and Smith, see John Millar, *An Historical View of the English Government from the Settlement of the Saxons in Britain, to the Revolution in 1688: To Which Are Subjoined, Some Dissertations Connected with the History of the Government, from the Revolution to the Present Time*, 4th ed., 4 vols. (London: J. Mawman, 1818), 2:429–30 (footnote). For the influence of Lafitau on Smith, see David L. Blaney and Naeem Inayatullah, *Savage Economics: Wealth, Poverty and the Temporal Walls of Capitalism* (Abingdon, Oxon, UK: Routledge, 2010), 27–57, and Ronald L. Meek, *Social Science and the Ignoble Savage* (Cambridge: Cambridge University Press, 1976).

22. For the disinterest of Montesquieu, Voltaire, and Jean-Jacques Rousseau, see the introduction by William N. Fenton and Elizabeth L. Moore to their translation of Joseph-François Lafitau, *Customs of the American Indians Compared with the Customs of Primitive Times*, 2 vols. (Toronto: Champlain Society, 1974–1977), 1: esp. lxxxiii.

23. Joseph-François Lafitau, *Moeurs des sauvages amériquains comparées aux moeurs des premiers temps*, 2 vols. (Paris: Saugrain l'aîné, 1724), 1:106. Millar, *Observations* (1771), 8–12. On p. 8 he has a footnote with a long quote from Lafitau.

24. For Montesquieu on climate, see esp. his books 14–17 of *The Spirit of Laws*; Millar, *Observations* (1771), 2 and iii.

25. John Pinkerton, *An Enquiry into the History of Scotland Preceding the Reign of Malcom III or the Year 1056. Including the Authentic History of That Period.* 2 vols. (London: Printed by John Nichols, for George Nicol, 1789), 1:340; Millar, *Observations* (1773), 249 (footnote). Silvia Sebastiani was kind enough to share her thoughts on this question with me.

26. For Millar's personal life, see John Craig, "Account of the Life and Writings of the Author," and Lehmann, *John Millar of Glasgow*, esp. 7–86.

27. The lecture notes come from National Library of Scotland, Advocates' MS 28.6.8 (1777–78), esp. p. 94 (I am using the page numbers penciled in).

28. For his expectations of students, see his lecture notes, Advocates' MS 28.6.8, p. 90, and also John Craig, "Account of the Life and Writings of the Author," xviii. In his remarks on the defects of law education of the time, Henry Home, Lord Kames, considered Millar the only exception. Lord Henry Home Kames, *Elucidations respecting the Common and Statue Law of Scotland* (Edinburgh: Printed for William Creech, 1777), viii–ix.

NOTES · **163**

29. The quotes from Frederick Lamb come from Lloyd C. Sanders, ed., *Lord Melbourne's Papers* (London: Longmans, Green, 1889), 5–6.

30. John Gregory, M.D., *A Father's Legacy to His Daughters*, 3rd ed. (Dublin: Thomas Ewing and Caleb Jenkin, 1774), 19. Gregory's manual went through at least six editions in 1774 and many others in the 1770s and 1780s. Craig remarks on Millar's habit of consulting his wife and reading his work to the family in the 1806 edition, John Craig, "Account of the Life and Writings of the Author," lxxiii. The quote from William Lamb comes from Sanders, *Lord Melbourne's Papers*, 7.

31. The distinctiveness of Scottish intellectual life has attracted increasing attention in the last twenty years. See, for example, John Robertson, *The Case for the Enlightenment: Scotland and Naples, 1680–1760* (Cambridge: Cambridge University Press, 2005), and Alexander Broadie, ed., *The Cambridge Companion to the Scottish Enlightenment* (Cambridge: Cambridge University Press, 2003).

32. R. A. Houston, "The Population History of Britain and Ireland, 1500–1750," in *British Population History: From the Black Death to the Present Day*, ed. Michael Anderson (Cambridge: Cambridge University Press, 1996), 95–190, esp. 122; Henry Hamilton, *An Economic History of Scotland in the Eighteenth Century* (Oxford: Clarendon Press, 1963), 404–5, 414, 419–20.

33. [Duncan Forbes], *Some Considerations on the Present State of Scotland: In a Letter to the Commissioners and Trustees for Improving Fisheries and Manufactures. To Which Is Subjoined, A Letter from the Annual Committee of the Convention of Royal Boroughs, to the Several Boroughs of Scotland, by Order of the General Convention, for Preventing the Pernicious Practice of Smuggling* (Edinburgh: Printed by Order of the Magistrates, 1744), 7. The term "tea table" can be traced through a Google Ngram. On tea drinking in Scotland, see Glover, *Elite Women and Polite Society in Eighteenth-Century Scotland*, esp. 82–87.

34. Elizabeth A. Foyster and Christopher A. Whatley, *A History of Everyday Life in Scotland, 1600 to 1800* (Edinburgh: Edinburgh University Press, 2010), 152.

35. Paul Hallberg and Christian Koninckx, eds., *Colin Campbell's Diary of the First Swedish East India Company Expedition to Canton, 1732–33* (Gothenburg, Sweden: Royal Society of Arts and Sciences in Gothenburg, 1996), xix–xxii, 96, 104. On Scandinavian trade, see Hanna Hodacs, *Silk and Tea in the North: Scandinavian Trade and the Market for Asian Goods in Eighteenth-Century Europe* (London: Palgrave Macmillan, 2016). I am grateful to Hodacs for sharing her work with me.

36. Meike von Brescius, "Worlds Apart? Merchants, Mariners, and the Organization of the Private Trade in Chinese Expert Wares in Eighteenth-Century Europe," in *Goods from the East: 1600–1800: Trading Eurasia*, ed. Maxine Berg et al. (New York: Palgrave Macmillan, 2015), 163–82, esp. 170. Figures of Swedish and Danish companies in the eighteenth century and the scale of smuggling are found in Janes, "Fine Gottenburgh Teas," 226.

37. Andrew Mackillop, "A North Europe World of Tea: Scotland and the Tea Trade, c. 1690–c. 1790," in Berg at al., *Goods from the East*, 294–308, esp. 301–3.

164 · NOTES

38. On literacy, see R. A. Houston, *Scottish Literacy and the Scottish Identity: Illiteracy and Society in Scotland and Northern England, 1600–1800* (Cambridge: Cambridge University Press, 1985), esp. 56.

39. David Hume, "Of Essay Writing [1742]," in *Essays, Moral, Political and Literary* (London: Grant Richards, 1908), 570; David Fordyce, *Dialogues concerning Education*, 2 vols. (London: n.p., 1745), 2:111.

40. Millar, *Observations* (1771), 19 and 75. For attitudes toward women of the Scottish Enlightenment, see Sebastiani, *The Scottish Enlightenment*, and O'Brien, *Women and Enlightenment*.

41. Millar, *Observations* (1771), 75–78.

42. Millar, *The Origin of the Distinction of the Ranks* (1779), 123–24. On Millar's views of the family, see Miller, *John Millar and the Scottish Enlightenment*.

43. Millar, *Observations* (1771), 234, 236–37. The modifications of Millar's position on slavery in the various editions are traced in detail in John W. Cairns, "John Millar and Slavery," in *MacCormick's Scotland*, ed. Neil Walker (Edinburgh: Edinburgh University Press, 2012), 73–106.

44. Lehmann, *John Millar of Glasgow*, 50–51.

45. Millar, *Observations* (1771), 113; Lehmann, *John Millar of Glasgow*, 68.

46. For the excerpt from the trial, see Peter Mackenzie, *The Life of Thomas Muir, Esq. Advocate, Younger of Huntershill, Near Glasgow, Member of the Convention of Delegates for Reform in Scotland, etc., etc.: Who Was Tried for Sedition before the High Court of Justiciary in Scotland, and Sentenced to Transportation for Fourteen Years: With a Full Report on His Trial* (Glasgow: W. R. MacPhun, 1831), 107. For the reactions of parents, see Lehmann, *John Millar*, 69.

47. Mackenzie, *The Life of Thomas Muir*, 1

CHAPTER TWO: REVOLUTIONARY IMAGERY AND THE UNCOVERING OF SOCIETY

1. Maurice Tourneux, ed., *Correspondance littéraire, philosophique et critique par Grimm, Diderot, Raynal, Meister, etc., revue sur les textes originaux, comprenant outre ce qui a été publié à diverses époques les fragments supprimés en 1813 par la censure, les parties inédites conservées à la Bibliothèque ducale de Gotha et à l'Arsenal à Paris*, 16 vols. (Paris: Garnier frères, 1872–77), 10:313–18.

2. Google Ngrams show the spike of "société" and "social" in the 1790s and the new usage of "organisation sociale."

3. Brian C. J. Singer, *Society, Theory, and the French Revolution: Studies in the Revolutionary Imaginary* (Houndmills, Hampshire, UK: Macmillan, 1986). Singer was interested in visibility but not visualization. Earlier versions of my interest in these questions can be found in Lynn Hunt, "La Visibilité du monde bourgeois," in *Vers un ordre bourgeois? Révolution française et changement social*, ed. Jean-Pierre Jessenne (Rennes, France: Presses Universitaires de Rennes, 2007),

NOTES • 165

371–81; and Lynn Hunt, "Envisioning Equality in the French Revolution," in *Imagining Unequals, Imagining Equals: Concepts of Equality in History and Law*, ed. Ulrike Davy and Antje Flüchter (Bielefeld, Germany: Bielefeld University Press, 2022), 71–102. For a general consideration of printmaking in the Atlantic world, see Ashli White, *Revolutionary Things: Material Culture and Politics in the Late Eighteenth-Century Atlantic World* (New Haven: Yale University Press, 2023), esp. 181–304.

4. To determine the number of prints at the French National Library (hereafter BNF), I used the online search function entering *estampe*, France as the place of publication, and the years. This gave 2,275 as the number of prints for the period 1757–1761, 2,999 for 1767–1771, 3,443 for 1777–1781, and 9,213 for 1787–1791. I compared revolutionary prints within and among different collections using Excel sheets. The eight volumes of the printed catalogue of the De Vinck collection are listed under a maddening variety of titles because their completion required decades and collaboration by many different people. Bibliothèque nationale (France). Cabinet des estampes. Collection de Vinck, *Un siècle d'histoire de France par l'estampe, 1770–1871*, 8 vols. (Paris: Imprimerie Nationale, 1909–1969). For the purposes of this study, volumes 2–4 are the relevant ones: *La Constituante* (1914), *La Législative et la Convention* (1921), and the first part of *Napoléon et son temps* (1969). Some 5,700 prints are listed in the De Vinck catalogue but at least 500 of them are duplicates. The other major collection is that of Michel Hennin (also in the BNF): Georges Duplessis, *Inventaire de la collection d'estampes relatives à l'histoire de France, léguée en 1863 à la Bibliothèque nationale par M. Michel Hennin*, 5 vols. (Paris: H. Menu; H. Champion, 1877–1884). The Musée Carnavalet also has many prints, but its collection has not been organized in the same fashion. Some of the prints in these collections were produced outside France, but the vast majority are French.

5. Some newspapers and pamphlets were illustrated, but not many. Most of these illustrations are included in the De Vinck and Hennin collections. John Lough, *Paris Theatre Audiences in the Seventeenth and Eighteenth Centuries* (London: Oxford University Press, 1957), 157; Emmet Kennedy et al., *Theatre, Opera, and Audiences in Revolutionary Paris: Analysis and Repertory* (Westport, CT: Greenwood Press, 1996), 379; Tony Halliday, *Facing the Public: Portraiture in the Aftermath of the French Revolution* (Manchester: Manchester University Press, 1999), 30; Richard Taws, *The Politics of the Provisional: Art and Ephemera in Revolutionary France* (University Park: Pennsylvania State University Press, 2013).

6. The number of portraits is given under the Topic tab in the French Revolution Digital Archive (hereafter FRDA). I limited the dates to 1789–99. The current version of the FRDA has 4,623 images for the period 1789–99, all derived from the collections of the BNF. The categories are those of the BNF.

7. Amy Freund, *Portraiture and Politics in Revolutionary France* (University Park: Pennsylvania State University Press, 2014), 49–80.

166 · NOTES

8. Freund, *Portraiture*, esp. 54.

9. My conclusions about chronology are based on putting the dates into the FRDA. The highest number of prints is listed for 1790, followed by 1789 and 1791.

10. F. A. Aulard et al., eds., *Recueil des actes du comité de salut public, avec la correspondence officielle des représentants en mission et le registre du conseil exécutif provisoire*, 37 vols. (Paris: Imprimerie Nationale, 1889–1999), 10 (1897): 187. The figures on the price of prints, bread, and daily wages can be found in Antoine de Baecque, *La Caricature révolutionnaire* (Paris: Presses du CNRS, 1988), 27. One of the few prints that shows the display of prints on the outside wall of a shop can be found at the BNF online site Gallica under the title *Le Joli Moine*. This print and the general meanings of revolutionary prints are discussed in detail in Rolf Reichardt and Hubertus Kohle, *Visualizing the Revolution: Politics and the Pictorial Arts in Late Eighteenth-Century France* (London: Reaktion Books, 2008); see p. 38 for the print in question. Reichardt and Kohle's book was an essential point of departure for me.

11. In her article on the social hermeneutics of suspicion, Carla Hesse shows that the question of legally defined suspects in 1793–94 created new tensions about understanding social identities. These tensions contributed to the uncertainties of social identification and may well have increased the pressure for a "social science," though that is not part of her argument. It is a reminder, nonetheless, that Mercier was commenting in a very different atmosphere from that analyzed by Boyer. Carla A. Hesse, "Law, Suspicion, and Social Hermeneutics at the Inception of the Terror, April 1793," *French History* 38, no. 1 (March 2024): 83–95.

12. The publication of the installments, their length and their cost, is announced as beginning in April 1792 by *Journal encyclopédique ou universel* 1, no. 5 (February 20, 1792): 274. The same journal advertised vol. 1 of the work in its issue of May 10 (vol. 4, no. 13), 127–28 (with no price). The *Journal de la cour et de la ville* gave 50 livres as the price for four volumes as well as the yearly subscription (no. 48, February 17, 1792), 378–79. The last date cited by Boyer is July 27, 1792. Jacques-Marie Boyer-Brun, *Histoire des caricatures de la révolte des Français, par M. Boyer de Nîmes*, . . . , 2 vols. (Paris: Impr. du Journal du peuple, 1792).

13. Boyer-Brun, *Histoire des caricatures*, 1:10. See also Champfleury, *Histoire de la caricature: Sous la République, l'Empire et la Restauration*, 2nd ed. (Paris: E. Dentu, 1877), 170–93. The prospectus is quoted in the important article by Annie Duprat, "Le Regard d'un royaliste sur la Révolution: Jacques-Marie Boyer de Nîmes," *Annales historiques de la Révolution française* 337 (2004): 21–39, quote on p. 23. In his *Histoire* (vol. 1, p. 134), Boyer claimed he had inserted a caricature in issue 17 of *Journal de Nîmes* dated February 28, 1790, but the BNF's copy of the journal does not include it. On Boyer, see also Claude Langlois, *Les Sept morts du roi* (Paris: Anthropos, 1993), esp. 146–65. Langlois questions whether Boyer overestimates the mobilizing power of caricatures and the ability to manipulate

them, yet Langlois's book is devoted to explaining how caricatures of the king undermined his position and therefore contributed to his demise; see esp. p. 152.

14. *Essai sur la régénération physique, morale et politique des Juifs; ouvrage couronné par la Société royale des sciences et des arts de Metz le 23 Août 1788, par M. Grégoire, curé du diocese de Metz* (Metz: Claude Lemort, 1789); Boyer-Brun, *Histoire des caricatures*, 1:247, 362.

15. Boyer-Brun, *Histoire des caricatures*, 1:69. Although the title does not appear on Boyer's reproduction in the book, he does discuss it in the text, noting that it appeared at the bottom of the image.

16. Boyer-Brun, *Histoire des caricatures*, 1:27–28, 70, 71; 2:72; Henri Wallon, *Histoire du Tribunal révolutionnaire de Paris avec le Journal de ses actes*, 6 vols. (Paris: Librairie Hachette, 1880–82), 4:12–13.

17. *Actes des apôtres*, vol. 7, chapter 201 (ca. November 1790), p. 12 [pagination and numbering seems to vary by collection]. The Rowlandson print, *Political Affection*, can be viewed online at the British Museum. The fox could easily be mistaken for a wolf. *Journal de la cour et de la ville*, no. 60 (June 30, 1791): 483. The complaint was shared by another royalist journal, *Les Sabats Jacobites*, no. 42 (1791, month unspecified but definitely after June): 270.

18. *Journal des révolutions de l'Europe en 1789 et 1790* 4 (1789): 77–78, 85. The author refers to a hare hanging from the pole of the peasant in one of the images. An example can be seen at BNF Gallica under the title "J'savois ben qu'jaurions not tour."

19. *Révolutions de Paris*, no. 105 (July 9–16, 1791): 33–35; *Courrier français*, no. 151 (May 30, 1792): 240.

20. The critic is quoted in Samuel Lutz, "Quelques échos," in *Louis-Sébastien Mercier, précurseur et sa fortune: Avec des documents inédits: Recueil d'études sur l'influence de Mercier*, ed. Hermann Hofer (Munich: Wilhelm Fink Verlag, 1977), 285–300, quote on p. 289. On licentious prints, see Louis-Sébastien Mercier, *Tableau de Paris*, 8 vols. (Amsterdam: n.p., 1783), 6:92; Louis-Sébastien Mercier, *Tableau de Paris*, 2 vols., ed. Jean-Claude Bonnet (Paris: Mercure de France, 1994), 1:1323. Bonnet's team has compared the various editions.

21. On Mercier's role in the trial of the king, see J. Mavidal and E. Laurent, eds., *Archives parlementaires de 1787 à 1860, première série (1787 à 1799)*, 90 vols (Paris: P. du Pont, CNRS, 1867–1990), 57:374; Marie-Jeanne Roland de la Platière, *Mémoires de Madame Roland* (Paris: Editions de Saint-Clair, 1967), 312.

22. Louis-Sébastien Mercier, *Néologie, ou Vocabulaire de mots nouveaux, à renouveler, ou pris dans des acceptions nouvelles*, 2 vols. (Paris: Chez Moussard, chez Maradan, 1801), 2:244. For his various publications and reactions to them, see Enrico Rufi, *Louis-Sébastien Mercier* (Paris: Memini, 1996). It is worth noting that the Goncourts attributed criticism of Mercier's stand on the arts in the Conseil des Cinq Cents to the fact that he "n'a guère voulu voir d'hiérarchie de genre dans l'art."

Edmond de Goncourt et Jules de Goncourt, *Histoire de la société française pendant le directoire*, 2nd ed. (Paris: E. Dentu, 1855), 279.

23. Louis-Sébastien Mercier, *Le Nouveau Paris*, 6 vols. (Paris: Fuchs, 1798). Although the publication date was given as 1798, it most likely appeared in 1799. See Louis-Sébastien Mercier, *Le Nouveau Paris*, ed. Jean-Claude Bonnet (Paris: Mercure de France, 1994), ccxcvi. Quotations from the work come from the Bonnet edition. For the quote about obscene books, see p. 430.

24. Mercier, *Le Nouveau Paris*, 625.

25. For the discussion of critical prints, see Mercier, *Le Nouveau Paris*, 623–25; for the vogue of caricatures, see Mercier, *Le Nouveau Paris*, 421.

26. Mercier, *Le Nouveau Paris*, 421–22.

27. Mercier, *Le Nouveau Paris*, 266 and 25. On *Chronique du mois*, see Gary Kates, *The Cercle Social, the Girondins, and the French Revolution* (Princeton, NJ: Princeton University Press, 1985), 195–220.

28. Mercier, *Le Nouveau Paris*, 868–69. Mercier did not use the term "social science" himself.

29. *Le Concert de la rue Feydeau; ou, La Folie du jour, comédie en un acte, en prose . . . Par les citoyens René Périn et Camille* (Paris: Chez les marchands de nouveautés, an III [1795]). Two different engravers did stippled prints titled *Folie du Jour* based on a painting by Louis-Léopold Boilly. By *The Danger of Wigs*, Mercier no doubt meant the print titled *L'Inconvénient des perruques* (The inconvenience of wigs) because the scene of the woman on a horse is quite precisely described by Mercier in his text. It, too, is a stippled engraving from 1797 based on a drawing by Carle Vernet, etched by Louis Darcis. According to the British Museum, the print *Folie du Jour* by Salvatore Tresca was registered at the BNF in February 1797. The version by J. P. Levilly can be seen in the online collections of the Musée Carnavalet. Both show the same scene in slightly different formats. A colored version of *L'inconvénient des perruques* can be seen in the online collection of the British Museum, which dates it as 1797.

30. On the fistfights at this play, see Edmond and Jules de Goncourt, *Histoire de la société française pendant le directoire*, 374–75. On the politicization of women's dress in the early years of the Revolution, see Dominique Godineau, "Costume, apparence et identité politique des citoyennes (1789–1794)," *Annales historiques de la Révolution française*, no. 409 (2022–23): 93–116.

31. Petit's etching seems the likely candidate, not only because of the title but also because like all the others referenced by Mercier as "naive depictions," it is stippled and dates from 1797. Only two of the prints mentioned by Mercier (*L'Anarchiste* and *Les Incroyables*) appear in the FRDA. For the use of "anarchist," see, for example, Antoine Jean Thomas Bonnemain, *Les Chemises rouges ou Mémoires pour server à l'histoire du règne des anarchistes*, 2 vols. (Paris: Du Roy, 1799); Mercier, *Le Nouveau Paris*, 44.

32. According to Aileen Ribeiro, ribbon garters like the one worn by the young man

NOTES • **169**

on the right in the etching were worn over pants (*pantalons*) to create the illusion of knee breeches. Aileen Ribeiro, *Fashion in the French Revolution* (New York: Holmes and Meier, 1988), 119; "La Mode des pantalons et des bottines se soutient," *Tableau général du gout, des modes, et des costumes de Paris*, no. II de Brumaire, an VII (October–November 1798): 108.

33. Mercier, *Le Nouveau Paris*, 453. On the political meanings of fashion in the French Revolution, see the invaluable Richard Wrigley, *The Politics of Appearances: Representations of Dress in Revolutionary France* (Oxford: Berg, 2002).

34. Mercier's comment is from a previously unpublished manuscript that is reproduced in the Bonnet edition of Mercier, *Le Nouveau Paris*, 1238. On the *frac*, see Philip Mansel, "Monarchy, Uniform and the Rise of the *Frac*, 1760–1830," *Past & Present* 96, no. 1 (August 1982): 103–32. Although it is true that the fashion journals paid more attention to women's dress than to men's, I do not agree with Ribeiro's contention that "with regard to the details of men's dress, there are few changes to chronicle in the last years of the eighteenth century." Ribeiro, *Fashion in the French Revolution*, 119.

35. Jean-Gabriel Peltier, *Paris pendant l'année 1799* (London: Bayliss, 1799), 394–401. With Peltier we come full circle, since he was one of the original collaborators on *Actes des apôtres*. For an example of a long review focusing on Mercier's politics, see from London *The Monthly Review; or Literary Journal* 30 (September–December 1799): 572–81; *La Décade philosophique, littéraire et politique*, 2nd trimester an V, no. 12 (January 19, 1797): 175; 2nd trimester an V, no. 14 (February 8, 1797): 305–6; Johann Wolfgang von Goethe, *Werke*, 133 vols. (Weimar: H. Böhlaus, 1887–1919), 47 (1896): 353–60.

36. Quote from Moratín in Amelia Rauser, *Caricature Unmasked: Irony, Authenticity, and Individualism in Eighteenth-Century English Prints* (Newark: University of Delaware Press, 2008), 131; British Museum, *Catalogue of Political and Personal Satires Preserved in the Department of Prints and Drawings in the British Museum*, 11 vols. (London: British Museum, 1870–1954), 7:1793–1800 (ed. Mary Dorothy George, 1942). It lists 9,692 prints. See also Diana Donald, *The Age of Caricature: Satirical Prints in the Reign of George III* (New Haven: Yale University Press, 1996).

37. George W. Stocking Jr., "French Anthropology in 1800," *Isis* 55, no. 2 (June 1964): 134–50; Jean-Luc Chappey, *La Société des observateurs de l'homme (1799–1804): Des anthropologues au temps de Bonaparte* (Paris: Société des études robespierristes, 2002), esp. 293–390.

CHAPTER THREE: ART, FASHION, AND ONE WOMAN'S EXPERIENCE

1. The terms can be followed through Google Ngrams.

2. Paris Spies-Gans, "Exceptional, but Not Exceptions: Public Exhibitions and the Rise of the Woman Artist in London and Paris, 1760–1830," *Eighteenth-Century Studies* 51, no. 4 (2018): 393–416, esp. 406. Paris was kind enough to provide me

170 · NOTES

the information about the 1770s and 1780s based on her compilation of lists of all women who displayed their art publicly in Paris in the years 1760–1830. The lists can be found in her PhD dissertation: "The Arts Are All Her Own: How Women Artists Navigated the Revolutionary Era in Britain and France, 1760–1830" (PhD diss., Princeton University, 2018), 612–26. Her findings are now available in Paris A. Spies-Gans, *A Revolution on Canvas: The Rise of Women Artists in Britain and France, 1760–1830* (London: Paul Mellon Centre for Studies in British Art, 2022).

3. The quote about Capet is from Leo R. Schidlof, *The Miniature in Europe in the 16th, 17th, 18th and 19th Centuries*, 4 vols. (Graz, Austria: Akademische Druck- und Verlagsanstalt, 1964), 1:126.

4. Laura Auricchio, *Adélaïde Labille-Guiard: Artist in the Age of Revolution* (Los Angeles: Getty Publications, 2009), esp. 91 and 107–8. On Capet's life, see Arnauld Doria, *Gabrielle Capet* (Paris: Les Beaux-Arts, 1934).

5. Spies-Gans, *A Revolution on Canvas*, 178.

6. For the figures on theatrical plays and performances, see Emmet Kennedy et al., *Theatre, Opera, and Audiences in Revolutionary Paris: Analysis and Repertory* (Westport, CT: Greenwood Press, 1996), 379; Charles Théremin, *De la situation intérieure de la République* (Paris: Maradan, pluviôse an V), 11.

7. The black-and-white photograph of the original oil painting (present location unknown), 72 × 58 cm, can be found in Doria, *Gabrielle Capet*, 70, plate II. Doria presumably saw the painting himself, as he describes the color of the dress, the hat, and the kerchief. For him the color is that of a pigeon's throat with variable reflections between violet, rose, and blue. My interest in the connection to fashion was stimulated by Susan L. Siegfried, "The Visual Culture of Fashion and the Classical Ideal in Post-Revolutionary France," *Art Bulletin* 97, no. 1 (2015): 77–99.

8. Marie-Jo Bonnet, "Femmes peintres à leur travail: De l'autoportrait comme manifeste politique (XVIIIᵉ–XIXᵉ siècles)," *Revue d'histoire moderne et contemporaine* 49, no. 2 (2002–3): 140–67; quote is on p. 141.

9. TheVigée Le Brun self-portait from 1782 is *Self-Portrait in a Straw Hat* (1782), held by the National Gallery in London. The Labille-Guiard self-portrait from 1782 can be seen in Auricchio, *Labille-Guiard*, 24 (its location is unknown). For the fashion prints, see Auricchio, *Labille-Guiard*, 45–46. Auricchio says that the prints date from around 1784. On the fashion press more generally, see Annemarie Kleinert, "La Naissance d'une presse de mode à la veille de la Révolution," in *Le Journalisme d'ancien régime: Questions et propositions*, ed. Pierre Rétat (Lyon: Presses universitaires de Lyon, 1982), 189–97. See also Annemarie Kleinert, *"Le Journal des dames et des modes" ou la conquête de l'Europe feminine (1797–1839)*, Beihefte der Francia, no. 46 (Stuttgart: Jan Thorbecke Verlag, 2001), esp. the graph on p. 16.

10. There is enduring uncertainty about just when the drawing was executed, whether in 1790 or in the mid-1790s as Christophe Marcheteau de Quinçay has suggested. He argues for the later date (1793–94) on the grounds of her thin face and especially the simplicity of her dress. But since the dress had already appeared in her

NOTES · 171

self-portrait of 1784, I would argue for the earlier date, given the emphasis then on simplicity of self-presentation in the new regime. Christophe Marcheteau de Quinçay, "Marie-Gabrielle Capet: Artiste et modèle dans l'atelier des Vincent," in *Marie-Gabrielle Capet (1761–1818): Une virtuose de la miniature* (Ghent: Snoeck Ducaju et Zoon, 2014), 10–25, but esp. the catalogue entry on p. 59.

11. Melissa Hyde makes a similar point about this drawing in her catalogue entry about it: "The Horvitz sheet thoughtfully engages with Enlightenment concepts of naturalness, transparency, and authenticity; ideas very much in step with the Revolutionary period in which Capet produced it." Alvin L. Clark Jr., ed., *Tradition & Transitions: Eighteenth-Century Art from the Horvitz Collection* (Paris: Horvitz Collection, 2017), 320. On the increase in female depictions of women artists, see Spies-Gans, *A Revolution on Canvas*, 186–99. On the smile in portraiture and its evolution at this time, see Colin Jones, *The Smile Revolution in Eighteenth-Century Paris* (Oxford: Oxford University Press, 2014).

12. Freund, *Portraiture and Politics*, 51, 68.

13. For the reference to nonchalance and reproductions of the painting and miniatures, see Marcheteau de Quinçay, *Marie-Gabrielle Capet*, 65–67. Capet's miniature is reproduced on p. 65. The prints of the duke as deputy can be found in the FDRA.

14. On the supposed royalism of Labille-Guiard and Capet, see Marcheteau de Quinçay, *Marie-Gabrielle Capet*, 16.

15. Bern Pappe, "Marie-Gabrielle Capet et la miniature sur ivoire," in Marcheteau de Quinçay, *Marie-Gabrielle Capet*, 36–44.

16. On the scandal of the Marie Antoinette portrait, see Mary D. Sheriff, *The Exceptional Woman: Elisabeth Vigée-Lebrun and the Cultural Politics of Art* (Chicago: University of Chicago Press, 1996), 165–72. See also Amelia Rauser, *The Age of Undress: Art, Fashion, and the Classical Ideal in the 1790s* (New Haven: Yale University Press, 2020).

17. Madame [Albertine] Clément-Hémery, *Souvenirs de 1793 et 1794* (Cambrai: Presses de Lesne-Daloin, 1832), 25–26. On Clément-Hémery's editorial role, see Kleinert, *"Le Journal des dames,"* 336–37.

18. On the general issue of dress, see Nicole Pellegrin, *Les Vêtements de la liberté: Abécédaire des pratiques vestimentaires en France de 1780 à 1800*, Librairie Du Bicentenaire de La Révolution Française (Aix-en-Provence: Alinea, 1989), 14–18, 151.

19. A full account can be found in François-Alphonse Aulard, *Le Culte de la raison et le culte de l'être suprême (1793–94)* (Paris: Félix Alcan, 1892). For the prints, see FDRA. David's plan for the Festival of the Supreme Being asserted that the young girls would be daughters who would promise to only marry men who had served the fatherland. M. J. Guillaume, *Procès-verbaux du Comité d'instruction publique de la Convention nationale*, 6 vols. (Paris: Imprimerie Nationale, 1891–1907), vol. 4 (1901), 350. White dresses had appeared in festivals in 1792 even

172 · NOTES

before the proclamation of the republic. See Mona Ozouf, *Festivals and the French Revolution*, trans. Alan Sheridan (Cambridge, MA: Harvard University Press, 1988 [1976]), 68.

20. On the multiple sources for Grecian-style dress, see Rauser, *The Age of Undress*. Her claim that Tallien wore a white dress as goddess of liberty in Bordeaux (p. 170) is contradicted by evidence provided in Maurice Ferrus, *Madame Tallien à Bordeaux pendant la Terreur: Étude historique et critique* (Bordeaux: Ferret et Fils, 1930), 128. The Bordeaux connection to Creole fashion remains speculative. It is asserted with no evidence provided by Madeleine Delpierre, *Dress in France in the Eighteenth Century*, trans. Caroline Beamish (New Haven: Yale University Press, 1997), 109.

21. For what is known about cotton textile use by the enslaved in the Caribbean, see Robert S. DuPlessis, "What Did Slaves Wear? Textile Regimes in the French Caribbean," *Monde(s)* 1, no. 1 (2012): 175–91. See also Robert S. DuPlessis, *The Material Atlantic: Clothing, Commerce, and Colonization in the Atlantic World, 1650–1800* (Cambridge: Cambridge University Press, 2015). For the Caribbean origins, see also Naomi Lubrich, "The Little White Dress: Politics and Polyvalence in Revolutionary France," *Fashion Theory* 20, no. 3 (2016): 273–96. On the dress of Creole women in Saint-Domingue, see Albert Savine, ed., *Saint-Domingue à la veille de la révolution (souvenirs du baron de Wimpffen). Annotés d'après les documents d'archives et les mémoires. Illustrations documentaires* (Paris: La Michaud, 1911), 160 (he also reports that enslaved women wore muslin skirts, p. 162). Rauser argues that "the experience of the Terror was widely aestheticized through fashion," but offers little evidence for this. Rauser, *The Age of Undress*, 173. On the Salon of 1796 reception, see Tony Halliday, *Facing the Public: Portraiture in the Aftermath of the French Revolution* (Manchester: Manchester University Press, 1999), 80–83.

22. The December 1798 quote comes from *Tableau général du goût, des modes et costumes de Paris*, no. 8 (2 nivôse an VII, December 22, 1798): 227. The subsequent quote comes from *L'Arlequin, ou Tableau des modes et des goûts*, 110. There is some uncertainty about the date of this journal, as none are given except on the first page, which indicates fall 1798, but according to Kleinert, "*Le Journal des dames*," it was published between August and October 1799 (p. 16). Muslin was an issue under the Old Regime, too, and the French crown tried to prevent its importation, finally giving up in the face of widespread smuggling in 1759. Hortense's account can be found in Jean Hanotaux, ed., *The Memoirs of Queen Hortense*, trans. Arthur K. Griggs, 2 vols. (New York: Cosmopolitan Book Corp., 1927), 1:33. On Napoleon's decree, see "Décret impérial relatif aux costumes de cour, et à ceux des membres des cours et tribunaux et des députations des colléges [sic] électoraux," January 4, 1811, in no. 342 of *Bulletin des lois de l'Empire français*, 4th series (Paris: L'Imprimerie Impériale, 1811), 14:3–4.

23. On the introduction of cashmere in France by the expedition to Egypt, see C.

Alexandre Le Goux de Flaix, "Mémoire sur les laines et les moutons de Cachemire et du Boutan," *La Décade philosophique, littéraire et politique*, nos. 13–18 (1801): 389–97, 458–566. See also Susan Hiner, *Accessories to Modernity: Fashion and the Feminine in Nineteenth-Century France* (Philadelphia: University of Pennsylvania Press, 2010), 83–84. For an example of another portrait with the white dress and red or orange shawl, see the portrait by François Gérard of Thérésia Cabarrus (Madame Tallien) ca. 1805 available online from the Carnavalet Museum in Paris.

24. On the Titus cut, see *Tableau général du goût, des modes et costumes de Paris*, no. 1 (1 vendémiaire an VII, September 22, 1798): 14; Edmond-Denis de Manne, *Galerie historique des comédiens de la troupe de Talma; notices sur les principaux sociétaires de la Comédie Françoise depuis 1789 jusqu'aux trente premières années de ce siècle* (Lyon: N. Scheuring, 1866), 111. Further information on Talma and Mars can be found on the online site for the Comédie Française.

25. On the replacement of blond wigs with dark-haired ones, see *Tableau général du goût, des modes et costumes de Paris*, no. 7 (1 nivôse an VII, December 22, 1798): 195. For Tallien's blond wigs, see Edmond de Goncourt et Jules de Goncourt, *Histoire de la société française pendant le directoire*, 2nd ed. (Paris, E. Dentu, 1855), 418; Louis-Sébastien Mercier, *Le Nouveau Paris*, ed. Jean-Claude Bonnet (Paris: Mercure de France, 1994), 404.

26. Auricchio, *Labille-Guiard*, 93.

27. Bonnet, "Femmes peintres à leur travail," 157; Auricchio, *Labille-Guiard*, 105. The portrait, in a private collection, can be seen in a black-and-white photograph on p. 104. Roger Portalis, *Adélaïde Labille-Guiard (1749–1803)* (Paris: Imprimerie Georges Petit, 1903), 93; Doria, *Gabrielle Capet*, 24. I identify it as the same dress because it has a distinctive seam down the sleeve that appears in Capet's self-portrait of 1790 but not in Labille-Guiard's *Self-Portrait with Two Pupils*. On the turn toward miniatures, see Halliday, *Facing the Public*, 27.

28. Even Auricchio has to admit that Labille-Guiard appears "quite plain," especially in comparison to Capet, who assigns "fashionable femininity" to herself. Auricchio, *Labille-Guiard*, 108. Heather Belnap Jensen wants to see this painting as a portrayal of rather pious father-daughter connections, including those of Joseph-Marie Vien with Labille-Guiard, who is painting his portrait, and of Vincent with Capet. Heather Belnap Jensen, "Picturing Paternity: The Artist and Father-Daughter Portraiture in Post-Revolutionary France," in *Interior Portraiture and Masculine Identity in France, 1789–1914*, ed. Temma Balducci, Heather Belnap Jensen, and Pamela J. Warner (London: Routledge, 2016 [2011]), 39–41.

29. *Explication des ouvrages de peinture, sculpture, architecture et gravure, des artistes vivans, exposés au Musée Napoléon, le 24 octobre 1808, second anniversaire de la bataille d'Iena* (Paris: Dubray, 1808), 13 (the parentheses in the quote are Capet's).

30. Paris Spies-Gans has helped me make sense of this painting. She shared with me her portfolio of images of women artists wearing white while working and also drew my attention to the disjointed temporal quality of the painting. See,

for example, Marie-Nicole Dumont, b. Vestier, *The Author at Her Occupations* (*L'Auteur à ses Occupations*), shown at the Salon of 1793. The downplaying of Labille-Guiard should not be exaggerated, however, since the dress she is wearing has a gauze collar and is not that different from the dress worn by Houdon's wife in Louis-Léopold Boilly's painting of 1804, *A Sculptor's Studio. Picture of a Family.* Emma Drouin has a different interpretation of Labille-Guiard's white dress; she finds it the "height of bourgeois fashion." Emma Rodney Drouin, "As the Eye Is Formed: Marie-Gabrielle Capet and the Artist in Her Studio," in *VERGES: Germanic & Slavic Studies in Review* 3, no. 1 (2020): 21, available online.

31. On the 1789 meaning of the plumed hat, see Freund, *Portraiture and Politics*, 64–65. For a description of the costume requirements for senators, see Frédéric Masson, *Napoleon and His Coronation*, trans. Frederic Cobb (London: T. Fisher Unwin, 1911), 333.

32. Capet's painting of Vincent, in a private collection, is reproduced in Marcheteau de Quinçay, *Marie-Gabrielle Capet*, p. 88. Capet's rendition in the studio scene is not identical, however; in the painting of Vincent alone, he is sitting, not standing, and he wears a strikingly ruffled jabot.

33. Analysis of the painting and identification of the figures and their ages can be found in Drouin, "As the Eye Is Formed." The fashion journal *L'Arlequin* claimed in the fall of 1799 that though wigs were still in use, they would soon fall victim to the "*cabal* hatched against [the fashion] by *hair worn in the Greek style*." *L'Arlequin, ou Tableau des modes et des goûts*, 81. Guérin does not have the high-collared vest that is seen on some of the men in the Capet painting. The Lefèvre painting is held by the Musée des Beaux-Arts of Orléans. The *jabot de point*, a fashion imported from England, was known as early as 1777. *Dictionnaire de l'Académie Françoise. Nouvelle Édition. Tome 1* (Nîmes: Chez Gaude, 1777), 628.

34. On the rivalry between Vincent and David, see Jean-Pierre Cuzin, *François-André Vincent (1746–1816): Entre Fragonard et David* (Paris: Arthena, 2013), esp. 281. On Capet's connection to Meynier, see Isabelle Mayer-Michalon, *Charles Meynier (1763–1832)* (Paris: Arthena, 2008), 102–3.

35. On the resistance of some critics to Boilly's success, see Halliday, *Facing the Public*, 140–42.

36. *Journal des dames et des modes* complained in December 1807 that "the fashion or rather the rage for cashmere continues to increase: a shawl costs 50, 80, 100 *louis* [1 *louis* was the equivalent of 20 francs], and what is even more surprising, a striped cashmere for a dress fetches up to 5000 francs." *Journal des dames et des modes*, no. 70 (December 20, 1807), 564. Quote is from *Tableau général du goût, des modes et costumes de Paris*, no. 1 (1 Vendémiaire, an VII, September 22, 1798): 8. For a similar waistline and ribbon marking it as shown on Vien's daughter-in-law, see *Journal des dames et des modes*, no. 2 (16 Vendémiaire, an VII, October 7, 1798): illustration 3, facing p. 37. For the commentary on wigs and hair, see *Journal des dames et des modes*, no.88 (December 10, 1806): 702.

NOTES · 175

37. For the trimmed redingote, see also plate 701 in no. 28 (February 10, 1806). It is called a Turkish-style padded dressing gown (*douillette turque*) and is shown over a white undergarment. For the collar, see plate 769 in no. 86 (November 30, 1806), plate 774 in no. 90 (December 20, 1806), plate 854 in no. 67 (December 5, 1807), plate 856 in no. 69 (December 15, 1807), and plate 858 in no. 70 (December 20, 1807).

38. For the complaint about the directors' costumes, see *Le Citoyen français, Journal politique, commercial, littéraire*, no. 3 (26 brumaire an VIII, November 17, 1799): 4. The emergence and growing dominance of colored fabrics as well as silk and wool can be readily traced in the issues of *Journal des dames et des modes*.

39. For Capet's last years, see Marcheteau de Quinçay, "Marie-Gabrielle Capet, artiste et modèle," 23–24.

CHAPTER FOUR: REVOLUTIONARY ARMIES AND THE STRATEGIES OF WAR

1. Some of the material in this chapter first appeared in Lynn Hunt, "The French Revolutionary Wars," in *Politics and Diplomacy*, ed. Michael Broers and Philip Dwyer, vol. 1 of *The Cambridge History of the Napoleonic Wars* (Cambridge: Cambridge University Press, 2022), 127–45. The essential source is Jean-Paul Bertaud, *La Révolution armée: Les Soldats-citoyens et la Révolution française* (Paris: Robert Laffont, 1979). It has been translated into English as *The Army of the French Revolution*, trans. R. R. Palmer (Princeton, NJ: Princeton University Press, 1988). For the figure on reserve muskets, see Georges Lefebvre, "Etudes sur le ministère de Narbonne: Troisième partie," *Annales historiques de la Révolution française* 19, no. 107 (1947): 193–217, esp. 195.

2. The quote about the state of the army comes from Robert Johnstone, "French Frontier 1790–1791" (folio 8) in British Library, Western Manuscripts, Add MS 69096, Dropmore Papers (Series II), Vol. LIX. He goes on, however, to contest the severity of this judgment. The government estimates are to be found in "Apperçu de la balance du commerce de la France, Année 1789–Ensemble le relevé de la population, des finances, et forces militaires des principales puissances de l'Europe," British Library, Western Manuscripts, Add MSS 74100. Needless to say, these figures were approximations and did not represent the size of armies that would be available for specific campaigns. For the number of nobles among the generals, see Jean-Paul Bertaud, Daniel Reichel, and Jacques Bertrand, *L'Armée et la guerre*, vol. 3 of *Atlas de la Révolution française* (Paris: Éditions de l'École des Hautes Études, 1989), 31.

3. For the number of cannons, see Matti Lauerma, *L'Artillerie de campagne française pendant les guerres de la Révolution* (Helsinki: Suomalainen Tiedeakatemia, 1956), 161. For the range of cannon, see Gunther E. Rothenberg, *The Art of Warfare in the Age of Napoleon* (Bloomington: Indiana University Press, 1978), 76. On the

176 · NOTES

battle itself, see Emmanuel Hublot, *Valmy, ou la défense de la Nation par les armes* (Paris: Fondation pour les études de défense nationale, 1987); Arthur Chuquet, *Valmy*, 11th ed. (Paris: Plon, 1927); and Jean-Paul Bertaud, *Valmy: La Démocratie en armes* (Paris: Julliard, 1970).

4. My translation from the German in Johann Wolfgang von Goethe, *Campagne in Frankreich (23 août–20 octobre 1792)*, ed. A. Chuquet (Paris: Ch. Delagrave, 1884), 93.

5. Because of these anticipations of later strategy, T. C. W. Blanning argues that "revolutionary warfare was not revolutionary." T. C. W. Blanning, *The French Revolutionary Wars, 1787–1802* (London: Arnold, 1996), 17. In this he follows Peter Paret, "Napoleon and the Revolution in War," in Peter Paret, Gordon A. Craig, and Felix Gilbert, *Makers of Modern Strategy from Machiavelli to the Nuclear Age* (Princeton, NJ: Princeton University Press, 1986), 123–42. For the most recent iteration of this view, see Jonathan Abel, *Guibert: Father of Napoleon's Grande Armée* (Norman: University of Oklahoma Press, 2016). On the ambiguities of Guibert's notion of a citizen army, see R. R. Palmer, "Frederick the Great, Guibert, Bülow: From Dynastic to National War," in Paret et al., *Makers of Modern Strategy*, esp. 107–8. Beatrice Heuser shows that Guibert gave up on the idea of a citizen army before his death in 1790; he preferred a small, well-trained professional force. Beatrice Heuser, "Guibert, Prophet of Total War?" in *War in an Age of Revolution, 1775–1815*, ed. Roger Chickering and Stig Förster (Cambridge: Cambridge University Press, 2010), 49–67.

6. Some nobles may well have masked their heritage. For the army, see Bertaud, *The Army of the French Revolution*, 182–84. For the navy, see Bertaud, Reichel, and Bertrand, *L'Armée et la guerre*, 29.

7. For the estimates of naval strength, see BL Additional Mss 74100. For the naval arms race, see Jonathan R. Dull, *The Age of the Ship of the Line: The British & French Navies, 1650–1815* (Lincoln: University of Nebraska Press, 2009), 119. On the general land-based strategy, see Arnaud Bernard, "Napoléon et la Marine ou l'histoire d'un malentendu," *Napoleonica. La Revue* 8, no. 2 (2010): 53–76. On the general background for the navy, see Kenneth Johnson, "The French Navy," in *Fighting the Napoleonic Wars*, ed. Bruno Colson and Alexander Mikaberidze, vol. 2 of *The Cambridge History of the Napoleonic Wars* (Cambridge: Cambridge University Press, 2023), 207–28.

8. For the size of the regular army, see Bertaud, *The Army of the French Revolution*, 16. On the volunteers and conscription in 1793, see Alan Forrest, *The Soldiers of the French Revolution* (Durham, NC: Duke University Press, 1990), esp. 64–82. On deserters, see Bertaud, *The Army of the French Revolution*, 259–60, and Alan Forrest, *Conscripts and Deserters: The Army and French Society during the Revolution and Empire* (New York: Oxford University Press, 1989), map facing p. 3. For an exemplary local study, see Annie Crépin, *Révolution et armée nouvelle en Seine-et-Marne (1791–1797)* (Paris: Éditions du CTHS, 2008).

NOTES · **177**

9. On the mutinies, see Samuel F. Scott, *The Response of the Royal Army to the French Revolution: The Role and Development of the Line Army 1787–1793* (Oxford: Clarendon Press, 1978). In addition to Bertaud, *The Army of the French Revolution*, see Jean-Paul Bertaud, *La Vie quotidienne des soldats de la Révolution* (Paris: Hachette, 1985). For the size of the cavalry, see Louis Auguste Picard, *La Cavalerie dans les guerres de la Révolution et de l'Empire*, 2 vols. (Saumur, France: 1895–96), 1:1, 28.

10. Ernest Picard, ed., *Au Service de la nation: Lettres de volontaires (1792–1799)* (Paris: Librairie Félix Alcan, 1914), 117–18.

11. Lorédan Larchey, ed., *Journal du cannonier Bricard, 1792–1802* (Paris: Librairie Ch. Delagrave, 1891), 11, 18, 49–62, 69.

12. Georges Six, *Les Généraux de la Révolution et de l'Empire* (Paris: Bordas, 1947), 5, 228–29.

13. Marc Martin, "Journaux d'armées au temps de la Convention," *Annales historiques de la Révolution française* 44, no. 210 (1972): 567–605; John Albert Lynn, *The Bayonets of the Republic: Motivation and Tactics in the Army of Revolutionary France, 1791–94* (Urbana: University of Illinois Press, 1984), 124–40.

14. Lorédan Larchey, ed., *Journal de marche du Sergent Fricasse de la 127e brigade, 1792–1802* (Paris: n.p., 1882), 29.

15. Étienne Jolicler, ed., *Joliclerc: Volontaire aux armées de la Révolution, ses lettres (1793–1796)* (Paris: Perrin, 1905), 141–43.

16. Thomas Dodman, "Ordinary Radicalization: Becoming a Citizen-Soldier during the French Revolution," *Journal of Modern History* 94, no. 4 (2022): 751–89.

17. Lucien Duchet, ed., *Deux volontaires de 1791: Les Frères Favier de Montluçon* (Montluçon, France: A. Herbin, 1909), quotes on pp. 55, 77, 93.

18. Letter of November 5, 1793 quoted in Arthur Chuquet, *Quatre généraux de la Révolution: Hoche & Desaix, Kléber & Marceau: Lettres et notes inédites suivies d'annexes historiques et biographiques*, 4 vols. (Paris: Fontemoing, 1911–12), 1:13–14.

19. Laurent de Gouvion Saint-Cyr, *Mémoires sur les campagnes des armées du Rhin et de Rhin-et-Moselle, de 1792 jusqu'à la paix de Campo-Formio*, 4 vols. (Paris: Anselin, 1829), 1:7. On Saint-Cyr's career, see Christian d'Ainval, *Gouvion Saint-Cyr: Soldat de l'an II, Maréchal d'Empire, Réorganisateur de l'armée* (Paris: Copernic, 1981).

20. For the three examples, see Xavier de Pétigny, *Un Bataillon de volontaires (3eme bataillon de Maine-et-Loire) 1792–96* (Angers, France: Germain et G. Grassin, 1908), 26–42. For the past experience of lieutenant colonels elected in 1792, see Bertaud et al., *Atlas de la Révolution française*, 28.

21. *Réimpression de l'ancien Moniteur*, 32 vols. (Paris: Bureau central, 1840–63), 23:608 (session of the National Convention of 14 ventôse an III reported in the issue of 16 ventôse an III, March 6, 1795).

22. *Mémoire adressé au public et à l'armée sur les opérations du conseil de la guerre, publié en 1789*, in *Oeuvres militaires de Guibert, publiées par sa veuve*, 5 vols. (Paris: Magimel, 1803), 5: esp. 201.

23. Dubois-Crancé presented the report of the war committee on February 7, 1793.

178 · NOTES

Rapport du Dubois-Crancé, au nom du comité de la guerre, sur l'organisation de l'armée (Paris: Imprimerie Nationale, 1793), esp. 8, 26.

24. Still essential on these questions is Lynn, *The Bayonets of the Republic*; on horse artillery, see esp. p. 204.

25. Especially important on the question of horse artillery is Lauerma, *L'Artillerie de campagne française* (see p. 42 on Gribeauval's unwillingness to take a firm stand on horse artillery and p. 126 on the reputation of the horse artillery). On the introduction of howitzers and improvement of mortars, see Ernest Picard and Louis Jouan, *L'Artillerie française au XVIIIᵉ siècle* (Paris and Nancy: Berger-Levrault, 1906), 73. On the cavalry, see Édouard Desbrière and Maurice Sautai, *La Cavalerie pendant la Révolution: Du 14 juillet 1789 au 26 juin 1794: La Crise* (Paris and Nancy: Berger-Levrault, 1907). For Murat's letter to his father about the cost of equipping himself, see Albert Lumbroso, ed., *Correspondance de Joachim Murat, chasseur à cheval, général, maréchal d'Empire, grand-duc de Clèves et de Berg (juillet 1791 à juillet 1808)* (Turin: Roux Frassati, 1899), 8. For Custine's view, see Arthur Chuquet, *L'Expédition de Custine* (Paris: Librairie Léopold Cerf, 1892), 235.

26. Antoine-Henri Jomini, *Précis de l'art de la guerre, ou nouveau tableau analytique des principales combinaisons de la stratégie, de la grande tactique et de la politique militaire*, 2 vols. (Paris: Anselin and Laguionie, 1838), 1:311.

27. For the April 1794 letter to two deputies on mission to the Army of the North, see Étienne Charavay, ed., *Correspondance générale de Carnot: Publiée avec des notes historiques et biographiques*, 4 vols. (Paris: Imprimerie Nationale, 1892–97), 4:326.

28. The Scharnhorst quote can be found in Peter Paret, *Yorck and the Era of Prussian Reform* (Princeton, NJ: Princeton University Press, 1966), 258 (from an essay of 1811 describing the fighting in 1793–94, emphasis in text); Saint-Cyr, *Mémoires sur les campagnes des armées du Rhin et de Rhin-et-Moselle*, 1:xliii.

29. For the 1791 regulation, see *Règlement concernant l'exercice et les manoeuvres de l'infanterie, du 1 août 1791* (Paris: Imprimerie Royale, 1791), esp. 51; Saint-Cyr, *Mémoires sur les campagnes des armées du Rhin et de Rhin-et-Moselle*, 1:xliv. For the comments of Noël, see Dodman, "Ordinary Radicalization," 771.

30. Lynn, *The Bayonets of the Republic*, esp. 241–300.

31. My argument about the importance of numbers does not mean that I endorse the idea that the French were fighting a "total war" in the sense laid out by David Bell. In any case, my interest here is quite different because I am trying to highlight the inevitable tensions between individual ambitions and the need for collective discipline and undertakings. David A. Bell, *The First Total War: Napoleon's Europe and the Birth of Warfare as We Know It* (Boston: Houghton Mifflin, 2007). A part of Grimoard's *Mémoire* is cited as the basis of a January 25, 1793, report to the National Convention by Edmond Dubois-Crancé on the state of the armies. P. J. B. Buchez and P. C. Roux, eds., *Histoire parlementaire de la Révolution française, ou Journal des Assemblées Nationales, depuis 1789 jusqu'en 1815, contenant la narration des évènements . . . précédée d'une introduction sur*

NOTES • **179**

l'histoire de France jusqu'à la convocation des Etats généraux, 40 vols. (Paris: Paulin, 1834–38), vol. 24 (1836), 414. The full text can be found in "Mémoire sur la force des armées françaises et étrangères," in Philippe-Henri de Grimoard, *Recherches sur la force de l'armée française* (Paris: Treuttel et Würtz, 1806), 152–57, quotes on p. 156.

32. J. Mavidal and E. Laurent, eds., *Archives parlementaires de 1787 à 1860, première série (1787 à 1799)*, 90 vols (Paris: P. du Pont, CNRS, 1867–1990), 76:316.

33. On the cult of the bayonet, see Lynn, *The Bayonets of the Republic*, esp. 185–91. On the slow recovery of cavalry, see Desbrière and Sautai, *La Cavalerie pendant la Révolution*, esp. 427–35. For Carnot's speech, see *Archives parlementaires*, 47:122.

34. According to Ken Alder, "Between 1700 and 1840, the design of the flintlock musket remained essentially constant." Ken Alder, *Engineering the Revolution: Arms and Enlightenment in France, 1763–1815* (Princeton, NJ: Princeton University Press, 1997), 192. The lighter Gribeauval cannon had been introduced in the late 1770s and 1780s. Jean-Lambert-Alphonse Colin, *La Tactique et la discipline dans les armées de la Révolution: Correspondance du general Schauenbourg du 4 avril au 2 août 1793* (Paris: Librairie militaire R. Chapelot, 1902), xiv–xv.

35. Still essential on Napoleon's education and early years is Jean-Lambert-Alphonse Colin, *L'Éducation militaire de Napoléon* (Paris: Librairie militaire R. Chapelot, 1901).

36. Karl A. Roider Jr., *Baron Thugut and Austria's Response to the French Revolution* (Princeton, NJ: Princeton University Press, 2014), quote on p. 204. On Bonaparte's strategy, see Gabriel Défossé, *Montenotte: La Première Victoire de Napoléon Bonaparte* (Cagnes-sur-Mer, France: EDICA, 1986), esp. 54 for his appointment as commander.

37. Michael Broers, *The Napoleonic Empire in Italy, 1796–1814: Cultural Imperialism in a European Context?* (New York: Palgrave Macmillan, 2005), 30–62; Larchey, *Journal du canonnier Bricard*, 189.

38. Bruno Colson, "Napoléon et la guerre irrégulière," *Stratégique* 93–94–95–96, no. 1 (2009): 227–58; H. Galli, ed., *L'armée française en Égypte, 1798–1801: Journal d'un officier de l'Armée d'Égypte* (Paris: G. Charpentier, 1883), 81; Paul Roussier, ed., *Lettres du Général Leclerc, Commandant en Chef de l'armée de Saint-Domingue en 1802* (Paris: Société de l'Histoire de Colonies Françaises, 1937), 238 (letter of September 17, 1802, to the minister of the Navy).

39. Isser Woloch, *Napoleon and His Collaborators: The Making of a Dictatorship* (New York: W. W. Norton, 2001); Wayne Hanley, *The Genesis of Napoleonic Propaganda, 1796–1799* (New York: Columbia University Press, 2005).

40. Wolfgang Kruse, "La Formation du discours militariste sous le directoire," *Annales historiques de la Révolution française*, no. 360 (April–June 2010): 77–102.

41. John A. Lynn, "Toward an Army of Honor: The Moral Evolution of the French Army, 1789–1815," *French Historical Studies* 16, no. 1 (1989): 152–73. Bertaud, *La Révolution armée*, 275. On the passivity bred by politicization, see Rafe Blaufarb,

180 · NOTES

The French Army, 1750–1820: Careers, Talent, Merit (Manchester: Manchester University Press, 2002), 163.

42. A. Hilliard Atteridge, *Joachim Murat: Marshall of France and King of Naples* (London: Methuen, 1911).

43. For Napoleon's views of Lannes in Italy, see *Correspondance de Napoléon 1er: Publiée par ordre de l'empereur Napoléon III*, 32 vols. (Paris: L'Imprimerie Nationale, 1858–70), vol. 1 (1858), 250–51, 261, 338–39; Margaret Scott Chrisawn, *The Emperor's Friend: Marshal Jean Lannes* (Westport, CT: Greenwood Press, 2001). For Napoleon's strong feelings about Lannes, see Brian Joseph Martin, *Napoleonic Friendship: Military Fraternity, Intimacy and Sexuality in Nineteenth-Century France* (Durham: University of New Hampshire Press, 2011), 40–67.

44. Victor Bernard Derrécagaix, *Le Maréchal Berthier, prince de Wagram & de Neuchatel*, 2 vols. (Paris: R. Chapelot, 1904–05), 1:107–9, 367–70. For the quote about Berthier, see *Correspondance de Napoléon 1er*, 1:261. See also François Houdecek, *Louis-Alexandre Berthier, Prince de Neuchâtel et de Wagram* (Rennes, France: Presses Universitaires de Rennes, 2022).

45. Charles Antoine Thoumas, *Le Maréchal Lannes* (Paris: Calmann Levy, 1891), 65 (December 1799 letter).

46. Thoumas, *Le Maréchal Lannes*, 205 (his disenchantment with Napoleon after the capitulation of Danzig in 1807).

CHAPTER FIVE: MONEY, SELF-INTEREST, AND MAKING A REPUBLIC

1. On the general issue of debt and representative government, see James Macdonald, *A Free Nation Deep in Debt: The Financial Roots of Democracy* (Princeton, NJ: Princeton University Press, 2006). On accountability, see Jacob Soll, *The Reckoning: Financial Accountability and the Rise and Fall of Nations* (New York: Basic Books, 2014). For Hume's views, see the essay "Of Public Credit," in *Political Discourses by David Hume, Esq.*, 2nd ed. (Edinburgh: R. Fleming, 1752), esp. 130–35.

2. *The Spirit of Laws, translated from the French of M. de Secondat, baron de Montesquieu [by Thomas Nugent]; with corrections and additions communicated by the author*, 2 vols. (Dublin: G. and A. Ewing and G. Faulkner, 1751 [1748]), 2:86 (book 22, chapter 17); Paul Leicester Ford, ed., *The Writings of Thomas Jefferson*, 10 vols. (New York: G. P. Putnam's Sons, 1892–99), vol. 8 (1801–1806), 185. For the French revolutionary language about the national debt, see FRDA under the rubric "Archives parlementaires." The same terms had appeared in the grievance lists submitted to the Estates General (they are available from the same source).

3. On the issuance of paper money in the United States, see William Watts Folwell, "Evolution of Paper Money in the United States," *Minnesota Law Review* 8 (1924): 561–78, esp. 570. The literature on John Law is extensive. The best introduction is François Velde, "John Law's System," *American Economic Review* 97, no. 2 (May

NOTES · 181

2007): 276–79. See also John Shovlin, "Jealousy of Credit: John Law's 'System' and the Geopolitics of Financial Revolution," *Journal of Modern History* 88, no. 2 (June 2016): 275–305. For a full account, see Bertrand Martinot, *John Law: Le Magicien de la dette* (Paris: Nouveau monde, 2015). On the vague character of memories about Law, see Rebecca L. Spang, "The Ghost of Law: Speculating on Money, Memory and Mississippi in the French Constituent Assembly," *Historical Reflections / Réflexions Historiques* 31, no. 1 (2005): 3–25.

4. Francesca Trivellato, *The Promise and Peril of Credit: What a Forgotten Legend about Jews and Finance Tells Us about the Making of European Commercial Society* (Princeton, NJ: Princeton University Press, 2019).

5. For the interest rate in Britain, see Nathan Sussman and Yishay Yafeh, "Institutional Reforms, Financial Development and Sovereign Debt: Britain 1690–1790," *Journal of Economic History* 66, no. 4 (2006): 906–35. On the Bank of England, see Patrick K. O'Brien and Nuno Palma, "Not an Ordinary Bank but a Great Engine of State: The Bank of England and the British Economy, 1694–1844," *Economic History Review* 76, no. 1 (February 2023): 305–29. For the proposals made in the eighteenth century, see Shovlin, "Jealousy of Credit." On the Discount Bank, see Robert Bigo, *La Caisse d'Escompte (1776–1793) et les origines de la Banque de France* (Paris: Presses universitaires de France, 1927). His estimate of French interest rates on the debt can be found on p. 43.

6. On the origins of life insurance and the differences between Britain and Catholic Europe, see Geoffrey Clark, *Betting on Lives: The Culture of Life Insurance in England, 1695–1775* (Manchester: Manchester University Press, 1999); *Arrêt du Conseil d'État du roi, Qui autorise à perpétuité l'établissement des Assurances sur la Vie, avec Privilege exclusive pendant quinze années, du 3 novembre 1787* (Paris: N. H. Nyon, Imprimeur du Parlement, 1788). A subsequent decree allowed the life insurance company to separate from the fire insurance company that provided its original organization. *Arrêt du Conseil d'État du roi, Relatif à la séparation des deux Compagnies d'Assurances, & au dépôt des sommes versées au Trésor Royale par celle des Assurances à Vie, du 27 juillet 1788* (Paris: N. H. Nyon, Imprimeur du Parlement, 1788). These were companies organized by Clavière and his associates.

7. For an overview of Clavière's remarkable life, see Édouard Chapuisat, *Figures et choses d'autrefois* (Paris: G. Cres, 1920), and Jean-Marc Rivier, *Étienne Clavière, 1735–1793: Un Révolutionnaire, ami des Noirs* (Paris: Panormitis, 2006). While I was writing this chapter, Mathieu Chaptal sent me a new doctoral thesis on Clavière that has proved invaluable: Mathieu Chaptal, "De Genève à la France, la pensée républicaine d'Etienne Clavière: Réforme financière, Souveraineté populaire et Révolutions (1735–1793)" (PhD diss., Aix-Marseille Université, December 2020). It is now published as *D'une révolution à l'autre: Étienne Clavière (1735–1793)* (Le Kremlin-Bicêtre, France: Mare & Martin, 2024).

8. Clavière's political philosophy was first emphasized by Richard Whatmore. See, for example, Richard Whatmore, "Commerce, Constitutions, and the Manners of

182 · NOTES

a Nation: Etienne Clavière's Revolutionary Political Economy, 1788–1793," *History of European Ideas* 22, nos. 5–6 (1996): 351–68. For the characterization of Clavière, see M. J. L. Duval, ed., *Souvenirs sur Mirabeau et sur les deux premières assemblées législatives par Étienne Dumont* (Brussels: P. J. Meline, 1832), 299–300. The more recent work of Rivier, Whatmore, and Chaptal counters the earlier negative judgments of Clavière, such as that found in Herbert Lüthy, *La Banque protestante en France de la Révocation de l'Edit de Nantes à la Révolution*, 2 vols. (Paris, 1959–61), esp. 2:715.

9. For Brissot's view of Clavière, see Claude Perroud, ed., *J.-P. Brissot: Mémoires (1754–1793)*, 2 vols. (Paris: Picard, 1911), 2:28. Robert Darnton has examined the indebtedness of Brissot to Clavière, who between the end of 1786 and the beginning of 1789 loaned Brissot more than 24,000 livres. Brissot paid back most but not all of it; he still owed nearly 3,700 livres. Robert Choate Darnton, "Trends in Radical Propaganda on the Eve of the French Revolution (1782–1788)" (PhD diss., University of Oxford, 1964), 416. I am indebted to Sarah Maza for this reference. Clavière figured out how to make the most of the liberalization of the stock market, which is analyzed by T. J. A. Le Goff, "An Eighteenth-Century Big Bang? The Liberalization of the Paris Stock Market, 1774–1793," in *The Cultural Life of Risk and Innovation*, ed. Chia Yin Hsu, Thomas M. Luckett, and Erika Vause (New York: Routledge, 2021), 123–49.

10. The letter to Delessert of June 27, 1781, can be found in Archives Nationales (herafter AN) T//*/646/1. On Clavière's financial difficulties, see the letter to Jacques-Antoine Du Roveray, one of his fellow agitators from Geneva forced into exile (but who landed on his feet as a professor of law in Dublin), dated November 17, 1783: "The mishap at the Discount Bank has taken from me all of my resources and menaces my fortune with such a reduction that I would be truly close to being ruined." AN T//*/646/1.

11. For the letter to Delessert, see AN T//*/ 646/1, letter of December 20, 1783.

12. Louis Petit de Bachaumont, *Mémoires secrets pour servir à l'histoire de la republique des lettres en France, depuis MDCCLXII jusqu'à nos jours; ou, Journal d'un observateur . . .* , 36 vols. (London: John Adamson, 1781–89), 28:54 (this is dated January 23, 1785, so before the government's decree annulling futures contracts). See also Jean Bouchary, *Les Manieurs d'argent à Paris à la fin du XVIIIᵉ siècle*, 3 vols. (Paris: M. Rivière, 1939–43), esp. vol. 1. Considerations of length precluded any consideration of Clavière's investments in the French India Company. On the company, see Elizabeth Cross, *Company Politics: Commerce, Scandal and French Visions of Indian Empire in the Revolutionary Era* (New York: Oxford University Press, 2023), esp. 112.

13. *De la Caisse d'Escompte. Par le comte de Mirabeau* (n. p., 1785), 82. *Mémoires secrets* says the tract appeared on May 25 (29:45).

14. AN T//*/646/2, letter of July 16, 1785, to Delessert & fils of Lyon. See Bouchary, *Les Manieurs*, I:46–52, for a much more detailed discussion. For a defense of Clavière's motives, see Richard Whatmore and James Livesey, "Étienne Clavière,

Jacques-Pierre Brissot et les fondations intellectuelles de la politique des girondins," *Annales historiques de la Révolution française*, 321 (July–September 2000): 1–26.

15. Bertrand Dardenne, *L'Eau et le feu: La Courte mais trépidante aventure de la première Compagnie des eaux de Paris (1777–1788)* (Paris: Editions de Venise, 2005). On the details of Clavière's actions in this regard, see Bouchary, *Les Manieurs*, 1:54–71.

16. AN T//*/646/3, letter of January 13, 1786.

17. On the intricacies of the life annuity, see George V. Taylor, "The Paris Bourse on the Eve of the Revolution, 1781–1789," *American Historical Review* 67, no. 4 (July 1962): 951–77. See also Bouchary, *Les Manieurs*, 1:80–88. For the amounts invested and owed in April 1786, see AN T//*/646/5, folios 1–9. These figures can only be considered approximations, as Clavière had mortgaged some of his investments.

18. In April 1784, Clavière volunteered to send to Étienne Delessert a study done by Cazenove in London on the relative advantages of life annuities based on one life and those based on many. In March 1786, he wrote to Cazenove asking for more precise information about life insurance practices in London. Letter to Delessert of April 25, 1784, in AN T//*/646/1. For the letter of March 23, 1786, see Bouchary, *Les Manieurs*, 1:89. Richard Price, *Observations on Reversionary Payments*, 4th ed. 2 vols. (London: T. Cadell, 1783). The 4th edition's tables were the attraction for British and French investors.

19. This summary can hardly do justice to the complexities of the negotiations involved. See Jean Bouchary, *Les Compagnies financières à Paris à la fin du XVIIIe siècle*, 3 vols. (Paris: Marcel Rivière, 1940–42), 3:9–58. On Condorcet's involvement with financiers and the general issue of life insurance, see Jean-Marie Thiveaud, "Condorcet: Prévoyance, finance et probabilités, entre raison et utopie," *Revue d'économie financière*, no. 49 (1998): 51–77. Clavière's behind-the-scenes role in setting up the competing fire insurance company is revealed by the fact that his son-in-law was named an administrator alongside Etienne Delessert, his banker. Bouchary, *Les Compagnies financières*, 3:15, footnote 12.

20. *Compagnie royale d'assurances, Prospectus de l'établissment des assurances sur la vie* (Paris: Lottin l'ainé, 1788), quote on p. 5. It is clear that Clavière is the author because his name and address are given for all inquiries at the end, on a page with no number. For the mutual aid society for servants, see *Compagnie d'assurances sur la vie, Extrait des registres de l'administration de ladite Compagnie, du mercredi 28 juillet 1790*, "Proposition pour l'établissement d'une caisse de secours en faveur des domestiques de tout age" (Paris: Lottin l'ainé, 1790).

21. On the fate of the insurance companies, see Bouchary, *Les Compagnies financières*, vol. 3.

22. For Clavière's investment in French government loans, see AN T//*/646/5, folios 2 and 3. On US debt issues, see James C. Riley, *International Government Finance and the Amsterdam Capital Market, 1740–1815* (Cambridge: Cambridge University Press, 1980), esp. 188.

184 · NOTES

23. Étienne Clavière and J. P. Brissot, *De la France et des États-Unis* (London: n.p., 1787); on paper money, see p. 318. The book was translated into English as *Considerations on the Relative Situation of France and the United States of America* (London: Logographic Press, 1788). Clavière noted his financial contribution of nearly 1,000 livres to the book's publication in London in his account book, AN T//*/646/5, folio 240 (March 14, 1788). On Brissot, see Régis Coursin, *Jacques-Pierre Brissot: Sociologie historique d'une entrée en révolution* (Rennes, France: Presses Universitaires de Rennes, 2023). Brissot is one of the most controversial and least studied of the major revolutionary figures.

24. See the preface by Marcel Dorigny to *De la France et des États-Unis: Étienne Clavière et J. P. Brissot de Warville* (Paris: Éditions du C.T.H.S., 1996), 7–29. On the utopian dimension, see also Darnton, "Trends in Radical Propaganda," 91–130. On the various networks interested in this part of the United States, see Marcel Deperne, "Le Réseau d'affaires francophone dans la haute vallée de l'Ohio et le Kentucky entre 1783 et 1815," *French Historical Studies* 46, no. 4 (November 2023): 525–58. On the US securities market, see Niccolò Valmori, "Looking for New Markets in a Time of Revolution: The U.S. Securities Market, 1789–1804," in Hsu, Luckett, and Vause, *The Cultural Life of Risk and Innovation*, 43–60.

25. [J. P. Brissot and Étienne Clavière], *Point de banqueroute, ou lettres à un créancier de l'État* (London: n.p., 1787), 5, 17, 18.

26. The question of a constitution is much more prominent in the longer version of *Point de banqueroute* published in London in 1788.

27. Quotes from *Discourse on the Necessity of Establishing in Paris a Society for. . . the Abolition of the Slave Trade and of Negro Slavery* in Lynn Hunt, ed., *The French Revolution and Human Rights: A Brief Documentary History* (Boston: Bedford/St. Martin's, 1996), 58–59.

28. The republican substrate of Clavière's views was emphasized by Whatmore, "Commerce, Constitutions," and Richard Whatmore, *Against War and Empire: Geneva, Britain, and France in the Eighteenth Century* (New Haven: Yale University Press, 2012), and then further elaborated in Chaptal, *D'une révolution à l'autre*, who emphasizes Clavière's indebtedness to his fellow Genevan Rousseau.

29. The register of the meetings of the society can be found in Marcel Dorigny and Bernard Gainot, *La Société des Amis des Noirs, 1788–1799: Contribution à l'histoire de l'abolition de l'esclavage* (Paris: Éditions UNESCO, 1998). See pp. 128–29 for Clavière's intervention on April 8, 1788.

30. On the proslavery agitation more generally, see Lauren R. Clay, "Liberty, Equality, Slavery: Debating the Slave Trade in Revolutionary France," *American Historical Review* 128, no. 1 (March 2023): 89–119. On Clavière's participation and Clarkson's attendance, see the register of the meetings in Dorigny and Gainot, *La Société des Amis des Noirs*, 243–70. In fact, Clavière did not attend much of the time that Clarkson was there, returning in March 1790. The register ends in May 1790, though the meetings continued. For the younger Mirabeau quotes,

NOTES · 185

see J. Mavidal and E. Laurent, eds., *Archives parlementaires de 1787 à 1860, première série (1787 à 1799)*, 90 vols (Paris: P. du Pont, CNRS, 1867–1990), 12:76.

31. On the debt more generally, see T. J. A. Le Goff, "Les Crises de la dette nationale en France, 1724–1815," in *Les Crises de la dette publique: XVIII*ᵉ*–XXI*ᵉ *siècle*, ed. Gérard Béaur and Laure Quennouëlle-Corr (Paris: Comité pour l'histoire économique et financière de la France, 2021), 263–86. I am grateful to the author for sending this chapter to me. [Étienne Clavière], *De la foi publique envers les créanciers de l'état. Lettres à M. Linguet sur le No CXVI de ses Annales par M. **** (London: n.p., 1788). The term "public confidence" (or "public faith") appears over and over again. Public confidence goes along with "all the truths that are useful to the grandeur of nations, to the peace of the human race, to the happiness of peoples" (quote from p. 149).

32. *De la foi publique*, quotes from pp. 76 and 31. The development of Clavière's republicanism is the major theme of Chaptal, *D'une révolution à l'autre*.

33. The importance of Clavière's residence is noted in M. J. L. Duval, ed., *Souvenirs sur Mirabeau*, 42. For Clavière's economic views ca. June 1789, see Étienne Clavière, *Opinions d'un créancier de l'État, sur quelques matières de finance importantes dans le moment actuel par M. Clavière* (London: n.p., June 1789). There are at least two versions of this pamphlet.

34. *Le Courrier de Provence, servant du suite des Lettres du Comte de Mirabeau à ses commetans*, no. 48 (29 September–1 October 1789), 18–24.

35. The complicated ins and outs of the financial issues are best followed in Marcel Marion, *Histoire financière de la France depuis 1715*, 6 vols. (Paris: Librairie Arthur Rousseau, 1914–31), esp. vol. 2 (1789–1792).

36. For a description of Clavière's ceaseless activity, see M. J. L. Duval, ed., *Souvenirs sur Mirabeau*, 300; Étienne Clavière, *Dissection du projet de M. l'Évêque a'Autun* [Talleyrand] *sur l'échange universel et direct des créances d'État contre les biens nationaux* (Paris: L'Imprimerie du Patriote Français, July 1790); *Le Patriote français* was Brissot's newspaper. At the same time, Clavière published a *Lettre de l'auteur à M. Cerutti* rejecting any negative comparison with the paper money set up by John Law.

37. Étienne Clavière, *Réponse au mémoire de M. Necker, concernant les assignats, et à d'autres objections contre une création qui les porte à deux milliards* (Paris: L'Imprimerie du Patriote Français, September 15 and 24, 1790), esp. p. 29 for the value of church lands and pp. 63 and 110–13 for the references to Smith and the English situation. This pamphlet was published in two parts but paginated consecutively.

38. *Le Courrier de Provence*, no. 193 (the previous number included discussions of the sessions of September 15–17, 1790), 320. On the Genevan collaborators with Mirabeau, see J. Bénétruy, *L'Atelier de Mirabeau: Quatre proscrits genevois dans la tourmente révolutionnaire* (Paris: A. and J. Picard, 1962).

39. *Archives parlementaires*, 19:264, 267. For the letter to J. Mauvillon about the assignats, see *Mémoires biographiques, littéraires et politiques de Mirabeau / écrits*

186 · NOTES

par lui-même, par son père, son oncle et son fils adoptif, 12 vols. (Paris: Delaunay, 1834–36), 8:78.

40. Étienne Clavière, *Réflexions sur les formes et les principes auxquels une nation libre doit assujétir l'administration des finances . . .* (Paris: Belin, Desenne, Bailly and Bureau du Patriot français, 1791), esp. 5–7. On the staggering difficulties faced by the National Assembly, see Marion, *Histoire financière de la France,* 2: esp. 245–52.

41. For Clavière's response to Dillon, see especially *La Société des Amis des Noirs à Arthur Dillon* (Paris: Imprimerie du Patriote Français, March 10, 1791), reprinted in *La Révolution française et l'abolition de l'esclavage,* 12 vols. (Paris: Éditions d'histoire sociale, 1968), 8: no. 7 (n.p.); Médéric Moreau de Saint-Méry, *Considérations présentées aux vrais amis du repos et du bonheur de la France: A l'occasion des nouveaux mouvemens de quelques soi-disant amis-des-noirs* (Paris: Imprimerie nationale, 1791).

42. Étienne Clavière, *Adresse de la Société des Amis des Noirs à l'Assemblée Nationale, À toutes les villes de commerce . . .* (Paris: Imprimerie du Patriote Français, March 1791), 4, 32, 42.

43. See, for example, *Archives parlementaires,* 34:526, 603, 721–23.

44. *La Chronique du mois ou les cahiers patriotiques,* November 1791 (Paris: L'Imprimerie du Cercle Social, 1791), 3–44. For the petition to the assembly on November 5, 1791, see *Archives parlementaires,* 34:642–49.

45. *La Chronique du mois,* November 1791, 4. For the estimates of the debt, see pp. 8–35.

46. *La Chronique du mois,* December 1791, 3. For the pamphlet in response to critics, "Réflexions sur les remboursements," see *Archives parlementaires,* 35:494–97. For the vote against suspension, see 35:677.

47. *La Chronique du mois,* January 1792, 105, 117–18, 129, 132, 134. Clavière added further reflections to this first essay in February and March 1792. In these he floated the ideas of an alliance with Great Britain and reminting of silver and gold coins. He then published all three parts in a 112-page pamphlet. *La Chronique du mois,* February 1792, 66–95, esp. 81; March 1792, 60–86.

48. On Clavière's challenges as minister, see Pierre-François Pinaud, "Clavière: Ministre des contributions et revenus publics, agioteur et réformateur," *Revue historique,* no. 289 (April–June 1993): 361–81. These issues are treated in much greater detail in Chaptal, *D'une révolution à l'autre,* 783–897.

49. On the impossibility of determining Clavière's role in the Batz conspiracy, see Chaptal, *D'une revolution à l'autre,* 864–65.

50. Étienne Clavière, *Suite du compte rendu à la Convention Nationale, par le Ministre, le 31 janvier 1793, l'an second de la République française* (Paris: Imprimerie Nationale Executive du Louvre, 1793), 3–19.

51. Clavière, *Suite du compte rendu à la Convention Nationale,* 26.

52. On the American debt, see F. A. Aulard, ed., *Recueil des actes du Comité de salut public: Avec la correspondance officielle des représentants en mission et le registre du*

Conseil exécutif provisoire, 2 vols. (Paris: Imprimerie Nationale, 1889–1923), 1:224–25; *Actes et mémoires concernant les négociations qui ont eu lieu entre la France, et les État Unis . . . depuis 1793, jusqu'à la conclusion de la convention du 30 septembre, 1800,* 3 vols. (London: J. B. G. Vogel, 1807), esp. vol. 1; Anne Cary Morris, ed., *The Diary And Letters of Gouverneur Morris: Minister of the United States to France . . . Etc.,* 2 vols. (New York: C. Scribner's Sons, 1888), 1:579. It should be noted that at this first attempt, Clavière sought money from the United States to help the French in Saint-Domingue. Despite the desperation for funds, Clavière advocated suppressing the lottery established by the monarchy; suppression was only voted several months after Clavière's departure. On reminting, see Chaptal, *D'une révolution à l'autre,* 889–96. On the 20 sous coin, see *Archives parlementaires,* 50:69. On the general question of coinage, see Charles Saunier, *Augustin Dupré: Orfèvre, médailleur et graveur général des monnaies* (Paris: Société de propagation des livres d'art, 1894).

53. Rebecca L. Spang, *Stuff and Money in the Time of the French Revolution* (Cambridge, MA: Harvard University Press, 2015), 120; Marion, *Histoire financière de la France,* 3:3–6.

54. On the proportion of taxes to expenses, see S. E. Harris, *The Assignats* (Cambridge, MA: Harvard University Press, 1930), 51. I have used Harris's figures for monthly revenue of taxes and those for yearly expenses, in both cases using the nominal value. If the depreciated values are used, the results would be virtually the same, 25 percent and 10 percent. Harris shows that tax revenue increased after the low point in 1790. Christian Aubin provides figures for the number of assignats printed and for their relative value: "Les Assignats sous la Révolution française: Un exemple d'hyperinflation," *Revue économique* 42, no. 4 (1991): 745–61, esp. 756 and 760. October 1794 was chosen for the sake of comparison because the number of assignats had doubled by then. A recent study has shown that hyperinflation occurred after the Jacobins fell from power in July 1794, in other words, long after Clavière's removal. Bryan P. Cutsinger, Louis Rouanet, and Joshua S. Ingber, "Assignats or Death: The Politics and Dynamics of Hyperinflation in Revolutionary France," *European Economic Review* 157 (August 2023), available online from Science Direct.

55. *Correspondance du ministre Clavière et le général Montesquiou, servant de réponse au libelle du général contre le ministre* (n.p.: n.d.), 66 pp. For a balanced view of Clavière's ambiguous position on Geneva, see Chaptal, *D'une révolution à une autre,* 897–930.

56. François-Alphonse Aulard, ed., *La Société des Jacobins; recueil de documents pour l'histoire du Club des jacobins de Paris,* 6 vols. (Paris: Librairie Jouaust, 1889–97), 5:77, 106, 136.

57. Étienne Clavière, *Exposé sommaire de la conduite de Clavière, ex-ministre des contributions fait par lui-même, Adressé à ses juges, ses concitoyens, et à ses ennemis* (Paris: n.p., an II [1793]), 1–19.

188 · NOTES

58. Clavière, *Exposé sommaire*, 19–54.
59. Clavière, *Exposé sommaire*, 35–37, 54.
60. For the fate of Clavière's relatives, see Chapuisat, *Figures et choses d'autrefois*, 164–66. For the Clavière quote, see Clavière, *Exposé sommaire*, 53.

EPILOGUE: SELF, SOCIETY, AND EQUALITY

1. Her evolution is most clearly traced in Arnauld Doria, *Gabrielle Capet* (Paris: Les Beaux-Arts, 1934), 70–79. The paintings can be seen in Christophe Marcheteau de Quinçay, *Marie-Gabrielle Capet (1761–1818): Une virtuose de la miniature* (Caen, France: Musée des Beaux-Arts de Caen, 2014), 79, 67, and 69.
2. For a picture of this miniature in a private collection, see Marcheteau de Quinçay, *Marie-Gabrielle Capet (1761–1818)*, 77.
3. Thomas Dodman, "Ordinary Radicalization: Becoming a Citizen-Soldier during the French Revolution," *Journal of Modern History* 94, no. 4 (2022): 751–89; quote on p. 773; Ernest Picard, ed., *Au Service de la nation: Lettres de volontaires (1792–1799)* (Paris: Librairie Félix Alcan, 1914), 31, 39, 62, 216.
4. Étienne Clavière and J. P. Brissot, *De la France et des États-Unis* (London: n.p., 1787), footnote on p. 96.

Index

Note: Page numbers in *italics* refer to illustrations.

abolitionist movement
  Brissot and, 129–30, 136
  Clavière and, 9, 125, 129–30, 136, 146, 152
  Condorcet and, 129, 130
  emergence of, 3
  Friends of Blacks, Society of, 129–31, 136, 137
  Millar and, 33–34
  Mirabeau and, 129
Actes des apôtres (newspaper), 47
actuarial tables, 6, 8, 9, 119, 125
Addison, Joseph, 13–14
Anarchist, The (Petit), 53, 58–59, *59*, 60
ancien régime, 37
Armand-Désiré, Duke of Aiguillon, 72–73
armed forces. *see* revolutionary armies
armies. *see* revolutionary armies
artillery, 91, 102–3, 107
assignats, 133–35, 138, 139–40, 141–44, 145, 146
  Augustus the Strong, 16
Auricchio, Laura, 69–70
autonomy
  increased, in revolutionary armies, 92
  social determinism *versus*, 1–2, 3, 4, 7, 19, 114, 148–49

Bache, Rose-Céleste, 80, 85–86
Bank of England, 118
Bank of Saint Charles, 123
Bastille prison, 34, 128, 132
Batz, Jean, Baron de, 140
Beauharnais, Hortense, 77
Beauharnais, Joséphine de (Joséphine Bonaparte), 76, 77, 87
Beaumarchais, Pierre Caron de, 123
Bentley, Thomas, 17
Berthier, Louis-Alexandre, 109, 110, 112–13
bills of exchange, 117–18, 119
Boilly, Louis-Léopold, 55, 85
Bonaparte, Caroline, 111
Bonaparte, Napoleon. *see* Napoleon Bonaparte
Boulton, Matthew, 17
Boyer de Nîmes (Jacques-Marie Boyer-Brun), 43–47, 49, 51
Bricard, Louis, 95, 96
Brissot, Jacques-Pierre
  abolitionist movement and, 129–30, 136
  arrest, 145
  Chronique du mois and, 54, 137
  criticism of speculators, 122, 123
  death, 146

190 · INDEX

Brissot, Jacques-Pierre (*continued*)
  deputy to Legislative Assembly, 137, 140
  Estates General and, 132
  friendship with Clavière, 8–9, 120
  Girondins and, 137, 140, 144
  interest in the United States, 127–28, 152–53
  on Louis XVI's execution, 140
  national debt and, 128, 139
  paper money and, 127
  republican political principles, 129–30
  transnational vision, 129–30
  transparency in government finance and, 129

Calonne, Charles-Alexandre de, 139
Calvinism, 27, 43, 119
Campbell, Colin, 29–30
Capet, Marie-Gabrielle
  as assistant to artist, 80, 81, 83–84, 88, 151
  attention to fashion, 82–83, 85, 86–87, 88, 151
  attention to generational change, 83, 85
  death, 88
  early career, 66–67, 68
  Labille-Guiard's paintings of, 67, 67–68, 79
  as Labille-Guiard's pupil, 7–8, 66, 72, 79, 83
  miniatures, 66, 71–73, *73*, 79–80, 83–86, 88, 151
  painting of Labille-Guiard (*Studio Scene*), 66, 80–84, *81*, 85–86, 88, 151
  Portrait of a Woman and Her Child, 151
  protégée of Vincent, 66
  rise from humble origins, 7, 65, 79, 151
  self-portraits, 68, 69, 70, 71, 79, 151

  in *Self-Portrait with Two Pupils* (Labille-Guiard), 67, 67–68, 79, 151
  Young Man in a Blue Jacket and Yellow Vest, 151
Caracalla cut for hair, 86
caricatures. *see* prints as revolutionary imagery
Caritat, Nicolas de. *see* Condorcet, Marquis de
Carnot, Lazare, 100–101, 104, 107
Carreaux de Rosemond, Marie Marguerite, 67, 67–68
cashmere shawls, 73, 77, 85–86
cavalry, 92, 94, 102, 103, 106, 111
Cazenove, Theophilus, 127
censorship in France, 37, 38, 39, 127, 153
Chronique du mois (Chronicle of the month), 54, 137
civilization
  stage theory, 20–22, 25
  women's status and level of, 7, 12, 19–20, 21–22
Clarkson, Thomas, 130
Clavière, Étienne
  abolitionist movement and, 9, 125, 129–30, 136, 146, 152
  arrest and interrogation, 145–46
  assignats and, 133–35, 138, 139, 140, 142–44, 145
  belief in equality, 152–53
  Chronique du mois and, 54, 137
  criticism of speculators, 121–22, 123, 139
  death, 9, 146
  Discount Bank and, 120–21, 133
  on disorder in state finances, 135–36, 141–42
  early career, 119
  Estates General and, 131–32
  as finance minister, 139, 140–45, 149

fire insurance company, 123, 125, 126
French politics and, 8–9
friendship with Brissot, 8–9, 120
friendship with Mirabeau, 8
Genevan politics and, 8, 119–20
Girondins and, 137, 138, 144, 147
interest in the United States, 127–28,
  152–53
on invasion and annexation of
  Geneva, 144
Legislative Assembly and, 138
life annuities and, 124–25, 126–27
life insurance company, 8, 119,
  123–24, 125–26, 140, 145
national debt and, 126–27, 128, 131,
  137, 138–39, 153
paper money and, 127, 132–34
Paris Water Company and, 123–24
republican political principles, 125,
  127, 129–30, 131, 138
on sale of church properties, 133–34,
  139
short selling and, 120, 139
support for war with Austria, 138, 139
transnational vision, 129–30
and transparency in government
  finance, 129, 137, 153
watchmaker colony proposed in
  Ireland, 120, 125
Clavière, Jean-Jacques, 146
Clément-Hémery, Albertine, 74
coffee, 11, 15
coffeehouses, 11, 13
Committee of Public Safety, 42, 100, 101
Comte, Auguste, 5, 62
Condorcet, Marquis de
  abolitionist movement and, 129, 130
  Chronique du mois and, 54, 137
  deputy to Legislative Assembly, 137
  Girondins and, 54, 137, 138
  Mercier and, 54
  on social science, 4–5, 62, 125

suicide, 5, 146
worries about assignats, 134
Courrier de Provence (newspaper), 133,
  134
Courrier français (newspaper), 49
Crèvecoeur, J. Hector St. John de, 127
Cruikshank, Isaac, 61
cultural relativism, 18, 22
Custine, General, 95–96, 99, 103

Danger of Wigs, The (print, Vernet), 53,
  55
Daunou, Pierre, 54
David, Jacques-Louis, 74–75, 78, 83
Décade philosophique, La (newspaper), 61
Delessert, Étienne, 120–21, 123
Destutt de Tracy, Antoine, 5, 62
De Vinck collection, 38
de Vinck de Deux-Orp, Eugène, 38
Dialogues concerning Education (Fordyce),
  31
Dillon, Arthur, 136
Discount Bank (*caisse d'escompte*), 118,
  120–21, 121, 123, 126, 133
  Clavière and, 120–21, 133
  establishment of, 118
  National Assembly and, 133
  paper money issued, 133
  Paris Water Company and, 123
  suppression of, 121, 126
*Discourse on the Origin and Foundation of
  Inequality among Men* (Rousseau), 3
Dodman, Thomas, 97
domesticity, 12–13, 14, 15
draft evasion, 94
Dubois-Crancé, Edmond, 102
Duboys, Jean-Jacques, 100
Ducancel, Charles-Pierre, 52
Dumouriez, General, 95, 98, 99, 140–41
du Pont de Nemours, Pierre Samuel,
  122, 134
Dutch VOC (East India Company), 16

INDEX

Edinburgh Musical Society, 30
Égalité (Quéverdo), 149–50, *150*
equality
  among soldiers, 151–52
  Boyer opposition to, 46
  Clavière's belief in, 152–53
  French Revolution and, 153, 154
  in French revolutionary prints,
    149–50, *150*
"Essay on the Physical, Moral and
    Political Regeneration of the Jews"
    (Grégoire), 45
Estates General
  called by Louis XVI, 131–32
  costumes of deputies, 40, 82
  elections, 43
  Friends of Blacks and, 130
  king's debt and, 117
  portraits of deputies, 40–41, *41*, 70
  see also National Assembly

Family of Three at Tea, A (Collins), *13*
fashion
  Capet's attention to, 82–83, 85,
    86–87, 88, 151
  Caracalla cut for hair, 86
  in caricatures and political prints,
    55–56, 58–60
  cashmere shawls, 73, 77, 85–86
  fashion plates, *84*, 85, 87
  fashion prints, 59, 61, 70, 87
  frock coats, 58, 60, 82, 83
  generational change in, 83, 85
  jabots, 83, 85
  knee breeches, 40, 58, 60, 82,
    85–86
  in Labille-Guiard's paintings, 69–70
  Napoleon's rules about, 77, 82, 87
  pantalons (nankeen trousers), 58,
    85, 86
  political and social meanings, 56, 60,
    70, 80

rapid changes during French Revolu-
    tion, 60, 70
  Titus cut for hair, 77–78, 83, 86
  white tunics and chemise dresses,
    73–77, 78, 86
  wigs, 56, 57, 60, 77–78, 82–83, 86
  see also incroyables; *merveilleuses*
Favier, Gilbert, 98
Female Spectator (Haywood), 14
Festival of Reason, 74–75
Festival of the Supreme Being, 74–75
fire insurance companies, 123, 125, 126
Folly of the Day, The (play), 56
Folly of the Day, The (print, Boilly), 53,
    55, 56
Forbes, Duncan, 28, 30
Fordyce, David, 31, 32
Frederick the Great, 102
French National Library, 38, 41–42
French Revolution
  beginning date, 4, 8, 37
  British reactions to, 34–35
  equality and, 153, 154
  social science birth during, 4–6, 37,
    61–63
  see also specific topics
French Revolution Digital Archive, 39, 42
Freund, Amy, 40, 71
Fricasse, Jacques, 97
Friends of Blacks, Society of, 129–31,
    136, 137
frock coats, 58, 60, 82, 83

Gérard, Michel, 40, *41*, 56, 70, 71
Gillray, James, 61
Girondins
  Brissot and, 137, 140, 144
  Clavière and, 137, 138, 144, 147
  Condorcet and, 54, 137, 138
  on Louis XVI's guilt, 140
  Mercier and, 49–50, 54
  opponents of Robespierre, 49

INDEX · 193

support for a republic, 138
support for war with Austria, 138, 139–40
Goethe, Johann Wolfgang von, 61, 91
Grégoire, Henri, 45
Gribeauval, Jean-Baptiste Vaquette de, 102–3
Grimoard, Philippe de, 106, 108
Group of Artists in Jean-Baptiste Isabey's Studio (Boilly), 85
Guérin, Pierre-Narcisse, 83
Guibert, Jacques, 92, 102, 104, 105
Guiut, Guillaume, 100

Hamilton, William, 75
Hart, Emma (Lady Hamilton), 75
Haywood, Eliza, 14
History of the Caricatures of the Revolt of the French (Boyer), 43–44
Hoche, Lazare, 99
Home, Henry (Lord Kames), 20, 25
horse artillery, 102–3
Hume, David, 25, 31, 116–17

ideology, defined, 5
I Knew We'd Have Our Turn (print), 48
incroyables (incredibles), 52–53, 56, 58–59, 61, 78, 83
see also fashion
Incroyables, Les (Vernet), 53, 55, 61
individualism
in art, 70, 88
individual autonomy *vs.* social determinism, 1–2, 3, 4, 7, 19, 114, 148–49
individual initiative in French army, 8, 105, 107, 113, 114, 152
tea and, 11–36
Inside the Revolutionary Committee (play and print), 50–52, 52
Irvine, Charles, 30
Isabey, Jean-Baptiste, 85

jabots, 83, 85
Jean-Jacques Rousseau Considered as One of the Authors of the Revolution (Mercier), 54
Jefferson, Thomas, 117
Jewish moneylenders in caricatures, 45
Joliclerc, François-Xavier, 97
Jomini, Antoine-Henri, 103–4
Joséphine, wife of Napoleon, 76, 77, 87
Journal de la cour et de la ville (newspaper), 47–48
Journal des dames et des modes (fashion journal), 74, 86, 87
Journal des révolutions de l'Europe (newspaper), 48
Journal du peuple (newspaper), 43
Julien, Joseph-Laurent, 56, 57

Kames, Lord (Henry Home), 20, 25
Kauffman, Angelica, 65
Kellermann, François, 91
knee breeches, 40, 58, 60, 82, 85–86

Labille-Guiard, Adélaïde
Capet as pupil, 7–8, 66, 72, 79, 83
Capet's oil painting of, 66, 80–84, 81, 85–86, 88, 151
death, 79
divorce, 72, 153
fashions and costumes in paintings, 69–70
marriage to Vincent, 66, 79, 153
paintings of Capet, 67, 67–68, 79
portraits of deputies to the National Assembly, 71–72
residences during Revolution, 72
in Royal Academy, 66, 71
scholarly attention to, 65
Self-Portrait with Two Pupils, 67, 67–68, 69–70, 79, 80
Lafayette, Marquis de, 48, 90, 98–99, 129

194 · INDEX

Lafitau, Joseph-François, 22–23
Lamb, Frederick and William, 26–27
Laneuville, Jean-Louis, 76
Lannes, Jean, 109, 110, 111–14
Lavoisier, Antoine, 129
Law, John, 117
Leclerc, General, 109
Lefèvre, Robert, 83
Legislative Assembly, 107, 137, 138, 139–40
Letters from an American Farmer (Crève-coeur), 127
lettres de cachet, 128
Levachez, Nicolas-François, 41
life annuities, 124–25, 126–27
life insurance
  actuarial tables, 6, 8, 9, 119, 125
  Clavière's company, 8, 119, 123–24, 125–26, 140, 145
  origins of, 118–19
  Paris Water Company and, 123–24
Linguet, Simon, 131
Locke, John, 14, 18
London East India Company, 30
Louis-Philippe, Duke of Orléans, 72
Louis XVIII, king, 99
Louis XVI, king
  condemned to death, 72
  declaration of war with Austria, 90, 139–40
  deposed, 90
  Estates General called by, 131–32
  execution, 140
  house arrest, 140
  National Convention and, 49–50
  portrait, *41*
  return to Paris after attempt to flee, 48
Lynn, John, 105

Marie Antoinette, 73–74, 76, 78, 90
marine insurance, 118, 119, 125

Mars, Mlle. (Anne Françoise Hyppolyte Boutet Salvetat), 72–74, *73*, 74, 77–79, 81, 85
Masséna, André, 8
Melbourne, Lady, 26
Mercier, Louis-Sébastien
  Chronique du mois and, 54
  Condorcet and, 54
  criticism of, 60–61
  on Louis XVI's guilt, 49–50
  political views and engagement, 49–50, 54, 61
  reaction to prints, 42, 49, 50–53, 55–60
  on rentiers who invested in state bonds, 56–57
  Rousseau and, 54
  on social systems and social mechanisms, 53–55, 62
  on styles associated with *incroyables*, 78
  support for the Girondins, 49, 54
  time in prison, 49, 50, 54
  "M . . . r [Mercier], An Ass Like No Other" (print), 50, *51*
merveilleuses (marvelous females), 52–53, 56, 61, 78
  see also fashion
Mérveilleuses, Les (Vernet), 53, 55, 55–56, 61, 78
Meynier, Charles, 83, 84, 85
Mill, John Stuart, 5
Millar, John
  abolitionist movement and, 33–34
  conversation as sign of civilization, 31–32
  family life, 25, 26–27, 36
  on Native Americans, 23–24
  nontraditional lectures, 7, 25–26, 35
  Observations, 20–21, 25–26, 27, 37
  stage theory and, 20–22, 32–33, 149
  status of women and level of civilization, 7, 21–22, 23, 25, 26–27, 31–32, 149

INDEX · 195

travel books and, 22, 23, 36, 62
Mirabeau, Comte de
 abolitionist movement and, 129
 as an agent of the court, 144
 on assignats, 135
 criticism of speculators, 122–23
 death, 137
 Estates General and, 132
 friendship with Clavière, 9, 120
 support of Panchaud, 126
"modernity," 19
Moeurs des sauvages amériquains
 (Lafitau), 22
Montesquieu
 on climate, 23
 danger of luxury and dissipation,
 32–33
 focus on the East, 22, 23, 32
 on national debt, 116
 Persian Letters, 19
 Spirit of Laws, The, 19, 116
 on status of women, 19–20
 "thrall of manners," 19, 33
 on types of political regimes, 19, 20,
 22
Montesquiou-Fézensac, Anne-Pierre,
 144, 146
Moratín, Leandro Fernández de, 62
Moreau de Saint-Méry, Médéric, 136
"Mountain" (Robespierre supporters),
 75, 144
Muir, Thomas, 34–35
Murat, Joachim, 8, 103, 109, 110, 111,
 112
Mure, Elizabeth, 15
mutinies, 93, 94

Napoleon Bonaparte
 ascent to power, 8, 87
 coronation, 82
 coup in 1799, 87, 109–11, 112, 113
 defeating 1795 insurrection, 111

First Consul, 109
 fostering individual talents, 8
 Italian campaign, 111, 112, 113
 patronage, 114
 populist authoritarianism, 110–11,
 114
 rapid rise in military, 107–8
 return to Paris from Egypt, 109
 rules about fashion and fabric, 77,
 82, 87
 Titus cut, 77–78
National Assembly
 on Discount Bank, 133
 formation from Estates General, 132
 Friends of Blacks and, 130
 political rights of free men of color,
 137
 portraits of deputies, 71–72
 reforms of army, 92
 Salon monopoly ended, 65
 theatrical monopolies abolished, 38
 see also Estates General
National Convention
 financial policies, 126, 141
 Girondins and Jacobins, 49–50, 54
 interactions with army, 95, 96, 101,
 106
 monarchy abolished by, 95, 140
national debt
 Brissot and, 128
 Clavière and, 126–27, 128, 131, 137,
 138–39, 153
 and development of representative
 government, 116
 Hume and, 116–17
 Legislative Assembly and, 139
 Montesquieu and, 116
 paper money and, 116, 117
 problems caused by, 116–17
 support by individuals buying bonds
 or shares, 115–16
National Institute, 4–5, 54, 62, 79, 82

196 · INDEX

Native Americans, 22–24
Necker, Jacques, 133, 134, 135
neoclassicism, 74, 86
Ney, Michel, 8
No Bankruptcy, or Letters to a Creditor of the State, 128
Noël, Gabriel, 105
Nouveau Paris, Le (Mercier), 50, 60–61, 78

Oath of the Horatii (David), 74
Observations concerning the Distinction of Ranks in Society (Millar), 20–21, 25–26, 27, 37
On the Bank of Spain, Called Saint Charles, 123
On the Shares of the Water Company, 123
Ostend East India Company, 29, 30

Panchaud, Isaac, 126
pantalons (nankeen trousers), 58, 85, 86
paper money
assignats, 133–35, 138, 139–40, 141–44, 145, 146
bills of exchange, 117–18, 119
Clavière and, 127, 132–34
France, early eighteenth century, 117
images on, 39
national debt and, 116, 117
as US legal tender, 117, 127
Paris Water Company, 123–24, 125
participatory democracy, development of, 1
Persian Letters (Montesquieu), 19
pikes, 107
Pinkerton, John, 24–25
Pitt, William, 139
Political Affection (Rowlandson), 47
Poor Ruined Rentier—Fish to Fry, to Fry (Julien), 53, 56–57, 57, 58, 60
populist authoritarianism, 110–11, 114
porcelain and china, 12, 14, 16–18, 29

Portrait of a Woman and Her Child (Capet), 151
Portrait of a Woman (Capet), 151
portraits
attention to fashion in, 8
of deputies to the Estates General, 40–41, 41, 70
of deputies to the National Assembly, 71–72
genre choice by French women artists, 66
miniatures, 66, 71–73, 73, 79–80, 83–86, 88, 151
self-portraits by women artists, 66–70, 71, 79–80, 151
Price, Richard, 125
prints as revolutionary imagery, 37–63
Anarchist, The (Petit), 53, 58–59, 59, 60
anonymous artists, 7
Boyer de Nîmes and, 43–47, 49, 51
Danger of Wigs, The (Vernet), 53, 55
English *vs.* French caricatures, 61–62
Folly of the Day, The (Boilly), 53, 55, 56
I Knew We'd Have Our Turn, 48
Incroyables, Les (Vernet), 53, 55, 61
Inside the Revolutionary Committee, 50–52, 52
"M . . . r [Mercier], An Ass Like No Other," 50, 51
Mérveilleuses, Les (Vernet), 53, 55, 55–56, 61, 78
newspapers and pamphlets compared to, 38–39
ordered for propaganda purposes, 42
overview, 38–42
Political Affection (Rowlandson), 47
Poor Ruined Rentier—Fish to Fry, to Fry (Julien), 53, 56–57, 57, 58, 60
portraits of deputies to the Estates General, 40–41, 41, 70, 71–72

INDEX · **197**

prices, 42
reaction to prints, 42–49
"They only wanted what was good for
us," 44, 44–46

Quéverdo, François, 149–51, *150*

Récamier, Juliette, 74
Regnault, Jean-Baptiste, 74
*Regulation concerning the Drill and
Maneuvers of the Infantry*, 104–5
revolutionary armies
artillery, 91, 102–3, 107
battle of Valmy, 90–91
cavalry, 92, 94, 102, 103, 106, 111
demi-brigades, 102
deployment of divisional formations,
92, 102, 106
discipline, 93, 94, 99
distrust of noble officers, 93, 94,
95–96, 98
draft evasion, 94
election of volunteer officers, 92,
99–100, 112
emigration of noble officers, 89, 92,
103, 111
equality among soldiers, 151–52
government interference, 101–2
government propaganda distributed
to, 96
increased autonomy, 92
increasing professionalism, 110, 113
individual initiative in, 8, 105, 107,
113, 114, 152
invasion of Egypt, 109
loyalty to comrades, 94, 98
mass army and attacks, 105–6, 114,
152
mutinies, 93, 94
numbers of men, 90, 93–94
occupation of conquered lands,
108–9, 114

offense *vs.* defense, 104
officer corps disintegration, 89, 90, 93
pace of march, 107
patriotism, 92, 94, 96–97
rapid advancement through ranks,
99–100, 111
reforms, 92–93
skirmishers, 103–4, 105
strategy and tactical innovation, 101,
102–8, 114
troops' affection gained by new
officers, 98
use of columns *vs.* firing lines, 92,
103–5
volunteers, at battle of Valmy, 91
see also war with Austria; *specific
individuals*
Révolutions de Paris (newspaper), 48–49
Riqueti, Honoré Gabriel. *see* Mirabeau,
Comte de
Robespierre, Maximilien, 49, 56, 71–72,
75, 76, 145
Roland, Marie-Jeanne, 50
Rousseau, Jean-Jacques, 3, 54, 152
Rowlandson, Thomas, 47, 61

Saint-Cyr, Laurent de Gouvion, 99–100,
104, 105
Saint-Domingue, 76, 109, 136, 137
Saint-Just, Louis de, 106
Salons
Salon of 1783, 73
Salon of 1785, 67
Salon of 1789, 39, 65
Salon of 1791, 39, 65, 71
Salon of 1796, 76
Salon of 1798, 84–85
Salon of 1800, 73
Salon of 1801, 83
Salon of 1808, 80
works by women, 65, 66, 67, 71, 76,
83, 84

Scharnhorst, Gerhard von, 104
Scottish philosophers
  on Highlands and Lowlands, 24–25
  rapid transformation in economy and,
    27–28
  societies compared and categorized,
    12, 20–25
  on women's status and level of civili-
    zation, 12, 20, 21, 27
  see also specific individuals
Self-Portrait with Two Pupils (Labille-
    Guiard), 67, 67–68, 69, 79, 80
short selling, 120, 121–22, 139
Sieyès, Emmanuel, 4, 5, 6, 54, 62
slaves and slavery, 2–3, 16, 76
  see also abolitionist movement
slippers, 56, 57, 58, 78, 85
Smith, Adam, 20, 22, 23–24, 25, 26, 134
Social Contract (Rousseau), 3
social determinism, 2, 3, 19
social organization, 5–6, 37, 148
social science
  Condorcet on, 4–5, 62, 125
  Destutt de Tracy on, 5, 62
  emergence in 1790s, 4–5, 148
  French Revolution and, 4–6, 37,
    61–63
  Mill on, 5
  Sieyès on, 4, 62
society as distinct entity, 1, 4, 37–38,
    131–32
Society of the Observers of Man, 62–63
sociology, emergence in 1840s, 4
South Sea Bubble, 29
Spectator, The, 13–14
Spies-Gans, Paris, 65
Spirit of Laws, The (Montesquieu), 19, 116
Stadnitski, Pieter, 124, 127, 128
stage theory, 20–22, 25
Steele, Richard, 13
Studio Scene (Capet), 66, 80–84, 81,
    85–86, 88, 151

sugar, 15–16, 28, 29
superiority of Western culture, belief in,
    18–19, 35–36
Swedish East India Company, 29–30

Tableau de Paris (Mercier), 49
Tallien, Jean-Lambert, 75, 76
Tallien, Thérèse (née Thérézia Cabar-
    rus), 75, 76, 78
Talma, François-Joseph, 78
tea, 11–36
  criticism of, 14
  effect on status of women, 2, 12–14,
    29, 30–31
  English and Scottish tea rituals, 27,
    28–29
  imports to Britain, 15, 28–30
  international trade, 15
  smuggling of, 28, 30
  tea paraphernalia, 11, 12
  women's new roles as tea servers, 2,
    11–12, 13, 13–15, 29, 30–31
tea tables, 2, 11–12, 13, 13–15, 29,
    30–31, 149
Thatcher, Margaret, 3
theaters during the Revolution, 38–39,
    66
Théremin, Charles, 66–67
"They only wanted what was good for
    us" (print), 44, 44–46
Thugut (Austrian chancellor), 108
Titus cut for hair, 77–78, 83, 86
Tournezy, Adèle, 74
travel books and travel accounts, 17–19,
    20, 22, 23, 36, 62

Valmy, battle of, 90–91, 95, 102, 104
Verger, Pierre, 100
Vernet, Carle, 52–53, 55, 55, 59, 61
Vien, Joseph-Marie (senator), 80, 81–82,
    83, 85
Vien, Joseph-Marie (son), 80, 85

Vieusseux, Pierre-François, 119
Vigée Le Brun, Élisabeth, 65, 68, 72,
73, 75
Vincent, François-André
Capet as protégée, 66
in Capet painting, 80, *81*, 82, 83, 151
death, 88
marriage to Labille-Guiard, 66, 79,
153
National Institute and, 79, 82
residences during Revolution, 72
Voltaire, 22

war with Austria and Prussia
battle of Valmy, 90–91, 95, 102, 104
beginning of war, 89–90, 103, 139–40,
153
early French losses, 90, 140
emigration of noble French officers,
89, 92, 103, 111
expansion in 1793, 91
Girondins' support for, 138,
139–40
government interference, 101–2
numbers of men, 90, 93–94, 106

shortage of men and equipment in
1792, 89, 106–7
strategy and tactical innovation, 101,
102–8, 114
use of columns *vs.* firing lines, 92, 103–5
as war of masses, 105–6, 114, 152
see also revolutionary armies
Wedgwood, Josiah, 16–17
What Is the Third Estate? (Sieyès), 4, 6
white tunics and chemise dresses, 73–77,
78, 86
wigs and fashion, 56, 57, 60, 77–78,
82–83, 86
women
artists, 64–88
domesticity and, 12–13, 14, 15
literacy, 30–31
new roles as tea servers, 2, 11–12, *13*,
13–15, 29, 30–31
status and level of civilization, 7, 12,
19–20, 21–22
see also specific women

*Young Man in a Blue Jacket and Yellow
Vest* (Capet), 151